HISTORICAL DICTIONARIES OF RELIGIONS, PHILOSOPHIES, AND MOVEMENTS
Jon Woronoff, Series Editor

1. *Buddhism,* by Charles S. Prebish, 1993
2. *Mormonism,* by Davis Bitton, 1994. *Out of print. See No. 32.*
3. *Ecumenical Christianity,* by Ans Joachim van der Bent, 1994
4. *Terrorism,* by Sean Anderson and Stephen Sloan, 1995. *Out of print. See No. 41.*
5. *Sikhism,* by W. H. McLeod, 1995. *Out of print. See No. 59.*
6. *Feminism,* by Janet K. Boles and Diane Long Hoeveler, 1995. *Out of print. See No. 52.*
7. *Olympic Movement,* by Ian Buchanan and Bill Mallon, 1995. *Out of print. See No. 39.*
8. *Methodism,* by Charles Yrigoyen Jr. and Susan E. Warrick, 1996. *Out of print. See No. 57.*
9. *Orthodox Church,* by Michael Prokurat, Alexander Golitzin, and Michael D. Peterson, 1996
10. *Organized Labor,* by James C. Docherty, 1996. *Out of print. See No. 50.*
11. *Civil Rights Movement,* by Ralph E. Luker, 1997
12. *Catholicism,* by William J. Collinge, 1997
13. *Hinduism,* by Bruce M. Sullivan, 1997
14. *North American Environmentalism,* by Edward R. Wells and Alan M. Schwartz, 1997
15. *Welfare State,* by Bent Greve, 1998. *Out of print. See No. 63.*
16. *Socialism,* by James C. Docherty, 1997
17. *Bahá'í Faith,* by Hugh C. Adamson and Philip Hainsworth, 1998
18. *Taoism,* by Julian F. Pas in cooperation with Man Kam Leung, 1998
19. *Judaism,* by Norman Solomon, 1998. *Out of print. See No. 69.*
20. *Green Movement,* by Elim Papadakis, 1998
21. *Nietzscheanism,* by Carol Diethe, 1999
22. *Gay Liberation Movement,* by Ronald J. Hunt, 1999
23. *Islamic Fundamentalist Movements in the Arab World, Iran, and Turkey,* by Ahmad S. Moussalli, 1999
24. *Reformed Churches,* by Robert Benedetto, Darrell L. Guder, and Donald K. McKim, 1999

Historical Dictionary of Epistemology

Ralph Baergen

*Historical Dictionaries of Religions,
Philosophies, and Movements, No. 70*

The Scarecrow Press, Inc.
Lanham, Maryland • Toronto • Oxford
2006

SCARECROW PRESS, INC.

Published in the United States of America
by Scarecrow Press, Inc.
A wholly owned subsidiary of
The Rowman & Littlefield Publishing Group, Inc.
4501 Forbes Boulevard, Suite 200, Lanham, Maryland 20706
www.scarecrowpress.com

PO Box 317
Oxford
OX2 9RU, UK

British Library Cataloguing in Publication Information Available

Library of Congress Cataloging-in-Publication Data

Baergen, Ralph.
    Historical dictionary of epistemology / Ralph Baergen.
        p. cm. — (Historical dictionaries of religions, philosophies, and
    movements ; no. 70)
        Includes bibliographical references.
        ISBN-13: 978-0-8108-5518-2 (hardcover : alk. paper)
        ISBN-10: 0-8108-5518-6 (hardcover : alk. paper)
        1. Knowledge, Theory of—Dictionaries. I. Title. II. Series.

    BD150.B34 2006
    121.03—dc22

                                                2006003761

∞™ The paper used in this publication meets the minimum requirements of
American National Standard for Information Sciences—Permanence of Paper
for Printed Library Materials, ANSI/NISO Z39.48-1992.
Manufactured in the United States of America.

This volume is dedicated to my wonderful wife and my three darling children. I know that I love them.

Contents

Editor's Foreword

Epistemology, or the theory of knowledge, lies at the root of philosophy and all the arts and sciences and is therefore a constant preoccupation. Like everything else, it has enjoyed periods of greater and lesser prestige, intensely absorbing the Greek philosophers, and dominating much of the seventeenth and eighteenth centuries; it has also concerned many more recent philosophers. It has also been studied beyond the Western tradition, in Asia and the Middle East. Yet, for all this activity, while epistemology has evolved and become immensely richer, it has failed to reach any final conclusions, and the range of views stretches from those who insist on certain points to those who remain fiercely skeptical. This is perhaps to the good since the existing range of beliefs—and even supposed facts—is still so broad that we obviously could not agree yet on what knowledge is, how to attain it, and how to confirm it. But we can continue seeking.

Historical Dictionary of Epistemology traces this long quest, starting with the ancients and coming up to the present. This is done first in a chronology and then the introduction, which describes the progression more analytically. It also tells us more about what epistemology is and why it is so difficult to agree on. The dictionary section, the core of the book, provides further information, with entries on the most notable philosophers from all periods and around the world, other entries on the key concepts, and yet others on the tasks and "problems" of epistemology. Together, they cover the field very broadly but obviously cannot go into all the details; this underlines the utility of the extensive bibliography.

This volume was written by Ralph Baergen, who is presently a professor of philosophy at Idaho State University. He wrote his dissertation on epistemic reliabilism and has continued writing on the topic of epistemology, including a number of papers and articles as well as the book

Contemporary Epistemology. But his interests are broader, having also written a book on ethics and currently doing research in medical ethics. Since epistemology is a particularly complicated field and those engaged in it often have very diverse and sometimes strongly held positions, the advantage to this volume is that it is amazingly easy to read and to follow and also allows the reader to draw his or her own conclusions. It is thus an excellent place to get started and later a resource for those who already know more but cannot quite remember it all.

Jon Woronoff
Series Editor

Acknowledgments

I gratefully acknowledge the assistance of Catherine Read Wallace in editing this manuscript.

Chronology

ca. 385 B.C.   Plato's *Republic* introduces the justified true belief theory of knowledge.

ca. 365–270 B.C.   Pyrrho of Elis defends skepticism, arguing that our senses are unreliable and that the world lacks determinate properties.

ca. 330 B.C.   Aristotle's *De Anima* explores the functioning of the sensory systems. His *Posterior Analytics* examines the nature of scientific knowledge.

ca. 280 B.C.   Epicurus presents an early version of empiricism, arguing that the senses are the source of all knowledge.

ca. A.D. 200   Sextus Empiricus formulates the case for skepticism and against dogmatism.

ca. A.D. 386   St. Augustine's *Contra Academicos* responds to skeptical arguments.

ca. 1265   St. Thomas Aquinas defends a foundationalist understanding of knowledge.

ca. 1300   Duns Scotus rejects Augustine's view that certainty is rooted in divine illumination, arguing that it leads to skepticism.

1637   René Descartes's *Discourse on Method* presents his "method of doubt," which is used in response to skepticism, removing all possible sources of error. This begins modern rationalism.

1641   Descartes's *Meditations on First Philosophy* employs his method of doubt in establishing a foundationalist account of knowledge.

1662   Antoine Arnauld and others publish the first edition of the *Port-Royal Logic*. Five more editions are published by 1685.

1670 Blaise Pascal's *Pensées* are published (posthumously), arguing that we can know that God exists even though we cannot be certain that this is so.

1674 Nicolas Malebranche's *The Search after Truth* argues that ideas perceived by humans are actually in the mind of God.

1675 Benedict Spinoza's *Ethics* presents a rationalist theory of knowledge and a coherence theory of truth.

1677 Benedict Spinoza's *Treatise on the Emendation of the Intellect* (published posthumously in the *Opera postuma*) identifies three levels of knowledge.

1690 John Locke's *Essay Concerning Human Understanding* attacks the claim that we have innate ideas and argues that all knowledge is rooted in experience (an empiricist view).

1705 Gottfried Leibniz's *New Essays* critically examines Locke's empiricism.

1713 George Berkeley's *Three Dialogues between Hylas and Philonous* attacks Locke's representative realism and defends an empiricist idealism.

1714 Leibniz's *Monadology* presents his metaphysic of monads and the accompanying rationalist theory of knowledge.

1728 Francis Hutcheson's *An Essay on the Nature and Conduct of the Passions and Affections with Illustrations on the Moral Sense* argues that sense perception provides knowledge of aesthetic and ethical properties.

1737 David Hume's *A Treatise of Human Nature* defends empiricism but draws skeptical conclusions about much of human "knowledge."

1751–1772 French publisher Le Breton publishes the seventeen-volume *Encyclopédie*, presenting the knowledge of the time.

1754 Étienne Bonnot de Condillac's *Treatise on Sense Perception* explores how perception and language contribute to knowledge. This work would later influence John Locke.

1764 Thomas Reid's *An Inquiry into the Human Mind on the Principles of Common Sense* criticizes Hume's skeptical empiricism and defends what has come to be known as commonsensism.

1781 Immanuel Kant's *Critique of Pure Reason* ("B" edition published in 1787) presents a rationalist account of human knowledge, arguing that synthetic propositions can be known *a priori*.

1794 Johann Fichte's *On the Concept of the Wissenschaftslehre* presents his "science of science," rejecting Kant's notion of things-in-themselves and defending a form of idealism.

1807 **13 October:** G. W. F. Hegel completes his *Phenomenology of Spirit*, explaining the use of his dialectical method to resolve contradictions in the application of philosophical concepts, attacking the empiricist's concept of the Given, and arguing that all knowledge is mediated by the application of concepts.

1812 Pierre Laplace's *Analytic Theory of Probability* introduces the principle of indifference, which requires that all possible outcomes should be regarded as equally probable.

1812–1816 Hegel's three-volume *Science of Logic* explores the nature of arguments, experience, being, essence, and appearance.

1818 Arthur Schopenhauer's *The World as Will and Representation* rejects both Kant's categories of judgment and Hegel's dialectic, arguing that reality is the manifestation of a single will.

1843 John Stuart Mill argues in his *System of Logic* that logic, arithmetic, and geometry are part of the natural sciences; thus, their principles are learned through experience.

1874 Franz Brentano's *Psychology from an Empirical Standpoint* argues that intentionality is the dividing line between the mental and the physical.

1877 C. S. Peirce's "The Fixation of Belief" examines the forms of reasoning employed in science, clarifying the hypothetico-deductive method. Science, he claims, applies the pragmatic maxim: The meaning of a statement lies in its testable consequences for experience.

1883 Ernst Mach's *The Science of Mechanics* argues that the external world is a logical construction of sensations.

1896 Henri Bergson's *Matter and Memory* presents epistemological issues in a biological light, rejecting what he regards as the overintellectual accounts of other theorists.

1897 William James's *The Will to Believe and Other Essays* argues that alternatives to religious and moral claims must be taken seriously and that certainty in such matters is undesirable.

1900–1913 Edmund Husserl develops phenomenology, the philosophical study of consciousness.

1905 C. S. Peirce's "Pragmatism" introduces the principle of pragmatism: meanings are conditional statements linking observations and experimental situations.

1907 William James's *Pragmatism* argues that the truth and falsehood of theories or propositions must be understood in terms of their role in experience. James's theory is a version of empiricism, combined with a version of the coherentist theory of truth.

1913 Edmund Husserl employs his method of *epoché* to identify and set aside all our presuppositions in order to study consciousness itself (in his *Ideas Pertaining to a Pure Phenomenology and Phenomenological Philosophy*).

1914 Bertrand Russell's *Our Knowledge of the External World* argues that physical objects are logical constructions of sense data.

1923 George Santayana's *Scepticism and Animal Faith* argues against skepticism, pointing out that it cannot be acted on in practice.

1926 Frank Ramsey's "Truth and Probability" argues that the calculus of probability should be used as a logic of partial belief.

1927 Martin Heidegger's *Being and Time* presents his phenomenology.

1928 Rudolf Carnap's *The Logical Structure of the World* examines the logical structure of experience and argues that we cannot be certain that scientific beliefs are true.

1929–1936 The Vienna Circle meets and develops logical positivism.

1931 Kurt Gödel proves the incompleteness of certain formal systems. Frank Ramsey's "Knowledge" defends an early form of epistemic reliabilism.

1932 Rudolf Carnap's *The Unity of Science* introduces protocol sentences, which record experiences while excluding presuppositions.

1933   G. E. Moore's "Proof of an External World" is published, defending commonsensism.

1939   Brand Blandshard's *The Nature of Thought* attacks empiricism and the correspondence theory of truth and defends rationalism and the coherence theory of truth.

1943   Jean-Paul Sartre's *Being and Nothingness* examines the nature of consciousness and self-knowledge.

1945   Maurice Merleau-Ponty's *Phenomenology of Perception* rejects traditional epistemology and defends his version of phenomenology.

1946   A. J. Ayer's *Language, Truth and Logic* endorses logical positivism and rejects traditional foundationalism.

1947   A. J. Ayer's *The Foundations of Empirical Knowledge* defends sense data.

1948   Bertrand Russell's *Human Knowledge: Its Scope and Limits* backs away from his earlier claims that the external world can be known with certainty. Human knowledge is significantly more limited.

1949   Gilbert Ryle's *The Concept of Mind* rejects Cartesian mind/body dualism and argues that epistemology overlooks the importance of procedural knowledge.

1952   P. F. Strawson's *Introduction to Logical Theory* uses ordinary language philosophy in an attempt to solve the problem of induction.

1953   W. V. O. Quine's "Two Dogmas of Empiricism" rejects the analytic/synthetic distinction and argues that all beliefs are subject to rational revision.

1955   Nelson Goodman's *Fact, Fiction and Forecast* examines the problem of induction and introduces the concept of projectible predicates.

1956   A. J. Ayer's *The Problem of Knowledge* presents an early version of epistemological reliabilism. Ludwig Wittgenstein's *Remarks on the Foundations of Mathematics* examines the nature of inference and its relationship to belief.

1959   Karl Popper's *The Logic of Scientific Discovery* (originally *Logik der Forschung*, 1934) argues that all observations are theory laden and that experience cannot establish the truth of scientific claims.

1960   Hans-Georg Gadamer's *Truth and Method* develops hermeneutics and explains its role in understanding knowledge.

1962   Jaakko Hintikka's *Knowledge and Belief* explores the modal logic of knowledge, initiating modal epistemology. Thomas Kuhn's *The Structure of Scientific Revolutions* introduces the concepts of paradigm shifts and scientific revolutions.

1963   Imre Lakatos's *Proofs and Refutations* examines the role of counterexamples in science and explores the nature of research programs. Edmund Gettier's "Is Justified True Belief Knowledge?" presents counterexamples showing that the tripartite "JTB" theory of knowledge is mistaken. This spawns many efforts to save or revise that theory. Wilfrid Sellars's "Empiricism and the Philosophy of Mind" argues against what he calls the "Myth of the Given."

1965   Nelson Goodman's *Fact, Fiction and Forecast* applies the method of reflective equilibrium to the task of establishing the criteria for knowledge.

1968   Curt Ducasse's *Truth, Knowledge and Causation* rejects sense data and defends the adverbial theory of perception. Jürgen Habermas's *Knowledge and Human Interests* examines the sociology of knowledge and defends a consensus theory of truth.

1969   Ludwig Wittgenstein's *On Certainty* (published posthumously) rejects both global skepticism and Cartesian foundationalism. A proper understanding of language, he argues, shows that many of our fundamental beliefs could not possibly be false. W. V. O. Quine's "Epistemology Naturalized" argues that epistemology should be reduced to or replaced by psychology.

1970   Jean Piaget's *Genetic Epistemology* and *Psychology and Epistemology* explore the stages of epistemic development. Paul Feyerabend's "Against Method" argues that there is no scientific method and that science is not clearly better than other epistemic approaches to the world.

1973   David Armstrong's *Belief, Truth and Knowledge* presents a causal theory of knowledge, an early version of reliabilism.

1979 Richard Rorty's *Philosophy and the Mirror of Nature* attacks the claim that minds represent the external world and is against the traditional epistemic enterprise. This is part of the "death of epistemology" movement.

1980 Isaac Levi's *The Enterprise of Knowledge* explores the relationships between knowledge, probability theory, and partial belief.

1981 Fred Dretske's *Knowledge and the Flow of Information* describes knowledge in terms of signals and information theory. This is linked to epistemic reliabilism. Hilary Putnam's *Reason, Truth and History* makes truth an epistemic concept by describing it as idealized warranted assertibility.

1984 Donald Davidson's *Inquiries into Truth and Interpretation* defends the principle of charity for interpretations and argues that when one's beliefs form a coherent system, many of them must be true.

1985 Laurence BonJour's *The Structure of Empirical Knowledge* presents a sophisticated formulation of epistemic coherentism.

1986 Alvin Goldman's *Epistemology and Cognition* presents a sophisticated form of the reliabilist theory of knowledge. Patricia Churchland's *Neurophilosophy* attacks traditional epistemology for not learning from the neurosciences. She defends eliminative materialism and argues that the traditional concept of belief will be replaced by something that fits better with neuroscience.

1987 Daniel Dennett's *The Intentional Stance* argues that belief attributions should be made whenever doing so gives one an explanatory or predictive advantage.

1988 William Lycan's *Judgment and Justification* examines the nature of beliefs and links this to work in the cognitive sciences. Justification is explained in terms of natural selection.

1989 Roderick Chisholm's *Theory of Knowledge* (third edition) takes the concept of epistemic justification to be fundamental and defines other epistemic concepts in terms of it. His theory of knowledge combines elements of foundationalism and coherentism. Paul Churchland's *A Neurocomputational Perspective* attacks folk psychology (including its concept of belief) and defends eliminative materialism.

1990   Jane Duran's *Toward a Feminist Epistemology* examines the role of feminist epistemology in post-Quinean naturalized epistemology.

1991   Lorraine Code's *What Can She Know?* provides a feminist critique of traditional epistemology and examines the social construction of subjectivity.

1992   Alvin I. Goldman's *Liaisons: Philosophy Meets the Cognitive and Social Sciences* marks an important advance in naturalized epistemology, applying the empirical sciences to individual and social epistemology. Frederick Schmitt's *Knowledge and Belief* argues against epistemic internalism and defends a reliabilist theory of knowledge.

1993   Alvin Plantinga's *Warrant: The Current Debate* and *Warrant and Proper Function* examine the nature of epistemic warrant and defend the rationality of belief in God.

1997   Keith Lehrer's *Self-Trust: A Study of Reason, Knowledge and Autonomy* examines the nature of metamental self-examination and the relationship between knowledge and self-trust.

2003   Michael Brady and Duncan Pritchard edit *Moral and Epistemic Virtues*, exploring the structural similarities between these two fundamental branches of philosophy.

2004   Luc Bovens and Stephan Hartmann's *Bayesian Epistemology* apply probability theory to a wide variety of epistemological issues. Martin Kusch's *Knowledge by Agreement* defends communitarian epistemology, arguing that knowledge is best understood as a form of social status.

2005   Paul Coates's *The Metaphysics of Perception* defends a version of Wilfrid Sellars's critical realism against the more common direct realist theories. Michael Bishop and J. D. Trout's *Epistemology and the Psychology of Human Judgment* presents strategic reliabilism, using empirical psychology as a basis for making normative recommendations about how we ought to reason.

Introduction

THE NATURE OF EPISTEMOLOGY

Epistemology is the branch of philosophy that investigates our beliefs, evidence, and claims of knowledge. It is a normative endeavor, asking how much we know and how we know it, whether our senses can be trusted to reveal the reality behind appearances, and how the value of evidence is to be determined. Epistemology is critical, raising objections to our ordinary, "commonsense" views, and finding flaws in the reasons we offer in support of our beliefs.

Epistemological questions play a central role in our everyday lives. In many situations, we recognize that there is a matter of fact, but we do not know what it is (Where did I leave the car keys? What is my dentist's telephone number?). We are particularly curious about the future (Will the price of this stock rise? Will this crime be solved?) and that which is difficult to observe (Is there intelligent life on other planets? What is the CIA really doing in Central America? Is there life after death?). Scholars and scientists spend their lives seeking evidence and answers (Which gene is linked to this cancer? Did Homer write all that is attributed to him? Why do electrons have this particular mass?). Epistemological issues are also key components of our entertainment, as we see in suspense stories, dramatic irony, and comedies of misunderstanding. There is even a chilling entertainment in the suggestion that we might be profoundly mistaken about everything, that the curtain of appearances might mask a vastly different reality.

The scope of epistemology is astonishingly wide. It encompasses nearly all branches of academia, covering abstract theory, practical application, literature, wild speculation, and mundane daily life. In all these areas, the epistemologist raises and attempts to quell skeptical challenges: there is always the possibility that we have it all wrong, that our reasons are flawed, that memory and experience are unreliable.

The concept of knowledge is central to epistemology. Epistemologists ask how this concept should be analyzed; what is knowledge, and what conditions must be met in order to possess it? Should the same analysis of and standards for knowledge be used in all contexts, or do different people or groups know things in different ways? There are also questions about the extent of our knowledge and about its sources. Skepticism presents us with the possibility that the standards of knowledge might be very demanding and that we might know little or nothing. It points out the flaws in our sources of belief and the shortcomings in our reasoning. In this way, much of epistemology has come to be a response to skepticism.

The history and development of epistemology mirrors the philosophical and scientific growth of cultures. Beginning with the dawning philosophical awareness and scientific curiosity of the ancient Greeks, one can trace the rise of mathematics and geometry, the growth of the natural sciences, changing attitudes toward religion and social institutions, and more recently the criticism of social structures and cultures. In many ways, the story of epistemology is the story of thought.

ANCIENT GREECE

The Greek tradition's earliest comments on epistemological issues come in the form of some rather disparaging remarks about the human *noûs* (soul or mind), particularly about the limits of human knowledge or understanding. Humans, they said, concern themselves only with what is presented to their senses today, with no understanding of what is to come. Indeed, a wise person will not seek to know too much; Epicharmus warns, "Mortals must think mortal things, not immortal ones" (DK 23 B20).[1] Xenophanes sees this as a part of the human condition, observing, "It is for god to know the truth, but for men to opine" (DK 21 A24). Thales sought to extend human knowledge of natural phenomena by investigating the material world's basic principles and substances. The evident presupposition in this undertaking that such knowledge was within the grasp of humans reveals a dawning optimism regarding our capacity to expand our knowledge. It is also noteworthy that this growth in knowledge would come not through revelation from the gods but by means of human inquiry. We also see here the origins of the assumption that nature is uniform: it is taken for granted that there are unchanging patterns or principles that govern not only observed instances but past, future, and unobserved ones as well. These patterns are sought through reasoning about what one observes in particular cases, although Heraclitus emphasized the role of the senses, while Parmenides emphasized reasoning.

Reflection on these issues led to reexamination of the distinction between the natural world and that which arises from convention or other human origin and between appearance and reality. The Sophists and others raised doubts about our commonsense beliefs, and skepticism emerged as a threat to our ordinary assessment of our intellectual hold on our world. It was against this background that the most notable thinkers of ancient Greece arose.

Plato

Plato's (ca. 429–347 B.C.) reflections on the nature of reality led him to believe that it must be perfect and unchanging. The material world around us clearly does not meet this standard, but the realm of Forms he posited does. Knowledge, he argued, can only be of what is real. Thus, one can know the Forms but not the world of our daily experience; the latter is the subject of mere opinion. Furthermore, our knowledge arises from our faculty of reason rather than from our senses. One is born with knowledge of the Forms, and this can be recollected through the process of *anamnesis*. A key feature of knowledge is that it is immune from error; this rules out knowledge of the ever-changing material world, or acquiring knowledge by means of the error-prone senses.

This is illustrated in the *Meno*, in which Socrates questions an untutored slave boy about geometry. When the boy eventually reaches the correct answer, Socrates argues that this indicates that the boy was actually remembering geometric Forms with which his soul was directly acquainted prior to birth. This dialogue also includes a discussion of the distinction between knowledge and true opinion. The former is said to be anchored in ways that the latter is not; this introduces the suggestion that knowledge may be true opinion conjoined with the believer's capacity to defend or provide an account of that belief.

This proposal is explored in detail in the last section of the *Theaetetus*. Here Plato considers the suggestion that knowledge consists in having a true belief along with the ability to provide a reason or defense (*logos*) for that belief. His examination of this approach covers the role of language in expressing and defending knowledge claims and the significance of grasping how the elements in a knowledge claim are interconnected. Although Plato ultimately seems to reject this account, it has been enormously influential as the justified true belief (JTB) or tripartite theory of knowledge. His conclusion seems to be that although one can have genuine knowledge of the Forms, only belief or opinion is possible regarding the material world. At some points (e.g., *Republic* 477e) Plato adds that while beliefs are fallible, knowledge is infallible. This differs interestingly from his earlier statements and introduces an epistemic desideratum that plays a large role in philosophy's modern era.

Aristotle

Rather than wrestling with the fundamental challenge of skepticism, Aristotle (384–322 B.C.) tended to take for granted that we know quite a lot and worked to understand what we know and how. He agreed with his teacher, Plato, that our knowledge is of universals, although he adds that one can know a universal in its particular instantiation. Contrary to Plato, Aristotle rejected the existence of a realm of Forms and argued that sense perception plays a key role in acquiring knowledge. Each sensory system passively receives impressions (confusingly described as sensible form without matter) about which it actively makes judgments. These judgments may result in error, although Aristotle sometimes suggested that there can be no error in the passive reception of forms.

Knowledge is produced by the faculty of judgment when one grasps a necessary connection among forms. For instance, one knows something about a dog when one grasps that it is essentially an animal and a mammal. Thus, knowledge consists in organizing and classifying universals as they are revealed through experience. Although knowledge requires one's capacity to provide a cause (in Aristotle's broad sense) of what is known, this does not apply to the most fundamental principles. For instance, the principle of noncontradiction is known, not because one can cite its cause but through a dialectical process. This involves using the skeptic's own presupposition of this principle to show that it can be regarded as knowledge. This fails, obviously, to take seriously the skeptical challenge.

In his *Posterior Analytics*, Aristotle presents scientific knowledge as a special case. He believed science to consist in a set of general claims, each supported by a demonstrative argument. The premises of such arguments are first principles, truths whose firm epistemic status provides a foundation for all scientific theorems based on them. The theorems thus established can then be used as premises in further scientific syllogisms, many of which have to do with causes and effects. This process allows epistemic support to flow from first principles to all subsequent claims. This foundationalist structure has exerted considerable influence on epistemic theorizing.

In *De Anima*, sense perception is used to distinguish between the common sensibles (qualities of objects that can be perceived by more than one sensory system, e.g., size and shape) and proper sensibles (qualities that can be perceived by only one sensory system, e.g., color and odor). This precursor of the distinction between primary and secondary qualities is used in arguing that observers may be mistaken about common sensibles but not about proper sensibles. Therefore, Aristotle seems to conclude, one has knowledge of an object's proper sensibles but only belief or opinion of its common sensibles.

Epicurus

Epicurus (341–270 B.C.) proposed a materialist view according to which even the soul is comprised of atoms. All knowledge is rooted in experience, the contact between the soul and the external world. The sensory experiences that result from this physical contact are sometimes classified into categories or taken as instantiations of abstract ideas; it is here that error typically arises. The sensations themselves, he argued, are always true and constitute the only standard for assessing judgments. His view might be better expressed by saying that only judgments are capable of truth or falsehood and that sensations involve no judgment. Thus, sensations would lack a truth value rather than always being true. Epicurus's view is often cited as an early exemplar of empiricism, the view that all knowledge is rooted in experience. This is true, although his position lacks much of the content and complexity of, for instance, the seventeenth-century British empiricists.

Epicurus followed the lead provided by Plato and Aristotle in claiming that true opinion by itself does not qualify as knowledge. In addition, the subject must be able to provide well-grounded arguments, typically with regard to the nature and causal connections of objects. Interestingly, Epicurus does not seem concerned with whether these arguments would survive skeptical counter-arguments.

The Stoics

The Stoic school of thought was diverse and long lived, so much of what can be said about their epistemological views applies to some but not others of their members. Like Epicurus, they held an atomistic view of the world and regarded experience as the source of knowledge. When material objects act on an observer, the result is a cognitive impression in the observer's soul (which is also material). Particularly clear and vivid impressions are veridical, but others may involve error. The soul registers or assents to these impressions, but they do not qualify as knowledge until the soul has grasped them in a process called *katalepsis*; this is a sort of apprehension whose nature is unclear.

Ordinary people will generally not possess knowledge of physical objects; this is seen as restricted to those with wisdom. This is a sort of skepticism, denying that most ordinary beliefs qualify as knowledge. Thus, the Stoics have a relatively pessimistic epistemology.

The Skeptics

Up to this point, one's capacity to provide an argument in defense of one's knowledge claims has been important, but the skeptics challenge this. For any argument that goes beyond the content of our sensory experiences (such as arguments about causes), they claim that an equally compelling argument can be devised to support the opposite conclusion. The only reasonable response to such pairs of arguments is to suspend judgment and refrain from claiming to know anything.

The gap between appearance and reality was emphasized by the skeptics, who argued that it is impossible to determine that any given appearance is veridical. Changes in observers or the circumstances of observation lead to changes in sensory experiences; how, then, can one defend the claim that a particular experience is veridical? Sense perception is not a source of knowledge; indeed, we must be content with mere appearance and give up any hope of knowing the underlying reality.

The skeptics also introduced the strategy of challenging others' theories of knowledge. How, they asked, can we be sure that this is the correct account of knowledge? The resulting disputes about the criteria for knowledge and epistemic justification are now a central feature of epistemology.

Those who defended knowledge claims were labeled dogmatists. In the first century B.C., the arguments (known as tropes) against dogmatists were collected and formalized. They emphasized the relativity of sense impressions, the possibility of error (as illustrated in cases of acknowledged illusion), and the lack of a defensible criterion of truth. Sextus Empiricus formulated the skeptics' position in its most mature form in the first century A.D.

EPISTEMOLOGY IN MEDIEVAL THOUGHT

Medieval epistemology was heavily influenced by religious matters and concerned largely with the nature of universals. Realists in this dispute argued that universals were existing entities, with the Platonists and Aristotelians disagreeing about the nature of that existence. Conceptualists believed that universals are mental entities, without independent existence. Nominalists held that although there are universal terms or words, they did not refer either to mental entities or substances. These disputes were aimed at working out the entities and processes involved in perception and cognition but surprisingly did not focus on accuracy or truth. Although Plato had been concerned with the pursuit of certainty and knowledge, these concerns would not reappear in full force until the work of Descartes.

St. Augustine

The thinking of St. Augustine (354–430) was strongly influenced by the theories of Aristotle. He understood perception to involve impressions on the soul resulting from stimulation of the body's sensory organs. These impressions are classified by the soul into general categories by a process of inference. These universals are Forms, although, unlike Plato, Augustine takes Forms to be thoughts in God's mind. It follows from this that all knowledge involves the individual's awareness of God. Although his *Contra Academicos* criticized the arguments of the skeptics, answering this challenge was not a central concern of medieval epistemology.

Abelard

Peter Abelard (1079–1142) held a conceptualist view of universals. He believed that they are concepts employed by the mind in judging that objects share common features. These mental concepts are rooted in the perception of particulars; it is from these that the mind abstracts common properties.

St. Thomas Aquinas

The epistemology of Thomas Aquinas (1225–1274) was closer to Aristotle's than that of Augustine. He was a conceptualist in the sense that he regarded universals as mental entities or functions. Even so, individuals that fall under the same universal share important properties; they share a common form. Thus, universals are not entirely in the mind. These objective similarities among external objects are taken by Aquinas as the basis of a form of realism regarding universals.

His account of scientific knowledge shares the foundationalist structure developed by Aristotle. This knowledge arises from demonstrative syllogisms, and the premises of these arguments must themselves be known. Aquinas argues that some of the most fundamental premises will be known immediately, without having to depend on any arguments. These premises, known as first principles, are necessarily true because of the relationship between the subject and predicate concepts (a view that influenced Immanuel Kant's account of analyticity). The epistemic regress argument that Aquinas used to defend this claim would later become an important element of modern foundationalism.

In sense perception, the soul's potentiality to receive Forms results in an image (*phantasma*), although the perceiver is not aware of it at this stage. The intellect then identifies the universals under which this particular image is subsumed. Aquinas is an empiricist in that all knowledge, even that of simple, necessary truths, has its origins in perceptual experience. Without experience, there would be no content on which the mind could operate. Thus, perception provides the ingredients of knowledge, although knowledge does arise directly from these experiences. Again, we see here an influential precursor of empiricism.

William of Ockham

The view of universals held by Ockham (1285–1349) came close to nominalism, the view that universals are general words. For him, words correspond to concepts, and concepts correspond to features of the external world. Both words and concepts can be general; both can refer to collections of things as well as to individual items. Universality is found in the way in which signs are related to that which is signified. In his later work, Ockham stated that universals are concepts in the mind; this move took him closer to conceptionalism.

Unlike his predecessors, Ockham argued that the mind can be directly acquainted with particular objects. The accepted view at that time was that although the senses may be stimulated by particular objects, the mind dealt only with abstractions or representations of those things. Although Duns Scotus (1265–1308) claimed that such representations always involved some degree of confusion, Ockham disagreed, arguing that the senses may pass perfectly clear representations along to the mind. This clarity did not, however, guarantee the accuracy of representations; error was always a possibility. Despite this risk, he claimed that perception could provide one with knowledge of an object's qualities. This is an important innovation: it allows knowledge to include contingent truths in addition to necessary ones. This is the first clear statement of fallibilism, the view that knowledge can arise from fallible sources. This position was not widely held, however, until much later.

SEVENTEENTH-CENTURY RATIONALISM

The skeptical elements of ancient thought had very little influence during the medieval period, but in the sixteenth century the works of Sextus Empiricus, Cicero, and others once again became available and were widely read by scholars. Initially applied to issues of religious doctrine, the arguments of the ancients were soon extended to all other areas of belief. This new skeptical challenge was addressed by both rationalists and empiricists in philosophy's modern period.

Descartes

René Descartes (1596–1650) was influenced both by developments in science and by the disputes and skeptical concerns that accompanied them. This concern with skepticism began a new age in epistemology, and he devised a method to address it. In his *Discourse on Method* (1637), Descartes introduced the "method of doubt," a means of identifying and eliminating all potential sources of error. Any idea or belief in which one can find any possibility of falsehood is to be set aside; one can be certain, then, that what remains is true. Descartes also employs the concept of a clear and distinct idea, one whose parts are all clearly delineated and that can be contemplated with no vagueness or confusion (and with no reliance on memory). Our ordinary beliefs about our surroundings, the past, and so forth are quickly ruled out because of the many possibilities for error. These beliefs might be based on dreams, madness, illusions, faulty memory, and the like. Even our beliefs about logic, geometry, and arithmetic are suspect; we might have a feeling of certainty when we contemplate a falsehood in these areas. The only belief that survives the winnowing process of the method of doubt is the belief that one's own mind exists; this is the famous *cogito ergo sum* ("I think, therefore I am"). On this slender foundation, Descartes planned to rebuild the edifice of knowledge.

In order to accomplish this, he needed to prove that God exists and is not a deceiver. His *Meditations on First Philosophy* (1641) employs versions of the cosmological and ontological arguments to this end and goes on to argue that a God who is a deceiver would therefore be imperfect. Thus, a perfect, nondeceiver God has endowed us with memory, sensory systems, and so forth, along with a strong predisposition to regard the products of these faculties as veridical. God would not have thus created us if our faculties were not generally dependable. The implication is that beliefs or judgments formed by means of these faculties generally *are* veridical; they can err, but only in ways we are capable of identifying and correcting for. Furthermore, God would not permit us to be mistaken about clear and distinct ideas.

Descartes is a substance dualist (it is his view that a human being comprises an extended, unthinking body and a thinking, unextended mind) and believes that the mind is only indirectly aware of objects in the external world. Mental representations of objects include both primary (size, shape, motion, and number) and secondary qualities (color, taste, smell, sound, and so on). We can have clear and distinct ideas of primary qualities, and this assures us that external objects really have size, shape, and so forth. Furthermore, because the primary qualities can be measured and quantified, they can be known by an intuition of the intellect. Our ideas of secondary qualities, however, are not clear and distinct, so we cannot be assured that external objects resemble these ideas.

Aristotle's approach of founding knowledge claims on arguments was influential here. Descartes's foundationalism adapts the system of intuitions and deductions, then in use in mathematics and geometry, to philosophy. A belief qualifies as knowledge if one can show that it is the product of a series of deductions all of whose premises can be traced back to indubitable foundations. This approach is very demanding, however, and opened up the issue of our knowledge of the external world to further investigation and debate.

Descartes is also the originator of modern rationalism, the philosophical school of thought that emphasizes the role of reason (as opposed to sense perception) in gaining knowledge. This approach is developed further in the work of Spinoza and Leibniz.

Malebranche

The epistemology of Nicolas Malebranche (1638–1715) was greatly influenced by that of Descartes. The distinction between primary and secondary qualities is preserved, along with the recognition that the senses are prone to error and thus unable to provide certainty about the world around us. Malebranche's contributions included introducing more fine-grained distinctions between different types of ideas, judgments, and sensations (particularly with respect to the role of the will in their formation) and in arguing that the human mind perceives ideas that are in the mind of God.

Spinoza

Benedict Spinoza (1632–1677) examined the question of whether ideas accurately represent their causes or other states of affairs in the world and took this issue in a new direction. Arguing that there is only one substance, God or Nature, of which both ideas and physical objects are modes, Spinoza concluded that ideas are true or false only from the perspective of an individual human mind. Insofar as all ideas refer to God, they are all accurate, but considered as ideas in a human mind (which is itself a mode of the one universal substance), ideas can be muddled or inaccurate. The truth of an idea or judgment arises not from its correspondence to some independent state of affairs but from its own internal coherence and completeness (which is very like the clearness and distinctness used by Descartes as a criterion of truth).

Knowledge is rooted in one's recognition that ideas follow from the necessity and perfection of God and that these ideas could not possibly be otherwise. What Spinoza labels "full" knowledge or intuition results from grasping how the essence of a thing results from the essence and perfection of God. Reason, a second kind of knowledge that he also calls opinion or imagination arises from sense perception. The ideas generated in this way are generally confused and inadequate, so they do not result directly in knowledge. Instead, our experiences form the basis for many of our universal concepts. Although these vary from person to person and cannot be relied on, a subset of them, called common notions, are shared by us all and form the foundation of science.

As envisioned by Spinoza, science would employ methods much like those of geometry or mathematics. This allows one to move beyond the confusion and inadequacy of particular ideas toward understanding the world as a coherent, necessary whole; thus, science can lead eventually to full knowledge.

Leibniz

Gottfried Wilhelm Leibniz (1646–1716) posited a metaphysic of monads, individual substances each of which reflects the entire cosmos from its own point of view. One's mind is a monad with the special property of self-awareness, and the physical world is (roughly) a set of appearances generated by monads. There are no causal interactions among these entities; monads are "windowless" in that all their properties, including relationships, are internal to them. Each monad "perceives" all the others, so any change in one is accompanied by noncausal changes in all the others. Therefore, one could say that all our ideas are innate and *a priori*.

Leibniz distinguished between necessary and contingent truths. The former, which he called truths of reason, are defined in terms of logical contradiction: each truth of reason is logically equivalent to an identity statement, and the negation of a truth of reason is contradictory.

Our awareness of the world is representative; we are aware of things because they are represented in our minds. Although our minds contain representations of everything that exists, many of these representations are unconscious, and many are vague or confused. Thus, perception is inherently unreliable and error prone.

BRITISH EMPIRICISM

Locke

Reacting against the rationalists, empiricists argue that ideas (and hence knowledge) originate in the senses rather than the mind. John Locke (1632–1704) began his *Essay Concerning Human Understanding* (1690) with an attack on the claim that we have innate ideas. At birth, he argues, the mind is a *tabula rasa* (blank slate), all of whose content originates in experience. His own positive account of human knowledge begins by examining our ideas. These are divided into ideas that originate in our sensory systems (ideas of sense) and ideas resulting from the mind's reflection on those sensory outputs (ideas of reflection). In addition, ideas can be either simple or complex. Locke's empiricism is seen in his claim that all our knowledge rests ultimately on simple ideas of sense.

Our ideas of sense make us aware of both primary and secondary qualities of objects in the external world. Like Descartes and others before him, Locke regards size, shape, motion, and number as primary qualities, noting that each of these can be observed by two or more sense modalities (an observation that can be traced back to Aristotle's discussion of common sensibles). These qualities are inseparable from the objects that possess them. Secondary qualities, which include taste, smell, sound, and color (Aristotle's proper sensibles), arise from the action of objects' primary qualities on the sensory systems of observers and do not resemble the objects that cause them.

Ideas of sense represent the objects that cause them, but our sensory systems are a worrisome source of error. Even when our senses provide us with an accurate likeness of physical objects, we are unable to observe the true nature of those objects, the particles (which Locke calls "corpuscles," following the science of the day) that make them up. As a result, we are generally aware only of objects' nominal essences, not their real essences. Locke's representative realism begins with the supposition that one is directly aware only of the contents of one's own mind; from these contents, one must try to work out whether there is an external world and what it is like. The "veil of perception" that hangs between the observer and the external world has been a potent image, influencing much subsequent epistemological thought.

Knowledge, Locke says, consists in one's recognition of relationships of agreement or disagreement among ideas. All knowledge is either intuitive (grasping at once the agreement or disagreement among ideas), demonstrative (grasping that an idea follows logically from other ideas), or sensitive (knowing through experience that particular, finite entities exist). The requirements for demonstrative knowledge are both stringent and familiar: one must have a clear grasp of the arguments that generate the belief in question as well as recognizing the deductive validity of the structure and the truth of the premises. He acknowledges that we cannot be certain that an external world exists or that its primary qualities are as they seem to be; therefore, we have no deductive knowledge of the world. We have sensitive knowledge of it, but this is a lower, less secure grade of knowledge. In this area, Locke does not take skeptical challenges as seriously as many of his colleagues. This is also seen in Locke's willingness to allow inductive arguments to generate sensitive knowledge despite the possibility of error such arguments introduce.

Berkeley

George Berkeley (1685–1753), troubled by what he regarded as encroaching atheism and skepticism, set out to defend certainty and common sense—with rather startling results. In Locke's theory, ideas of sense represent external objects, and this raises the question of whether these representations are veridical. Berkeley rejects this approach, arguing that ideas can resemble only other ideas, not material objects. Locke's theory also showed that the real essences of mind-independent material substances were largely beyond the limits of human knowledge, and even our limited mental representations of them were prone to error. Therefore, Berkeley chose to do away with material objects altogether, leaving an ontology of only minds and ideas. Physical objects are preserved, but only as clusters of ideas in minds. These ideas are caused in our minds by God (who is also a mind) rather than by the action of matter on observers' sensory surfaces. These radical changes were motivated by the skepticism Berkeley believed must follow from Locke's approach.

This view of physical objects enables Berkeley to conclude that we can be certain that objects are as they appear to us. After all, objects are nothing more than those appearances. The object/representation distinction drawn in Locke's theory is eliminated and along with it the central source of perceptual error and uncertainty. Errors arise only as a result of flawed judgments. The notion of certainty is itself modified in Berkeley's theory. For Locke and Descartes, certainty required ruling out the logical possibility of falsehood, but Berkeley sees it as requiring only the absence of grounds for doubt. This makes certainty easier to attain and thus lightens the burden of proof empiricists have undertaken in defending inferential beliefs.

Hume

David Hume (1711–1776) began with many of the same empiricist underpinnings as Locke and Berkeley but reached very different conclusions about the extent of human knowledge. On Hume's view, sensory experience produces sense impression; imagination and memory produce ideas. Each simple idea has a corresponding sense impression, so all mental contents originate in the senses. Ideas can be related to one another by means of their content; such "relations of ideas" can produce certainty when the mind grasps the necessity of the connection. Ideas can also be related in ways related to how they arise in experience; these "matter of fact" relations often carry considerable conviction, but careful examination reveals that we actually have no compelling reason for accepting these relationships.

This is clearest in the case of causality. We often see event *A* followed by event *B* and conclude that *A* causes *B*. We confidently accept this causal conclusion and even regard the connection between *A* and *B* as necessary; *A* must, we think, be followed by *B*. This is an impression of reflection. Hume argues, however, that this confidence is misplaced and results from a "habit of mind" developed by the constant conjunction of *A* and *B* in our experience. Our beliefs about causal connections are epistemically unjustified. Similarly, although we generally believe in a world of mind-independent material objects, our experience provides us with no compelling evidence to support this view. Again, Hume's views lead to skepticism. Furthermore, Hume raised the problem of induction, pointing out that nothing in our experience justifies our confidence in the uniformity of nature; it may be that unobserved instances are quite unlike the observed ones. Our beliefs about physical objects cannot be deduced from our sense impressions (and we are unable to defend our inductive practices), so Hume's position leads to skepticism regarding the physical world. So limited is human knowledge on Hume's account that one might regard his position as a *reductio ad absurdum* of empiricism.

Although all the arguments point to skepticism, Hume acknowledges that human psychology will not permit us to take this conclusion seriously. We continue using induction, forming beliefs about causation, believing in a world of physical objects, and so forth. This is an interesting development because it suggests separating epistemic evaluations of our beliefs from our voluntary control over them. That is, Hume suggests that many of our beliefs are unjustified despite the fact that we cannot prevent ourselves from believing these things; we are unjustified but blameless. This is an early form of epistemic externalism.

Reid

Thomas Reid (1710–1796) rejected Hume's skeptical conclusions as absurd and set out to defend our commonsense beliefs. He argued that the problem with previous theories lay in the ways in which mental contents had been understood, and he proposed a new distinction between sensations and perceptions. Sensations, exemplified by pain, are phenomenal states with no other object. Perceptions involve a phenomenal experience (a sensation) as well as an object of that experience and a belief in its existence. With this apparatus established, he was able to argue that perceptions do indeed provide compelling evidence about the existence and properties of objects in the external world. This is a form of direct realism and allows sense perception to provide us with knowledge.

KANT AND POST-KANTIAN IDEALISM

Kant

Immanuel Kant (1724–1804), spurred by his reading of a translation of some of Hume's work, set out to explore the nature and extent of human knowledge along with an examination of the metaphysical and psychological issues involved. His *Critique of Pure Reason* (1781, second edition 1787) defends the claim that synthetic *a priori* judgments can yield knowledge. This would show that not all knowledge is rooted in experience and thus that empiricism is mistaken.

Hume had allowed that we have knowledge of relations of ideas (which Kant calls analytic *a priori* truths) but took a skeptical position on at least some matters of fact (which Kant calls synthetic *a posteriori* truths). But Kant argues that Hume has missed an important category of knowledge: that of synthetic *a priori* propositions. This includes propositions about geometry, arithmetic, and some very general truths about the nature of the physical world we experience. For instance, we know that for any two events, either they occur simultaneously or one occurs before the other. Similarly, we know that for any two objects in space, there is a pathway leading from one to the other. This move allows Kant to save more of our knowledge from Hume's skeptical attacks.

Our perceptual experiences (sensible intuitions) necessarily present themselves to us in a spatiotemporal form, but objects as they exist in themselves may not have this structure. Kant expresses this by saying that spatiotemporal qualities are empirically real but transcendentally ideal. Something is said to be objective if it is a feature of how anyone must experience it; objectivity is not to be understood in terms of things-in-themselves. The truth of judgments arises not from their correspondence with mind-independent reality but from their correspondence with the necessary and intersubjective nature of experience. To qualify as knowledge, a judgment must be objectively valid; it must conform to the principles and categories of the understanding. Thus, we have knowledge of the ordinary, physical world of our experience although not of objects as they are in themselves. Our knowledge of our world is saved at the expense of introducing skepticism about a new and mysterious realm.

Post-Kantian Idealism

Johann Fichte (1762–1814) criticized Kant's claim that things-in-themselves are unknowable, arguing that this leaves us with no reason for thinking that things-in-themselves exist. Fichte's response was to reject the notion of things-in-themselves, leaving only experiences; from this starting point, he developed his own idealist position. This was combined with a coherence theory of truth: experiences are regarded as true if they form a coherent, united system.

G. W. F. Hegel (1770–1831) also defended a version of the claim that the world in which we live is one of appearances. Criticizing Kant for restricting the proper functions of reason, Hegel defends the use of reason (in the dialectical method) to resolve the contradictions that arise when philosophical categories are applied. When concepts are applied to experience, a contradiction arises between the immediacy and particularity of what is experienced and the inescapable generality of the concepts under which experience is subsumed. Reason resolves this by invoking a higher-level universal, that of law-likeness. Our knowledge of reality is not direct but is mediated by the application of these concepts or universals.

This position leads Hegel to challenge the claim that one can be certain of the nature of one's current experiences. This attack on the doctrine of the given is important because this is a central component of most empiricist positions. His *Phenomenology of Spirit* (1807) points out that the given is thought to be passive and unmediated and that no knowledge fits that description. Instead, all knowledge is mediated by concepts. This view was very influential in much Continental epistemology in the twentieth century.

Arthur Schopenhauer (1788–1860) found a middle ground between Kant and Hegel, maintaining Kant's insights into the nature of reason and Hegel's idealism, but rejected Kant's categories of judgment and Hegel's dialectical method. Schopenhauer argued that the world is made up of ideas and experiences and that these are linked by various versions of the principle of sufficient reason. On this view, the thing-in-itself is the will; reality is the manifestation of a single, unitary will.

LATE NINETEENTH-CENTURY PHILOSOPHY

Franz Brentano (1838–1917) examined the intentionality of mental acts and argued that the objects or contents of these acts must be real. But what is the object of the mental act when one imagines a nonexistent object? Alexius Meinong (1853–1920) posited nonexistent objects to fill this role; although these do not exist, they "subsist." This was a move back toward realism, led by a linguistic theory according to which the meaning of an expression is given by that to which it refers. Edmund Husserl (1859–1938) also studied consciousness and its objects. His method of *epoché* was intended to identify and set aside all our presuppositions so that consciousness itself could be isolated and examined. All else is studied by the ways in which it manifests itself to consciousness.

In Britain, John Stuart Mill (1806–1873) extended his father's attempt to reduce all knowledge to basic sensations and the ideas we associate with them. The result was a form of phenomenalism, the reduction of all statements about physical objects to ones about "permanent possibilities of sensation." He extended his empiricist approach to our knowledge of mathematics, arguing that mathematical truths are simply generalizations from experience.

Henri Bergson (1859–1941) led an anti-intellectualist response that emphasized our biological nature and needs. The mind divides the contents of consciousness into objects and events according to our biology. For example, the mind's role is to show how one can physically move in relation to an object and to store in memory only that which could be of practical value. There are, he argued, no basic, atomistic experiences as discussed by other theorists.

William James (1842–1910) agreed and argued that the stream of consciousness is more fundamental than the particular ideas abstracted from it. Indeed, all that we take to exist is constructed from fragments drawn from consciousness. He endorsed a form of empiricism combined with a coherentist theory of truth. Because the world is constructed from consciousness and we are directly aware of our own mental contents, we have knowledge by acquaintance of the world. Knowing *about* the world requires selecting portions of one's experience and analyzing it further.

The rise of pragmatism was led by C. S. Peirce (1839–1914) and John Dewey (1859–1952), who linked meaning (and, in James's case, truth) to the practical issues of prediction and explanation. The indicator of knowledge is practical success in scientific endeavors. Peirce attacked foundationalism, arguing that no belief is immune from error or revision. Thus, there can be no absolutely certain basis on which the rest of knowledge can rest. The theory he proposes is fallibilist in that knowledge can arise from sources prone to error. Descartes's method of doubt is also criticized for being psychologically unrealistic. Epistemology, Peirce thought, should examine how we actually form and revise beliefs; this is a significant component in naturalized epistemology.

EPISTEMOLOGY IN NON-WESTERN TRADITIONS

Epistemic issues have certainly been widely examined in non-Western traditions throughout history. Many of the concerns and questions are similar across cultures and eras, although there are important differences in the means by which solutions are formulated and defended. For instance, virtually all cultures and traditions include skeptical challenges and seek adequate responses to them. This often comes up in discussions of history, sense perception, ethics, and the desire to resolve conflicts between opposing views or judgments. Some of these traditions have been substantially influenced by Western thought; for instance, Arabic epistemology is linked with the work of Aristotle and the neo-Platonists.

There are a number of distinct philosophical traditions in Indian thought, and these present different views of the structure of thought, the nature of true or proper thinking, and the nature of the reality we seek to know. Some give an important place to divine revelation and our knowledge of God, while others focus on the nature and significance (or, rather, *in*significance) of the physical world. Many Buddhist traditions, for example, hold that everything in the physical world is ephemeral and insignificant. The epistemic challenge, then, is to dispel ignorance and illusion and grasp the true nature of reality. This may require a sort of mystic enlightenment that goes beyond the reach of ordinary experience and evidence.

The Chinese philosophical traditions also offer a variety of epistemic views and concepts. Once again, the central questions involve responding to skepticism, attaining moral knowledge, settling disputes between opposing views or judgments, and understanding the true nature of reality. The tradition that begins with Confucius emphasizes the existence of a sort of truth that is incapable of illusion or error and seeks sincerity and the means of grasping knowledge. Taoist traditions, by contrast, emphasize that every view is inextricably rooted in a perspective; it may be that there are no absolute truths that apply to all perspectives.

TWENTIETH-CENTURY EPISTEMOLOGY

Moore

G. E. Moore (1873–1958) clarified (but later rejected) the view that beliefs are propositional attitudes and that concepts are components of propositions. He also used an act/object analysis of consciousness in his arguments against idealism. Moore believed that attempts to dissect and refute arguments for skepticism were an unnecessary distraction for philosophers. Instead, he endorsed a commonsense approach according to which one begins with the presupposition that people generally know the things they take themselves to know. Rather than regarding the external world of physical objects as presenting an epistemic challenge (as Locke, Russell, and many others had), he argued that many propositions about external objects are known immediately and with certainty. He famously illustrated this by claiming to know unquestionably that "this is one hand, and this is another." Thus, Moore's position is a form of direct realism.

In analyzing sense perception, Moore endorsed a theory involving sense data although he was unable to provide satisfactory answers to questions about how sense data are related to external, physical objects or how our awareness of sense data can result in knowledge of our surroundings. His is one of the few sense-data approaches that rejected the foundationalist structure endorsed by Bertrand Russell, A. J. Ayer, and others of that period.

Russell

Bertrand Russell (1872–1970) was influenced by the realism of G. E. Moore and the early work of Ludwig Wittgenstein, with the result that his own views further explored propositions, sense data, and the nature of knowledge. He is particularly noted for his distinction between knowledge by description and knowledge by acquaintance. Knowledge by acquaintance is fundamental and provides the basis for all of our knowledge by description. This is essentially a foundationalist structure; Russell argues that knowledge by acquaintance is immune from error, although falsehood can be introduced into the knowledge by description that is based on it. Sense data are known immediately, by acquaintance, and this provides a basis of certainty for beliefs about the external world. Propositions about physical objects get their meaning not from mind-independent lumps of matter but from collections of actual and possible sense data. These collections of sense data are subsumed under concepts or universals when we make statements about them. This view was later attacked by Roderick Chisholm (1916–1999), who pointed out that propositions about physical objects do not entail propositions about sense data (so the two cannot be equivalent).

Logical Positivism

Members of the Vienna Circle, influenced by Wittgenstein's *Tractatus Logico-Philosophicus* (1921) and Ernst Mach's philosophy of science, devised the verification theory of meaning according to which a statement is meaningful only if it is either analytic or empirically verifiable. This was the cornerstone of a new movement known as logical positivism and was intended to preserve mathematics and science while rendering metaphysics and other areas of discussion meaningless. This project soon faced barriers, however. For instance, the verification principle itself is neither analytic nor verifiable but was regarded by most logical positivists as meaningful. There were also disputes within this group about the nature of verification, truth, and science itself. Moritz Schlick (1882–1936) argued that all meaningful statements must be capable of direct verification in one's own experience, but A. J. Ayer (1910–1989) was willing to allow for indirect confirmation of many statements. In addition, Schlick defended a version of the correspondence theory of truth, while Otto Neurath (1882–1945) argued for a coherence theory and Rudolf Carnap (1891–1970) for a conventionalist theory.

Logical positivism exerted a considerable influence on those outside of that movement. For instance, Karl Popper (1902–1994) reversed the notion of verifiability and argued that the role of scientific evidence is to falsify theories. From this he drew a broader account of the nature of science and the hypothetico-deductive method. This implies a form of skepticism in that we can never be certain of what is true; we can know only that certain theories or hypotheses are false.

Ordinary Language Philosophy

The ordinary language movement in philosophy, which is linked chiefly with Oxford University and Wittgenstein (who was at Cambridge), was in large part a response to the challenges of skepticism. As a rough approximation, an ordinary language philosopher might argue that skepticism is unacceptable because it violates the standards for the application of such concepts as knowledge as these are reflected in how we ordinarily think and speak of knowledge. Although J. L. Austin (1911–1960) presented arguments along these lines, he acknowledged that ordinary language alone cannot decisively settle the issue of skepticism; these arguments are to be part of a broader response to that challenge. He also raised influential arguments against the claim that sense data can be known with certainty; instead, all empirical beliefs are corrigible. Moreover, he argued that this need not imply skepticism; knowledge does not require certainty, so its loss does not lead to lost knowledge. Gilbert Ryle (1900–1976) used ordinary language to draw and show the significance of the distinction between propositional knowledge (knowing *that*) and procedural knowledge (knowing *how*).

The Gettier Cases and Responses

For the first half of the twentieth century, it was generally accepted that justified true beliefs qualify as knowledge. This JTB theory of knowledge, which can be traced back to Plato, was challenged by Edmund Gettier's 1963 article "Is Justified True Belief Knowledge?" This presented two cases in which subjects hold justified true beliefs that we clearly do not want to classify as knowledge. In the resulting discussion, some responded to these cases on the anecdotal level, arguing that the beliefs described were not justified and thus did not constitute evidence against the JTB theory of knowledge. Once Gettier had shown the way, however, it was clear that many other examples could be generated, meeting any of the then current claims about the nature of epistemic justification. Many epistemologists then turned their attention to working out what additional criterion must be added to justification and truth to be sufficient for knowledge.

Fred Dretske sought to rule out beliefs that are only accidentally true by adding the requirement that the subject's reasons for holding the belief be conclusive; that is, there must be no possible world in which the subject possesses those reasons and in which that belief is false.[2] Alvin Goldman proposed a criterion that focused on the causal connections between the subject's evidence and the truth of the belief: the evidence and the state of affairs that makes the belief true must be causally linked.[3] Keith Lehrer, Thomas Paxson, David Annis, and others argued that the subject's justification must be undefeated; that is, there must be no additional true proposition that, if added to the subject's stock of beliefs, would undermine the justification for the belief in question.[4] These and other inventive proposals met with only limited success; none was generally accepted as having solved the problem revealed by the Gettier cases. This debate also fueled the rise of externalist theories of knowledge and epistemic justification.

Criteria for Knowledge

The examination of the criteria of knowledge generally begins with the following skeptical challenge. We can claim to know something only if we are absolutely sure about it, only if there is no possibility of error. Because the vast majority of our beliefs could be mistaken in some way, we have little or no knowledge. Most of what we think we know faces the possibility of memory lapses, misinterpretations, and even deceiving demons.

A typical response to this line of skeptical argument is to identify a foundation of certain, error-proof knowledge and build on this a defense of the truth of our other beliefs. These foundations generally include straightforward truths of logic, arithmetic, and geometry and perhaps the current contents of one's phenomenal experience. The skeptic's riposte exploits the difficulty of using the narrow, sterile foundation of absolute certainty as a grounding for all the content and complexity of our ordinary beliefs. A much more promising epistemological strategy has been to argue that certainty is not a necessary condition for knowledge; much of the debate now centers on how to work out criteria of knowledge that strike the right balance between preserving the high epistemic status of knowledge and allowing for the messiness and imperfection of ordinary belief.

Theories of Epistemic Justification

The views of René Descartes and the empiricists illustrate a common foundationalist structure for transmitting epistemic justification from basic beliefs to inferentially justified ones. Justification is thus seen as something anchored in certainty and transmitted by (more or less) truth-preserving pathways to other beliefs. One of the difficulties faced by this approach is the problem of finding enough beliefs of which we are certain and enough strong connections between them and the rest of our beliefs to yield plausible epistemic evaluations. For instance, is one well justified in believing that the container on the table holds salt? Certainty about geometric principles, sense data, and a few other matters does not seem to be linked in the right ways to this commonplace belief, and foundationalists risk succumbing to skepticism about many beliefs we confidently regard as true.

Inspired in part by a growing recognition of the relevance of empirical psychology to epistemological issues, a number of twentieth-century theorists turned to reliabilism. This approach links a belief's degree of epistemic justification to the reliability of the process by which it was formed or maintained. Reliabilist theories are typically externalist; the subject need not be aware of the belief-forming process or its reliability. This is a significant development in that it draws the concept of epistemic justification away from the concept of ethical justification by undermining the former's traditional connection with the view that subjects have voluntary control over their beliefs and can thus be held accountable for them.

Reliabilism has been subjected to two types of criticisms. The first arises from its departure from the traditional epistemic internalism (the view that epistemic evaluations should be undertaken from the subject's own point of view). Reliabilist theories yield intuitively implausible assessments of some beliefs, as is illustrated by cases in which the subject is unaware that she is reliably clairvoyant. Beliefs formed by means of this clairvoyance are highly justified according to reliabilism, but we are inclined to regard them as poorly justified because the subject cannot successfully defend them. While some reliabilists have sought to align themselves with these inclinations, others argue that internalism is flawed and that cases that depend on it can be dismissed.

The second type of criticism addresses technical issues involved in determining reliability and individuating belief-forming processes. Although the measurement of reliability plays a central role in reliabilism, surprisingly little technical work has been done in working out the details. In addition, before the reliability of a belief-forming process can be measured, that process must be clearly identified. This has proved to be very challenging because an instance of belief formation seems to instantiate many different belief-forming processes, each with its own level of reliability. There has been difficulty in finding a clear, principled, and psychologically plausible means of deciding which process to select for the purpose of epistemically assessing a belief.

Naturalized Epistemology

Beginning with W. V. O. Quine's 1969 article "Epistemology Naturalized" (in his *Ontological Relativity and Other Essays*), the relationship between epistemology and the empirical sciences—particularly empirical psychology and the neurosciences—has been a source of considerable debate. Some, like the reliabilists, seek to incorporate findings in cognitive science and the neurosciences into their theories, while others, notably Patricia and Paul Churchland, argue that the entire epistemic enterprise should be replaced by (or at least fundamentally revised in light of) a completed neuroscience. Radical forms of naturalized epistemology, such as that proposed by Quine, eliminate the normativity of traditional epistemology, replacing it with purely descriptive science.

Social Epistemology

The concern with social epistemology began in nineteenth-century continental philosophy and social theory. Its roots can also be traced to Thomas Reid (1710–1796) and his claim that social factors play an important role in belief. This movement lays particular stress on the social context in which authority figures are identified, research programs are developed, and beliefs are transmitted. This has led to compelling criticisms of epistemology's tendency to examine the individual believing subject, abstracted from the social, political, and institutional context as though these were irrelevant and distracting factors. Social epistemology has brought greater understanding of the nature of testimony, common sense, consensus, and the cognitive division of labor. It also sheds light on the workings of science.

Feminist Epistemology

Another recent development in epistemology is the emergence of a diverse and growing body of feminist epistemological theory and criticism. This movement shares some important concerns with social epistemology, notably a sensitivity to the social, political, and institutional context in which beliefs are formed and assessed. To this basis, feminist epistemologists add a particular concern with women, minorities, and other oppressed groups. Particular attention has been paid to the ways in which social and political power are used to legitimate the experiences and knowledge claims of some while dismissing or marginalizing those of others. The traditional epistemological project of finding *the* criteria for knowledge or epistemic justification is criticized as reflecting only the perspectives and concerns of the white, male, wealthy elite and dismissing all other groups and ways of knowing. An important aspect of this is the criticism of the traditional ideals of rationality, truth, objectivity, and value neutrality.

THE FUTURE OF EPISTEMOLOGY

The criticisms of the traditional epistemological project and the insights offered by new approaches suggest that considerable changes are in store. As epistemology continues to evolve, believers will be placed in a rich sociopolitical context whose influence on evidence, authority, and inquiry will be better understood. Developments in the neurosciences will continue to challenge traditional assumptions about propositional attitudes and mental processes, profoundly affecting our understanding of epistemology's essential normativity. People will continue to believe that Elvis is alive and that space aliens are living among us, but we will have an improved understanding of why they *think* their beliefs are justified. And we will still have a lingering suspicion that the skeptics might be right after all.

NOTES

1. Citations for pre-Socratic sources are to H. Diels, *Die Fragmente der Vorokratiker*, 6th ed., 3 vols., rev. W. Krantz (Berlin, 1952). Information about the pre-Socratics is drawn from J. H. Lesher, "Early Interest in Knowledge," in *The Cambridge Companion to Early Greek Philosophy*, ed. A. A. Long (Cambridge: Cambridge University Press, 1999), 225–49.

2. Fred Dretske, "Conclusive Reasons," *Australasian Journal of Philosophy* 49 (1971): 1–22.

3. Alvin Goldman, "A Causal Theory of Knowing," *Journal of Philosophy* 64, no. 2 (1967): 355–72.

4. Keith Lehrer and Thomas Paxson, "Knowledge: Undefeated Justified True Belief," reprinted in *Essays on Knowledge and Justification*, ed. G. Pappas and M. Swain (Ithaca, N.Y.: Cornell University Press, 1978), 146–54; David Annis, "Knowledge and Defeasibility," reprinted in Pappas and Swain, *Essays on Knowledge and Justification*, 155–59.

The Dictionary

– A –

A *POSTERIORI* KNOWLEDGE. *See* A *PRIORI/A POSTERIORI* KNOWLEDGE.

A *PRIORI/A POSTERIORI* KNOWLEDGE. Although the *a priori/ a posteriori* distinction can be applied to **propositions, concepts, truths,** and so on, the focus here is on its application to **knowledge.** Knowledge is *a posteriori* when it is based on **experience.** The most common definition of *a priori* knowledge is **Immanuel Kant**'s: knowledge that is independent of **experience.** The *a priori* side of this distinction is more complex and has been the subject of more debate. This distinction is significant because the justification for *a priori* beliefs is generally held to be less vulnerable to **skeptical** attack.

A priori knowledge may still involve experience. As Kant has suggested, it may be that experience is required to acquire the concepts involved in the *a priori* knowledge or that experience is required to entertain the proposition.

The independence of *a priori* knowledge from experience can be formulated negatively or positively. A common negative formulation states that a **belief** is independent of experience if its **justification** is independent of experience; nothing is said about what this justification *would* depend on. A positive formulation would state the type of experience-independent justification a belief would require in order to qualify as *a priori* knowledge. This evidence might include the belief's being logically **necessary** or its being rationally unrevisable. When simply understanding the believed proposition is enough to make clear that it must be true, the resulting knowledge is said to be *a priori*. This view has been criticized for not providing a sufficiently detailed explanation of what is meant by understanding a proposition in such a way as to "see" that it must be true. Knowledge might also be said to be *a priori* if its justification arises from **intuition** or intuitive apprehension. Here again, questions arise about what this mental faculty is and how it is able to generate justification.

Although intuition and intuitive apprehension may be types of experience, knowledge that is based on them still qualifies as *a priori*. Therefore, a distinction must be drawn among types of experience, showing which types make resulting knowledge *a posteriori* and which do not. As this line is usually drawn, **sense perception** and **memory** are types of experience that result in *a posteriori* knowledge. **Introspection** is the subject of continuing debate, with some arguing that it can be a source of *a priori* knowledge, while others maintain that it cannot.

The debate surrounding *a priori* knowledge includes **arguments** about whether *a priori* knowledge is limited to necessary truths or whether **contingently** true propositions can be known *a priori* as well. It seems clear, however, that the necessity or contingency of the proposition alone cannot settle the question of whether knowledge is *a priori*; one would have to examine the way in which this belief is justified as well.

A priori knowledge has also been formulated in terms of rational unrevisability. A belief is said to be rationally unrevisable if it would be irrational to revise it in the light of any future experience (weak unrevisability) or perhaps in the light of any future evidence of any sort (strong unrevisability). This approach has been criticized for confusing the relationship between justifying evidence with **defeating** evidence.

Defenders of *a priori* knowledge often argue as follows: A particular set of propositions (e.g., necessarily true propositions or **analytic** propositions) cannot be known *a posteriori* (i.e., on the basis of experience), but we do know these propositions, so this knowledge must be *a priori*. For instance, Kant argues that although experience might show us that a particular arithmetic proposition is true, it cannot show us that it is *necessarily* true; therefore, if we know it is necessarily true, this knowledge must be *a priori*. Furthermore, it is often argued that no experience could qualify as compelling evidence against such beliefs; this is another aspect of the belief's independence from experience.

Critics argue that certain kinds of experience *could* qualify as compelling evidence against hitherto accepted mathematical propositions. This is linked to arguments by **W. V. O. Quine** and **Hilary Putnam** that *no* proposition is immune from rational revision. Defenders of *a priori* knowledge respond that knowledge may be *a priori* even though it may be subject to later rational revision. *See also* ANALYTICITY; EMPIRICISM; RATIONALISM.

ABDUCTION. The **logic** of abduction, first described by **Charles S. Peirce** and later developed by N. R. Hanson, is used to establish and evaluate the standards for determining whether a **hypothesis** is worth testing at a given stage of an investigation as well as to establish standards for determining what insights can be salvaged from rejected **theories** in order to produce improved theories. Abduction seeks to explain how we formulate hypotheses that are worth testing; thus, this is a logic that is more fundamental than that which governs empirical **induction**. **Hans Reichenbach** distinguishes between the sort of logic used in the context of **justification** and that used in the context of **discovery**. His view is that philosophy has much to contribute regarding the former but that the latter requires a different approach, dominated by **psychology**.

Some critics argue that although there may be a psychology of discovery and of the formulation of hypotheses, this is not correctly described as a form of logic. Others argue that the abductive **logic of discovery** is not genuinely distinct from the logic of justification. *See also* HYPOTHETICO-DEDUCTIVE METHOD; SCIENCE; TESTABILITY.

ABSTRACT ENTITY. An entity having no spatiotemporal characteristics and having no **causal** efficacy. The existence of abstracta is disputed, but defenders argue that they exist and include such things as universals, pure sets, numbers, geometric figures, **propositions**, relations, and other entities. Abstract entities are sometimes linked to the process of abstracting features shared by particular entities; for example, greenness can be abstracted from the set of all green things.

The debate regarding the existence of abstract entities can be traced back to **Plato**'s claim that the **Forms** (a type of abstract object) exist as well as **Aristotle**'s denial of this claim. In modern philosophy, **rationalists** tend to defend abstract entities, and **empiricists** tend to reject them. **W. V. O. Quine** argues that we should conclude that abstract entities exist only if their existence is required for the **truth** of an accepted **theory**. *See also* REALISM/ANTIREALISM; THEORETICAL ENTITY.

ACCESS. *See* EXTERNALISM/INTERNALISM; INTROSPECTION.

ACQUAINTANCE, KNOWLEDGE BY. *See* KNOWLEDGE.

ACT/OBJECT ANALYSIS. This **analysis** states that every **experience** with content includes an object of that experience and a subject who is having that experience. The subject is related to the object by an act of awareness. The object of an experience might be a physical object (as in the experience of seeing a table), but experiences such as hallucinations or dreams have some other sort of object. There is disagreement among act/object **theories** about what this sort of object might be; suggestions include properties, Meinongian objects, and **sense data**. The nature of the relationship between the objects of experience and the objects of **sense perception** is also disputed. **Representative realists** argue that these objects are usually distinct, while **direct realists** and others deny this. *See also* ADVERBIAL THEORY OF PERCEPTION; EXPERIENCE; GIVEN, THE.

ADORNO, THEODOR (1903–1969). German philosopher and social theorist. He rejects the claim that there can be a privileged standpoint from which to conduct epistemic evaluation. Socioeconomic conditions prevent us from understanding our situation and from being free. In rejecting the **logic** of identity (and the modern **science** that relied on it), he emphasizes the importance of developing a form of **dialectical** thought that encompassed the acceptance of some negative contradictions. Logic and Enlightenment reasoning are part of a system of sociopolitical domination. *See also* CONTINENTAL EPIS-

TEMOLOGY; DEATH OF EPISTEMOLOGY; EPISTEMIC RELA-
TIVISM; FEMINIST EPISTEMOLOGY; MARXISM.

ADVERBIAL THEORY OF PERCEPTION. The view that the
act/object analysis of **experience** is mistaken and that the **grammatical** object of statements describing experiences can be **analyzed**
as an adverb. For **example**, "*S* sees something red" would be rewritten as "*S* sees redly," and "*S* sees a red rectangle" would be rewritten
as "*S* sees red-rectangularly." This approach has the advantage of doing away with the necessity of finding, for every experience, an object that the subject is experiencing. This is particularly valuable
when the subject is dreaming or hallucinating. Instead of focusing on
the object of such experiences, we should think of the grammatical
object of descriptions of experience as functioning as a modifier explaining the *way* in which the subject is experiencing.

The adverbial **theory** faces the **many properties problem**, which
points out this theory's apparent inability to provide an adequate adverbial account of complex experiences. If I see a red circle and a
blue square, the adverbial analysis might be that I see redly-circlely-
bluely-squarely. The difficulty is that this description would also
seem to describe my experience of a red square and a blue circle. Defenders of the adverbial theory reply that adverbial descriptions can
be adapted to make clear the scope of each adverb and thus make the
required distinctions. *See also* REPRESENTATIVE REALISM;
SENSE PERCEPTION.

ALETHIC MODALITIES. In the history of philosophy, the four
modes in which a **proposition** can be true or false: **necessity, contingency**, possibility, and impossibility. In effect, a proposition might
be true but possibly false (contingently true), false but possibly true
(contingently false), true and not-possibly false (necessarily true), or
false and not-possibly true (necessarily false). *See also* POSSIBLE
WORLDS; TRUTH.

al-FĀRĀBĪ, ABU NASR (870–950). Also called Abunaser; known in
Latin as Alpharabius. Islamic philosopher; born in Turkestan, taught
in Baghdad. He played a key role in introducing Greek philosophy,
particularly that of **Aristotle** and **Plato**, into Islamic thought.

al-GHAZĀLĪ, ABU HAMID (1058–1111). Islamic philosopher, born in Khurasan and educated in Nishapur. He taught law and theology at the seminary he headed in Baghdad. His quest for **certainty** eventually led him to resign his position, abandon his family, and embark on a solitary quest for truth (*al-Haqq*). Documented in his *The Deliverance from Error* (ca. 1100), this search led him to regard **sense perception** and reasoning as prone to error and certainty as dependent on divine grace. *See also* REVELATION.

ALGORITHM. A finite procedure for generating an appropriate symbolic output from a symbolic input such that no step of the procedure requires any understanding or insight. The Church–Turing thesis states that an algorithm comprises a finite instruction set; a computational system for computing in accordance with those instructions, including methods for computing, storing, and recalling information; and computations that are carried out in a determinate, discrete, and stepwise fashion. A Turing machine is an abstraction of a system capable of carrying out algorithmic calculations.

A function is algorithmic if at least one algorithm exists that will yield the correct output given any acceptable input for that function. Such functions are also said to be algorithmically computable, effectively computable, or simply computable. *See also* CHURCH'S THESIS.

al RĀZĪ, ABU BAKR (ca. 854–932). Persian philosopher and physician; he practiced medicine in Rayy and Baghdad. In **epistemology**, he warns against reliance on **revelation**, maintaining that **rationality**, which has been given by **God** to everyone, is enough to yield **knowledge**.

ALSTON, WILLIAM P. (1921–). American philosopher; he taught at Syracuse University. William P. Alston has made significant contributions to **epistemology** in many areas, including the **analysis** of **justification** and **knowledge**, **epistemic principles**, the **foundationalism/coherentism** debate, the **externalism/internalism** debate, **perception**, and **religious knowledge**. Many of the distinctions he introduced now occupy important places in the literature.

Alston's understanding of **epistemic levels** makes clear, for instance, that one might be justified in believing that *p* without being justified in *believing* that one's **belief** that *p* is justified. This has been useful in explaining and defending **foundationalist theories** of **epistemic justification**. He also makes clear the difference between **deontological** views of justification (according to which justification results from fulfilling epistemic duties) and "strong position" views (according to which justification indicates that the subject is in a good position to be correct in believing that *p*). This, in turn, helps clarify the disagreement between internalist and externalist views of justification. Roughly put, the internalists evaluate beliefs from the standpoint of the subject, whereas the externalists evaluate beliefs from the standpoint of an **omniscient observer**.

Alston's **theory** of justification combines elements of internalism and externalism: *S* is justified in believing that *p* if and only if *S* has appropriate introspective **access** to the grounds of this belief, and these grounds place *S* in a strong position with respect to believing that *p* (i.e., these grounds make it likely that *S*'s belief that *p* is true). In general, he takes this condition to apply to knowledge as well, although he argues that in some cases *S* can know that *p* without justification (and therefore without introspective access to the grounds of that belief).

In exploring the role of **perception** in justification and knowledge, Alston makes clear the nature of **epistemic circularity**. He argues that *S* can know that *p*, where the belief that *p* is based on perception, even though *S* does not know that perception is **reliable**. Although some attempts to establish the reliability of perception involve a species of circularity, this need not prevent one from being justified in believing—or even knowing—that perception is reliable. This, of course, plays an important role in refuting certain forms of **skepticism**.

Alston's recent work includes defending the **theory of appearing** as an account of perception and developing an account of **doxastic** practices. The latter falls within the boundaries of **metaepistemology** and explains that justification is based in certain social practices. He has also developed an account of perception according to which **God** can be perceived; this allows religious beliefs to be justified and to qualify as knowledge. *See also* INTROSPECTION.

ALTERNATIVE COHERENT SYSTEMS OBJECTION. *See* CO-HERENTISM.

AMBIGUITY. A word, sentence, structure, or figure for which two or more interpretations are available. Homonymy is ambiguity arising from different words with the same sound, such as read (verb: reading a book) and reed (noun: a plant). Polysemy is ambiguity arising from a single word with different meanings, such as lead (verb: to guide) and lead (noun: a dense metal). Structural ambiguity arises in sentences when they may be parsed in two or more ways, such as "He cut down the tree with an orange ribbon." (Does the orange ribbon identify the tree that was cut, or is it the implement used to do the cutting?) This ambiguity may arise because the scope of an operator is unclear, such as "Illegal drug test." (Is this a test for illegal drugs, or is the testing itself illegal?) There can also be ambiguity in interpreting drawings, such as **Ludwig Wittgenstein**'s duck/rabbit figure.

AMPLIATIVE INFERENCE. Any **inference** whose conclusion goes beyond the content of the premises. Such inferences are **inductive** rather than **deductive**; they do not guarantee the **truth** of their conclusions. *See also* INDUCTION; LOGIC.

ANALOGY, ARGUMENT FROM. An **argument** from analogy is a form of **inductive** argument and may have categorical or statistical forms. The categorical argument from analogy has this form:

1. All *f*s that have been examined have characteristic *g*.
2. This *f* that has not been examined has characteristic *g*.

The statistical argument from analogy has this form:

1. *N* percent of the *f*s that have been examined have characteristic *g*.
2. There is a **probability** of *N* percent that this *f* that has not been examined has characteristic *g*.

Arguments from analogy provide stronger support for their conclusions if the objects (or classes of objects) that are described in the premises share many characteristics with the objects (or classes of objects) referred to in the conclusions. It is important that these shared characteristics stand in a **causal** or other **explanatory** relationship to the characteristic, *g*, about which the conclusion is drawn. The presence of significant points of disanalogy weakens this support.

A noteworthy application of the argument from analogy is in providing support for the **belief** that there are **other minds**. Although we interpret many of our **experiences** as interactions with other minds, skeptics point out that this belief could be false; it could be that other human beings have no mental states, and their behavior could arise from some mindless reaction to stimuli. One response to this challenge is to note the many features that one has in common with other human beings. We have many physiological similarities (including neurological similarities), we exhibit complex behaviors that are sensitive to circumstance, we can respond well to novel situations, and so forth. The subject presenting this argument has a mind, so it is likely that others have minds as well. This argument is weakened by the **fact** that it must begin with only a single case of a mind and from this infer the existence of millions of others; this seems to be a **hasty generalization**. *See also* INDUCTION; OTHER MINDS, PROBLEM OF; PRIVACY OF MENTAL STATES; SKEPTICISM; SOLIPSISM.

ANALYSIS. The process of breaking down a **concept, proposition, fact**, or statement into its simplest component parts. That which is analyzed is the analysandum, and the result of the analysis is the analysans. Some philosophers, notably **Bertrand Russell**, argue that analysis is the primary methodology of philosophy.

The **paradox of analysis** expresses a fundamental difficulty faced by this approach. In an adequate analysis, the analysandum and the analysans will be equivalent. If this is so, why do some cases of apparently successful analysis produce an analysans that does not seem to be equivalent to the analysandum? In addition, if the analysans is equivalent to the analysandum, why is the result not trivial and uninformative?

ANALYTIC/SYNTHETIC DISTINCTION. *See* ANALYTICITY.

ANALYTICITY. In his *An Essay Concerning Human Understanding* (1690), **John Locke** states that a **proposition** is analytic either if it states an identity (e.g., a cat is a cat) or if the predicate is contained in the subject (e.g., a cat is an animal). He contrasts analytic propositions with synthetic ones, which convey new, instructive information. **Immanuel Kant**'s explanation of analyticity, presented in his *Prolegomena to Any Future Metaphysic* (1783), focuses on **concept** containment and adds that a proposition is analytic if its denial results in a logical contradiction. Kant understands concept containment as a logical relationship: To say that the consequent of a **conditional proposition** is contained within its antecedent is to say that the consequent can be logically derived from the antecedent.

Analyticity can also be defined in terms of **logic**; one might argue that a proposition is analytic if it is true in virtue of its logical form (e.g., any proposition of the form "*p* or not-*p*" is analytic). **Gottlob Frege**, in his *Foundations of Arithmetic* (1884), resists Kant's **psychological** approach to understanding analyticity and defends logical containment as the most helpful understanding. His view makes analytic propositions the logical consequences of definitions and the laws of logic. **Rudolf Carnap** extends this view, replacing Frege's use of definitions with what he called "meaning postulates." These universally quantified logical statements spell out the content of concepts, such as $(\forall x)$ (x is a cat $\rightarrow$ x is an animal).

The distinction between analytic and synthetic propositions is attacked by **W. V. O. Quine**, notably in his "Two Dogmas of Empiricism" (1953). He rejects Carnap's meaning postulates, arguing that they cannot readily be generalized to other languages and that they still do not explain what it really means for a proposition to be analytic. Quine also argues that this distinction cannot be successfully drawn. This argument accompanies **Hilary Putnam**'s attack on Frege's traditional theory of meaning. Putnam also attacks the concept of analyticity, arguing that it cannot be understood as a logical concept. *See also* EMPIRICISM; RATIONALISM.

ANAMNESIS. Anamnesis is a form of recollection or **memory** and plays a central role in **Plato**'s **epistemology**. In the *Meno*, anamnesis is used to explain how an uneducated slave boy is able to answer **Socrates**' questions about geometry. In the *Phaedo*, anamnesis is used to explain how we uncover our **knowledge** of the **Forms** and hence how we possess various **concepts** that we could not have gained through **experience**. Interestingly, anamnesis is not employed in Plato's discussion of epistemology in the *Republic*. *See also A PRIORI/A POSTERIORI* KNOWLEDGE.

ANIMAL FAITH. *See* SANTAYANA, GEORGE.

ANSELM, SAINT (1033–1109). Italian-born English philosopher and theologian, also known as Anselm of Canterbury. He is noted for his ontological **argument** for **God**'s existence. This begins with an **idea** of a being greater than which none can be imagined. Because a being that exists in **reality** is greater than one that exists merely in the intellect, God must exist in reality. Anselm's *Proslogion*, his most notable philosophical work, attempts to demonstrate that God exists and possesses certain properties. *See also* RELIGIOUS KNOWLEDGE.

ANTINOMY. An antinomy is a situation in which both a **proposition** and its negation are presented as conclusions of **arguments** and our inspection of these arguments gives us no indication that either is unsound. An antinomy would be solved by showing that at least one of these arguments is unsound. **Zeno of Elea**, for example, argues that motion is impossible, but we also have arguments for the conclusion that motion is possible. If neither argument seems flawed, then we have an antinomy. In his *Critique of Pure Reason* (1781), **Immanuel Kant** argues that the world has a beginning in space and time and that it does *not* have such a beginning. He attempts to solve this antinomy by arguing that both arguments are flawed in that they employ "pure reason" and fail to take **sense experience** properly into account. *See also* APORIA.

ANTIREALISM. *See* REALISM/ANTIREALISM.

APODEICTIC. A **proposition** is said to be apodeictic when its **truth** can be demonstrated in such a way that it rules out even the possibility of that proposition being false. In the *Posterior Analytics*, **Aristotle** defines an apodeictic proposition as one that is logically deduced from premises that are guaranteed to be true. This term may be used more loosely to describe a proposition that could not reasonably be denied or one that must be true (regardless of any **argument** we may have for it). *See also* CERTAINTY; DEDUCTION; LOGIC; REASONS FOR BELIEF.

APORIA. Any very difficult problem facing our attempts to extend our **knowledge**, especially when there are equally strong **arguments** both for and against any solution to that problem. An **antinomy** is an **example** of an aporia. *See also* PARADOX.

APPEARANCE/REALITY. The distinction between what is (and what it is like) and what appears to be. **Realism** traditionally describes the relationship between the two this way: Appearances do not determine the nature of reality, and reality need not generate any appearances. The central epistemic question, then, is whether the appearances we **experience** justify our **beliefs** regarding reality. **Idealism** and **phenomenalism** hold that all statements about reality are reducible to statements about appearances. *See also* BERKELEY, GEORGE; EMPIRICISM; EPISTEMIC JUSTIFICATION; EXPERIENCE; LOCKE, JOHN; REALISM/ANTIREALISM; REPRESENTATIVE REALISM; SENSE PERCEPTION; SKEPTICISM.

APPERCEPTION. Introduced by **Gottfried Leibniz**, this term refers to one's inner awareness, or **self-consciousness**, as contrasted with **perception**, or outer awareness. Leibniz holds that one might have **experiences** or mental states of which one is unaware. **Immanuel Kant** describes the transcendental unity of apperception as the unity of one's experience, one's recognition of all of one's experiences as belonging to one. (This unity is transcendental rather than **empirical** because it is presupposed by **consciousness** and cannot be gained through consciousness.) This transcendental unity of apperception plays an important role in Kant's **arguments** against **skepticism** about the **external world**. *See also* APPEARANCE/REALITY; INTROSPECTION; PRIVACY OF MENTAL STATES.

AQUINAS, THOMAS (1225–1274). Thomas Aquinas, a theologian and philosopher, was born near Naples. In his work on **epistemology**, he began with the study of cognition. In his *Summa Theologica* (ca. 1267–1274), he agrees with **Aristotle** that in cognition the soul is assimilated to the object of cognition; that is, the soul takes on the characteristics of the object of cognition. The soul's activity of understanding involves grasping objects by means of **sense perception** (which involves the soul's taking on the properties of that object) and linking the natures of subjects and accidents into subject–predicate structures (or **propositions**). In addition to taking in new information through sense perception, the soul can also draw **inferences** from past **observations** to gain **knowledge**.

Aquinas argues that the clearest cases of knowledge involve the **propositional attitude** of *scientia*. To have *scientia* with respect to something is to have a complete grasp of it and be **certain** of its **truth**; it is to regard a proposition as true on the basis of grounds that guarantee its truth. He agrees with Aristotle that only demonstrative syllogisms can provide such a ground (*Sententia libri Ethiconrum* [*Commentary on Aristotle's Posterior Analytics*], ca. 1248). Thus, to have *scientia* with respect to some proposition, one must be in possession of premises that are well grounded epistemically. This view has a **foundationalist** structure: Some of these premises will themselves have an inferential epistemic basis, but others will have their positive epistemic status by their very nature. In describing these epistemic first principles, he claims that some get their epistemic status because we recognize that the predicate of the proposition is contained within the subject, and we recognize that this guarantees the proposition's truth. Some such propositions are too complex for their **necessary** truth to be apprehended by the cognizer. In addition, such propositions will generally be about **abstractions**, such as **logic** or mathematics; finding first principles regarding the material world is much more difficult.

Aquinas also addresses the question of how our **sense experience** of particular objects can lead to our understanding of universals. He rejects **Plato's theory** that we have direct acquaintance with the **Forms** and claims that sense perception provides the content for all human cognition. Our experiences are always of particulars, but our active intellect enables us to produce intelligible universals from this. These universals can then form the subjects and predicates of propositions that can function as epistemic first principles, or foundations.

We can have *scientia* with respect to only a limited range of propositions. A somewhat lower level of positive epistemic status results from **dialectical** reasoning. Conclusions drawn in this way are **probable** but not certain. The dialectic process may begin with premises that are **justified** but not certain and may use argument forms that cannot ensure that true premises would lead to a true conclusion (e.g.,

arguments from analogy, enumerative induction). Conclusions formed in this way are not *scientia* but opinion or **belief**.

To his account of strict demonstrative reasoning, Aquinas adds that some propositions about sensible objects may have high epistemic status for us simply because our senses play a central role in providing content for cognition; we find such propositions easiest to accept. When such propositions are used as premises in a **deductive** argument, the result is not unqualified *scientia* but a "factual demonstration" that fails to guarantee truth. **Natural science** provides this qualified form of knowledge about the corporeal world. Similarly, since we cannot grasp **God**'s essence, our theological knowledge is also a qualified form of *scientia*. *See also* EPISTEMIC LEVELS; EPISTEMIC PRINCIPLE; INDUCTION.

ARABIC EPISTEMOLOGY. Philosophers in the Arab world who dealt with epistemological questions represent a number of different ethnic and religious backgrounds (although much of this work is linked with Islam). It is greatly influenced by the late period of Greek philosophy and in turn influenced later medieval philosophy.

Major figures in this tradition include some who were heavily influenced by **neo-Platonism**, including al-Kindī (d. 873), as-Sarakhsī (d. 889), Abū-Zayd al-Balkhī (d. 934), and al-'Āmirī (d. 992). Others were more influenced by **Aristotle** and his commentators; these include Mattā Ibn Yūnus (d. 940), **al-Fārābī** (870–950), Yahyā Ibn 'Adī (d. 974), and 'Īsā Ibn Zur'a (d. 1008). The central issues they addressed include the nature of **rationality** and proper thought, **revelation** and **knowledge** of **God**, and the role of **sense perception**.

ARGUMENT. An argument is a series of statements (the premises) presented in support of another statement (the conclusion). Arguments are commonly classified by the degree of support they can provide for their conclusions. **Deductive** arguments can provide conclusive support for their conclusions, and **inductive** arguments provide substantial but inconclusive support. A valid deductive argument is one that preserves **truth**: If the premises are all true, then the conclusion is guaranteed to be true as well. A valid deductive argument comprised of premises that are all true is said to be sound. If the premises of an inductive argument are all true, the conclusion is only **probably** true. Deductive **logic** provides techniques for determining whether a deductive argument is valid, and inductive logic provides techniques for determining how much support the premises of an inductive argument provide for its conclusion. *See also* INDUCTION; INFORMAL FALLACIES; LOGIC; PROOF; TRANSCENDENTAL ARGUMENT.

ARGUMENT FROM ANALOGY. *See* ANALOGY, ARGUMENT FROM.

ARGUMENT FROM AUTHORITY. *See* INFORMAL FALLACIES.

ARGUMENT(S) FROM EVIL. Arguments drawn from **observations** of evil in the world for the conclusion that the all-knowing, all-powerful, all-benevolent **God** described in Judeo-Christian theology does not exist. The **deductive** version of the argument seeks to show that the existence of evil is **logically** inconsistent with the existence of God. The **inductive** version seeks to show that the existence of evil makes the existence of God very improbable. *See also* RELIGIOUS KNOWLEDGE.

ARGUMENT FROM ILLUSION. *See* RELEVANT ALTERNATIVES; SKEPTICAL ALTERNATIVES; SKEPTICISM.

ARGUMENTUM AD BACULUM. *See* INFORMAL FALLACIES.

ARGUMENTUM AD HOMINEM. *See* INFORMAL FALLACIES.

ARGUMENTUM AD IGNORANTIAM. *See* INFORMAL FALLACIES.

ARGUMENTUM AD MISERICORDIAM. *See* INFORMAL FALLACIES.

ARGUMENTUM AD POPULUM. *See* INFORMAL FALLACIES.

ARGUMENTUM AD VERECUNDIAM. *See* INFORMAL FALLACIES.

ARISTOTLE (384–322 B.C.). Aristotle, a Greek philosopher born in Stagira, addresses various epistemological issues. In the *Posterior Analytics*, he describes the nature of scientific **knowledge** (*epistêmê*).

Demonstrative **sciences** deduce theorems from **necessarily** true first principles. I know some **proposition** only if I can present a **justification** for that proposition and explain why it is a satisfactory justification. Ultimately, the justification must be anchored in a proposition that does not require any further justification. The first principles in this **foundationalist** structure are not **observations** or propositions whose **truth** is immediately obvious to **intuition**; instead, they are fundamental principles of that science.

The **epistemology** of **sense perception** is discussed in his *De Anima*. Perception is a capacity of the soul by which the perceiver becomes like the object perceived. In becoming like the object, the perceiver takes on the form (but not the matter) of that object. Aristotle claims that each sense is **infallible** about the qualities that are peculiar to that sense; for example, vision is infallible about color, and hearing is infallible about sounds. Qualities such as size, shape, and number are detected by a "**common sense**," or a unified perceptual faculty. Perception seems to be regarded as a **reliable** foundation for knowledge.

Scientific investigation (*historia*) begins with observations or **appearances** (*phainomena*), which are employed in **induction** (*epagôgê*) and which result in experience (*empeira*). Experience, in turn, provides the first principles of the science. Observation and experience are used both in formulating **theories** and in testing them.

Philosophical inquiry is a **dialectical** process. It begins with appearances and "common **beliefs**" (*endoxa*); appearances are not the only foundations here. It may be that some common beliefs must be rejected in forming the best theory. This seems to be closer to a **coherentist** approach rather than a foundationalist one; justification here is not put in terms of linking beliefs to an infallible foundation.

Aristotle addresses **skeptical** challenges in his *Metaphysics*. The skeptic might argue that appearances sometimes conflict with one another in situations in which we have no (nonarbitrary) **reason** to accept one appearance and reject the other. In these situations, we should suspend **judgment** about which appearance is correct. Aristotle argues that, in general, we do have reasons for preferring one appearance over another. He claims that the skeptic is insisting on a foundationalist-style **proof** of a proposition when it is inappropriate and unreasonable to expect this. Instead, we can have reasons for accepting justifications that are compelling because of their fit with other beliefs we hold; again, this is a coherentist approach rather than a foundationalist one. *See also* EPISTEMIC PRINCIPLE; REASONS FOR BELIEF; SEXTUS EMPIRICUS; SKEPTICISM.

ARITHMETIC. *See* MATHEMATICAL KNOWLEDGE.

ARMSTRONG, DAVID M. (1926–). Australian philosopher who was educated at the University of Sydney and Oxford University. He has taught at the University of Melbourne and the University of Sydney. He is a Foundation Fellow of the Australian Academy of the Humanities and is an Officer of the Order of Australia. Armstrong developed **reliabilism** (found earlier in the work of **F. P. Ramsey**), the view that whether a **belief** is **justified** or qualifies as **knowledge** is determined by the reliability of the way in which that belief is formed. This reliability arises from law-like relationships between the subject and the world, analogous to the law-like relationship between ambient temperature and the reading on a thermometer. Because the subject may not be aware of the reliability of the means by which a belief is formed, this view fits naturally with **externalist** views of **epistemic justification** and knowledge.

Armstrong defends scientific **induction** by **inference to the best explanation**. If we observe many *f*s that are *g* and never observe an *f* that is non-*g*, then the best **explanation** for our **observations** is that all *f*s are *g*. This rejection of **Humean skepticism** regarding **induction** follows from his view that there are strong **laws of nature**; these are **contingent** relationships among universals. These laws are not the result of inductive generalizations and so can provide a foundation for our scientific inductions. The property of being a *g* is universally but contingently linked to the property of being an *f* and so provides a reasonable basis for our assertion that all *f*s are *g*.

In responding to **skepticism**, Armstrong argues that some of our beliefs are so fundamental that they cannot reasonably be challenged. He adopts a strategy similar to that of **G. E. Moore** in arguing, for instance, that one cannot reasonably argue that one does not have a physical body. For us to take such a skeptical challenge seriously, it would have to present us with an **argument**, each of whose premises commands stronger belief than the belief being challenged. Such an argument, Armstrong claims, is not forthcoming. *See also* BELIEF-FORMING PROCESS; CAUSAL THEORIES OF KNOWLEDGE AND JUSTIFICATION; COMMONSENSISM; EXTERNALISM/INTERNALISM; REASONS FOR BELIEF; RELIABILISM.

ARNAULD, ANTOINE (1612–1694). French philosopher and theologian. One of the most acute commentators on the Meditations on First Philosophy of **René Descartes**, he points out the circularity of the **argument** for **God**'s existence and criticized the explanation of the representational properties of **ideas**. Despite these criticisms, Arnauld became a strong supporter of Descartes's philosophy. *See also* CARTESIAN CIRCLE; CIRCULAR REASONING; RELIGIOUS KNOWLEDGE.

ASSOCIATION OF IDEAS. When two or more **ideas** are associated in the mind, the **appearance** of one of them naturally leads the mind to consider the other(s). **John Locke** argues that the association of ideas in the mind explains certain **errors** to which the mind is prone: Errors result from associating ideas incorrectly. **David Hume** argues that repeated **experience** leads to the mind's association of ideas and that there is nothing in the content of the ideas themselves that dictates how they should be associated. He claims that the flow of ideas in human thought is explained by our associating ideas in accordance with principles of resemblance, contiguity, and **causation**. *See also* ANALYTICITY.

ATARAXIA. This Greek word, often translated as "tranquillity," denotes the mental state of being free from anxiety. **Pyrrhonian skeptics** regard this state as highly desirable and as the goal or *telos* of their **skepticism**. *Ataraxia*, they believe, results when one manages to suspend all **belief** about the world and its nature. Thus, their skepticism is a way of life and not just a philosophical position. *See also* PYRRHO OF ELIS; SEXTUS EMPIRICUS.

AUGUSTINE, SAINT (354–430). A theologian and philosopher, Augustine was Bishop of Hippo (North Africa). He divides our **beliefs** into those based on our mental grasp of **necessary** truths illuminated by the intelligible light of **truth** (these beliefs qualify as **knowledge**) and beliefs **justified** in other ways (which can qualify as knowledge only in a broader, weaker sense).

Fundamental truths of **logic** and arithmetic (e.g., p or not-p; $1 + 3 = 4$) can be known with **certainty**. This also applies to some basic **propositions** regarding ethics (e.g., that which is incorruptible is superior to that which is corruptible). In these cases, we can be directly aware of the proposition's necessity and truth. There are also some **contingent** propositions that can be known with certainty (e.g., I exist; I seem to feel pain). These cases show, contrary to the **skeptic**, that at least some knowledge is possible.

Augustine argues that truth can be grasped by the mind but that our senses cannot generate knowledge. Our senses reveal only things that are contingent and subject to change, so beliefs formed in this way cannot qualify as knowledge (compare **Plato**). Our knowledge of necessary truths arises from the mind's direct acquaintance with intelligible objects. **God** is said to be truth itself, so our knowledge of truth is grounded in divine illumination.

When one grasps a necessary truth, one possesses **evidence** of the immutability and necessity of that truth; thus, this belief qualifies as knowledge. Beliefs formed in other ways lack this type of evidence. Instead, the evidence is **external** to the believed proposition. This results in a different, weaker type of justification; such beliefs do not qualify as knowledge. Although we are justified in holding many beliefs that are based on testimony, for example, these beliefs differ fundamentally from the **paradigmatic** cases of knowledge.

Augustine claims that in matters of theology, one ought to believe in order that one may gain understanding. Many religious beliefs are based on the testimony of the Church and of Scripture, but history and miracles show that this is **reliable**; therefore, we are warranted in holding these beliefs. Once these beliefs are held, one can examine them and, in gaining understanding of them, provide them with an even more solid epistemic basis. *See also A PRIORI/A POSTERIORI* KNOWLEDGE; CONTINGENCY; EXTERNALISM/INTERNALISM; NECESSITY; RELIGIOUS KNOWLEDGE; REVELATION; SENSE PERCEPTION.

AUSTIN, JOHN L. (1911–1960). English philosopher who was educated at Oxford University and later taught there. Rather than directly addressing the traditional epistemological issues, Austin typically makes his contributions by attempting to show that these questions were confused or insignificant. His **arguments** usually draw on ordinary language and our usage of epistemological terms.

In addressing **skepticism** about other minds, Austin begins by examining how we usually use the phrase "I know" in order to work out what the conditions for **knowledge** are and how properly to respond to challenges to our claims of knowledge. This approach is also employed to show how "I know" differs from "I believe" and how it resembles "I promise."

Austin argues that traditional epistemological **theories** err in assuming that expressions such as "I know" and "I believe" describe mental states; he calls this "the descriptive fallacy." Epistemologists commonly supposed that a mental state qualifies as knowledge only if it is **infallibly** true. Austin denies this, saying that we cannot avoid the possibility of **error** and that theories that ignore this are inadequate.

Some of Austin's critics argue that he has done no more than explain the conditions in which one is entitled to make the claim that one knows that *p*. This, however, may be perfectly consistent with one not knowing that *p*. Thus, an account of being entitled to make a claim of knowledge is not equivalent to an account of knowledge. Austin and his defenders respond that he makes clear his understanding of this distinction and that rather than being confused about the project of developing a theory of knowledge, he is simply not interested in developing such a theory. Instead, his interest lies in understanding how we use "know" and other epistemological terms; he views this as exchanging a futile task for a rewarding one.

His most notable works were published posthumously by his students. The first of these volumes was *Philosophical Papers* (1961). This was followed by *Sense and Sensibilia* (1962), in which Austin examines and rejects **A. J. Ayer**'s *Foundations of Empirical Knowledge* (1947) and the **phenomenalism** it presents. Ayer's phenomenalism requires the introduction of **sense data**, and Austin argues that this is based on confusions and leads to further errors. Austin contends that the **argument from illusion** used in attacking **direct realism** fails to take proper account of our ordinary use of words such as "looks," "seems," and "real." Because the rejection of direct realism led to phenomenalism and the introduction of sense data, this theory and its new sort of entity are unmotivated. *See also* PRIVACY OF MENTAL STATES.

AUTHORITY. In the epistemic sense, a source or individual is authoritative (or is an authority) if it is a suitable epistemic basis for **belief** and overrides the individual **judgment** of others. An authority is highly **reliable** or **infallible**. This latter qualification is usually attributed to religious sources or **God**. Once a source or individual has been identified as authoritative, there is generally little or no further investigation regarding the **truth** of the claims made by that authority. *See also* FEMINIST EPISTEMOLOGY; SOCIOLOGY OF KNOWLEDGE.

AVENARIUS, RICHARD (1843–1896). German philosopher who developed a form of **positivism** that sought to base philosophy on scientific principles. In his *Critique of Pure Experience* (2 vols., 1888–1890), he endeavors to explore the form and content of "pure **experience**" and rejects distinctions between subject and object and between inner and outer experience. Although brain states may be correlated with conscious states, he denies that the latter could be reduced to the former. *See also* ACT/OBJECT ANALYSIS; CONSCIOUSNESS.

AVIDYA. Sanskrit word meaning "ignorance" or "lack of wisdom." In **Indian epistemology**, *avidya* is chiefly ignorance of **reality**'s true nature and results in karmic bondage. *Avidya* is dispelled by wisdom.

AXIOMATICS. In "Axiomatic Thinking" (1971), **David Hilbert** describes a method for organizing a **theory**. From the large body of statements that make up the theory, one selects a small subset from which the remaining statements can be derived. The statements in this subset are called axioms, and the theory organized in this way is an axiomatic theory. Hilbert argues that such theories can be studied and that the structure of axiomatic theories can itself be the subject of a theory. **Kurt Gödel** argues in his "On Formally Undecidable Propositions of Principia Mathematica and Related Systems I" (1931) that mathematics and even elementary number theory cannot be axiomatized. *See also* MATHEMATICAL KNOWLEDGE.

AYER, ALFRED JULES (A. J.) (1910–1989). British philosopher who was educated at Oxford University and was later a professor there. In *Language, Truth and Logic* (1946), Ayer objects to traditional formulations of **foundationalism**, arguing that there is no set of **propositions** made **certain** by **intuition** and thus that empirical **knowledge** cannot be established on such a basis. This work also uses **logical positivism** to dismiss the epistemological question of our knowledge of **other minds**: No **experience** could verify claims about private states of other minds, so these claims are meaningless.

In *The Foundations of Empirical Knowledge* (1947), Ayer uses the **argument from illusion** to support his claim that **sense data** are the objects of **sense perception**. Sense data are then used to address **David Hume**'s claim that we have no compelling **evidence** that physical objects persist when they are not observed. Ayer's position is that all we mean by the claim that these objects persist is that certain sense data can **reliably** be experienced in predictable situations, and experience provides us with evidence for this.

In *The Problem of Knowledge* (1956), Ayer's primary epistemological work, he proposes that requirements for knowledge should include a reliabilist component: The **belief** must be formed in a way that is generally reliable. The reliability of a process is relevant to circumstances: A **belief-forming process** might be reliable in one situation but unreliable in another. In applying this to the **Gettier cases**, he argues that the belief-forming process at work is that of using **logic** to draw **inferences** from true beliefs and that this process is unreliable in these particular circumstances. Critics point out that this confuses the belief-forming process with the content on which it operates.

Ayer also espouses a form of foundationalism that does not require that **basic beliefs** be **infallibly** true. **Inferential beliefs** are **justified** because of their links to experiences, but these experiences are not infallible. He acknowledges that this gives **skepticism** a foothold, but Ayer says the skeptical challenge can be answered by descriptive **analysis**. This involves giving an account of the procedures one follows in forming a belief, although this does not provide **proof** that the foundation of a belief is true. The skeptic's suggestion that experience provides inadequate evidence of our ordinary physical-object beliefs is unreasonable or incoherent. Critics point out that skeptical challenges seem to meet Ayer's requirements for meaningfulness, so his response to skepticism is inadequate. *See also* GETTIER CASES; OTHER MINDS, PROBLEM OF; RELIABILISM.

– B –

BACON, FRANCIS, LORD VERULAM (1561–1626). Francis Bacon, an English philosopher, rejects appeals to **authority** and traditional Scholasticism and seeks a method for investigating the world that would avoid the **errors** inherent in **experience**, language, **memory**, and so forth. Impressed by the gains made by **science**, he proposes a method of **induction** that would generate **knowledge** and help us control our environment. This is a **hypothetico-deductive method** that proposes causal **hypotheses** (or forms) that can then be tested. Testing involves the careful collection of the "histories" of the relevant phenomena. **Theories** can be regarded as correct if they yield practical success. He believes that the purpose of gaining **knowledge** is to benefit humanity and declared, "Knowledge is power." *See also* CAUSATION; INDUCTION, PROBLEM OF; SCIENTIFIC METHOD.

BASIC BELIEF. In **foundationalism**, a **belief** that is noninferentially justified and on which other beliefs depend for their **epistemic justification**. These beliefs are held to be **self-evident**, requiring no other support or justification in order for them to qualify as **knowledge**. They are sometimes called **protocol sentences**. *See also* EMPIRICISM; EXPERIENCE; GIVEN, THE; INFERENTIAL BELIEF; REGRESS ARGUMENT.

BASING RELATION. *See* BASIC BELIEF; EPISTEMIC REGRESS ARGUMENT; EVIDENCE; FOUNDATIONALISM; GROUNDS.

BAYESIANISM. Named for English Nonconformist minister and mathematician Thomas Bayes (1702–1761), this view begins with the claim that **beliefs** are held to different degrees and that the degree to which a rational person will hold or accept a belief will be guided by the mathematical principles of **probability**. Some epistemological difficulties are said to arise from the mistaken view that belief is an all-or-nothing affair and can be resolved by applying the probabilistic **logic** of **partial belief**.

Bayes's theorem states that the probability of H, given the assumption that E is true, is equal to the probability of H multiplied by the probability of E, given the assumption that H, divided by the probability of E:

$$\text{Prob}(H/E) = [\text{Prob}(H) \times \text{Prob}(E/H)] \div \text{Prob}(E)$$

Bayesianism holds that the beliefs of a rational person would be guided by this equation:

$$b(H/E) = [b(H) \times b(E/H)] \div b(E)$$

For example, if H is a **hypothesis** and E is **evidence** supporting that hypothesis, then $b(H/E) > b(H)$. In other words, a rational person will believe a hypothesis to a greater degree when it is supported by evidence than when it is not. Similarly, E qualifies as evidence for H only if, for a rational person, $b(H/E) > b(H)$. If E is a true prediction generated by hypothesis H, then this explains why successful predictions should increase our belief in a hypothesis. Bayesians argue that their approach can explain many features of **scientific** investigation and solve many of the problems that face it. In **decision theory**, Bayes's rule states that one ought to choose so as to maximize expected utility.

Critics of Bayesianism argue that, contrary to this approach's assumption, it is **psychologically** implausible that anyone's degree of belief can be represented with mathematical precision. Defenders of this approach suggest that mathematical representation be understood as a helpful model and not as implying such psychological detail in how we assent to beliefs. Critics also argue that our ordinary understanding of rational behavior need not always fit with the requirements of the logic of probability. For example, one might fail to recognize that a complex **proposition** is **tautologous** (or contradictory), so one's degree of belief might be somewhere between 1 (which would be required for tautologies) and 0 (which would be required for contradictions). *See also* PROBABILITY; SCIENTIFIC METHOD.

BEGGING THE QUESTION. *See* CIRCULAR REASONING.

BEHAVIORISM, ANALYTIC. The view that all sentences apparently about an individual's mental phenomena can be paraphrased as sentences about that individual's actual or dispositional behavior. This position arose partly in response to the **privacy of mental states** and the resulting difficulty in obtaining **evidence** about others' mental states. Analytic behaviorism is defended by B. F. Skinner. Critics point out that analytic behaviorism must abandon the commonsense view that mental states cause our **voluntary** behavior. *See also* OTHER MINDS, PROBLEM OF; PSYCHOLOGY.

BEHAVIORISM, METHODOLOGICAL. The widely held view that scientific **psychology** is based on publicly **observable** data about subjects' behavior rather than on **introspective** reports of mental states or events. *See also* PRIVACY OF MENTAL STATES; TESTIMONY.

BELIEF. A belief is the **propositional attitude** of accepting a **proposition** as true. **Epistemology** deals largely with the evaluation of these mental states, examining the **evidence** that supports beliefs and determining which beliefs are **justified** or qualify as **knowledge**. Beliefs are generally regarded as mental states that play a central role in guiding behavior. Most beliefs are **introspectively** available, although there may be some that are not.

Propositions are the objects of beliefs. It is propositions that are true or false, and they are typically expressed using sentences. This has led some, such as Jerry Fodor, to suggest that beliefs have a sentential structure, part of a "language of thought," although this approach has numerous critics.

Although beliefs are traditionally understood to be real mental states with real **causal** connections to behavior, **W. V. O. Quine**, **Donald Davidson**, and others defend an **antirealist** approach, arguing that an agent's behavior can be explained equally well by several very different belief attributions. This view is generally tied to a view of language according to which the meanings of sentences are inextricably linked to context.

Daniel Dennett argues that our belief attributions should be understood in terms of the **"intentional stance,"** in which we regard individuals or systems as having beliefs and other mental states when such attributions provide a predictive or **explanatory** advantage. These attributions are not dependent on what the **internal** states of the individual or system are. In such cases, the beliefs we attribute are genuine beliefs; it is not merely "as if" these are beliefs.

Beliefs are usually understood to be all-or-nothing attitudes toward propositions; either one accepts the proposition as true, or one rejects it as false. However, it may be more helpful to understand beliefs as admitting of degree. **Bayesianism** provides a mathematical account of the connection between **probabilities** and degree of belief.

There is some debate about whether believing is voluntary. **Voluntarism** is the view that our beliefs are under our voluntary control, although that control may be indirect or incomplete; this view is held by **René Descartes** and **Blaise Pascal**. Others, such as Bernard Williams, argue that beliefs are not (and perhaps could not be) controlled voluntarily.

Gilbert Ryle and others have argued that there is no compelling reason to suppose that there really are such things as beliefs. In *The Concept of Mind* (1949), Ryle argues that sentences that seem to refer to beliefs or other mental states can be paraphrased so that these references are replaced by descriptions of actual or dispositional behavior. Therefore, beliefs have no causal role in explaining our behavior and no place in our fundamental ontology.

Recent attacks on **folk psychology** include the claim that beliefs do not exist. Stephen Stich, **Patricia Churchland**, and **Paul Churchland** argue that our traditional, commonsense understanding of our **psychology** is fundamentally mistaken and that our current **science** does not support the existence of such mental entities as beliefs. Known as **eliminativism**, this view recommends that we replace our current terms for propositional attitudes, desires, and so forth with new descriptions that fit with our emerging scientific understanding of ourselves. Eliminativism's critics argue that science may improve our understanding of beliefs and other mental states but will not lead to their elimination. *See also* ACCESS; CAUSATION; COLLECTIVE BELIEF; EXTERNALISM/INTERNALISM; MENTALISM; PARTIAL BELIEF; PRIVACY OF MENTAL STATES;

PROPOSITIONAL ATTITUDE; QUINE, W. V. O.; REASONS FOR BELIEF; WEB OF BELIEF.

BELIEF-FORMING PROCESS. A **psychological** (or perhaps social) process that generates a **belief**. The nature and reliability of such processes plays a central role in **causal theories of knowledge and justification**, notably **reliabilism**. Belief-forming processes may include the psychological processes that maintain or revise beliefs, determine the degree to which a belief is accepted, or connect beliefs with changing **evidence**. There is no general agreement about how these processes should be individuated or evaluated. *See also* DENNETT, DANIEL; ELIMINATIVE MATERIALISM; NATURALIZED EPISTEMOLOGY.

BELIEF IN/BELIEF THAT. **Epistemology** generally focuses on propositional **belief** or "belief that," and this is contrasted with a sort of nonpropositional belief called "belief in." The latter resembles **faith** and describes one's attitude when one has **confidence** in someone or something; one might believe in **God**, in one's spouse, or in the city council. Although some argue that all cases of nonpropositional belief can be reduced to propositional belief, this strikes others as implausible. H. H. Price and others argue that "belief in" is a combination of propositional belief and some further attitude, a sort of commitment or trust. This trust is often less influenced by **evidence**, particularly evidence against the belief, than a propositional belief would be. *See also* EPISTEMIC OPERATOR; PROPOSITION.

BERGMANN, GUSTAV (1906–1987). Austrian philosopher, the youngest member of the **Vienna Circle**. He initially accepted **logical positivism**, then **phenomenalism**, but ultimately rejected both. He argues that the **external world** is independent of what we sense, think, or say and argues that even such things as propositional connectives and quantifiers are independent of our minds. This form of **realism** was met with widespread criticism. **Epistemologically**, he shows little interest in addressing skeptical challenges; he takes for granted that we have **knowledge** and focuses on what we know and how we know it. Bergmann believes that an ideal language would include terms that refer to objects or characteristics with which we are directly acquainted (through **sense perception** or **introspection**).

BERKELEY, GEORGE (1685–1753). Irish philosopher and Bishop of Cloyne (Anglican Church of Ireland). He believed that the philosophies of **John Locke, René Descartes**, and others made **skepticism** a serious threat and devised an idealist **theory** to combat this. Rejecting the notion of material substance as incoherent and unnecessary, Berkeley argues that only mental substance exists. Physical—but not material—objects exist as clusters of **ideas** dependent for their existence on the minds that perceive them. He argues that a physical object is a set of sensible qualities and that sensible qualities are ideas in minds; thus, physical objects are ideas in minds. Ideas cannot exist without being perceived (i.e., without being in a mind), so physical objects cannot exist without being perceived. Because we are directly aware of the physical world (and not, as Locke would have it, indirectly aware of it), there is no danger that the world is otherwise than it appears to be.

Berkeley argues that our ideas of sense cannot be **caused** by material substances; only a mind can cause an idea. Our own minds cannot be that cause, and the organized nature of our ideas indicates that the causing mind is powerful and benevolent. Berkeley infers from this that **God** is the cause of our physical-object ideas. Berkeley criticizes Locke's account of **abstract** ideas, arguing that the mind cannot perform the task of abstraction that Locke describes, that some abstract ideas are impossible, and that abstract ideas have no role to play in language.

Berkeley's epistemological stance is a form of **foundationalism**, although it has unusual features. **Beliefs** that Berkeley regards as basic include beliefs about physical objects; other foundationalists would regard these as inferential. *See also* APPEARANCE/REALITY; BASIC BELIEF; IDEALISM; INFERENTIAL BELIEF; PERCEPTION; SENSE DATA.

BLANDSHARD, PERCY BRAND (1892–1987). An American philosopher who was educated at the University of Michigan and Oxford University; he taught at Swarthmore College and Yale University. Blandshard opposed **positivism** and linguistic philosophy and defended **idealism**. His *The Nature of Thought* (1939) attacks **empiricism** and the **correspondence theory of truth**, defending **rationalism** and the coherence theory of **truth**. He argues that because coherence plays an important role in **epistemic justification**, it should also play an important role in understanding truth; failure to connect these gives rise to skeptical challenges. *See also* COHERENTISM.

BONAVENTURE, SAINT (ca. 1221–1274). Italian theologian, member of the Franciscan order; later cardinal bishop of Albano. He believes that our minds begin as a *tabula rasa* and that all **knowledge** of the world is gained through the senses. Divine illumination also contributes to knowledge by enabling one to acquire universal or abstract **concepts** from particular sensory **experiences** and gives our faculty of intellectual **judgment** its **certainty**. *See also* EMPIRICISM; REVELATION; SENSE PERCEPTION.

BONJOUR, LAURENCE (1943–). American philosopher and professor at the University of Washington (Seattle, Wash.). BonJour's contributions in **epistemology** include work on the **externalist/ internalist** debate and a notable defense of **coherentism** (*The Structure of Empirical Knowledge*, 1985). His recent work defends **foundationalism**.

BOUWSMA, OETS KOLK (O. K.) (1898–1978). American philosopher and **ordinary language philosopher**. He taught at the University of Nebraska and the University of Texas. O. K. Bouwsma is noted for his ability and humor in exposing incoherency and nonsense in the **theories** and **arguments** of others. Heavily influenced by **Ludwig Wittgenstein**, his contributions lie chiefly in his criticisms of others and his great skill as a teacher.

BRAIN IN A VAT. Often employed in explaining the challenges posed by **skepticism**, this is a hypothetical situation in which one's brain is removed from one's body and kept alive in a vat. In this situation, all of one's **experiences** are generated, not by the usual functioning of one's sensory systems but by a computer connected to one's brain. This is an updating of **René Descartes**'s discussion of deceiving demons; the evil demons are replaced by nefarious neuroscientists. Brain-in-a-vat situations, with numerous variations, have been a persistent theme in literature and motion pictures. *See also* RELEVANT ALTERNATIVES; SKEPTICAL ALTERNATIVES.

BRENTANO, FRANZ CLEMENS (1838–1917). German philosopher and psychologist. Brentano argues that one's conscious mental states are examined by a faculty of inner perception and that this perception yields **certainty** that one is in that particular state. He distinguishes between "physical" or sensory states and intentional conscious states. Unlike sensory states, intentional states are nonsensory, and each has an intentional object toward which the thought is directed. These intentional objects need not exist; one can desire or fear something that does not exist.

Brentano claims that we can be certain of our conscious states and we can have *a priori* certainty about necessary **truths**, although these are different types of certainty. He claims that these foundational **beliefs** can make other beliefs probable, but critics argue that there are no appropriate inferential connections between his **evidence** base and the other beliefs said to be supported by them. *See also* BASIC BELIEF; CONSCIOUSNESS; INFERENCE.

BROAD, CHARLIE DUNBAR (C. D.) (1887–1971). English philosopher; he was Knightsbridge Professor of Moral Philosophy at Trinity College, Cambridge. C. D. Broad's writings address many issues, including the nature of **sense perception**, *a priori* **knowledge**, and the problem of **induction**.

Broad defends **sense data** (which he calls "sensa") and employs them in his formulation of the causal **theory** of **perception**. He also rejects **empiricism**, arguing that reason can find synthetic connections between properties or characteristics. Broad connects the **problem of induction** to general claims about the **uniformity of nature**, although these turn out to be unclear and difficult to justify. *See also* ANALYTICITY.

BROUWER, LUITZGEN EGBERTUS JAN (1881–1966). Dutch mathematician and philosopher, Brouwer founded the **mathematical intuitionism** school of mathematical thought. He argues that **intu-**

ition and not traditional logical reasoning should be central to mathematics. The logical structures employed in traditional reasoning focus on the linguistic representations of mathematics and not on the true nature of mathematics. Therefore, using logical principles such as noncontradiction (no proposition can be both true and false) and excluded middle (every proposition is either true or false) in mathematics can lead to false conclusions. Like **Immanuel Kant**, Brouwer claims that mathematics is an activity of the mind that does not involve language. *See also* LOGIC; MATHEMATICAL KNOWLEDGE.

BUDDHAGOSA (fourth–fifth century A.D.). Theravada **Buddhist** philosopher. His primary work, the *Visuddhimagga* (*Path of Purification*), adopts the traditional Buddhist doctrine that everything is ephemeral (excepting only Nirvana) and argues that all physical objects and even the mind are collections of only momentary states. **Sense perception** yields **knowledge** of the existence of objects in the **external world**. *See also* BERKELEY, GEORGE; PHENOMENALISM.

BUDDHISM. A religion founded by Siddhārta Gotama Buddha; now dominant in eastern and central Asia. One of its central doctrines is the claim that there are no substances or enduring entities. Instead, all existence is ephemeral and imperfect. Even so, **sense perception** generates **knowledge** of the **external world**. In **epistemology**, the Theravada ("Doctrine of the Elders") school of Buddhism includes forms of both **representative realism** and **direct realism**. The Mahayana ("Greater Vehicle") school holds that our senses are unreliable and systematically illusory. Knowledge of the true nature of **reality** is said to require a mystic enlightenment. *See also* ILLUSION; MYSTICISM; REVELATION.

BURDEN OF PROOF. In a philosophical dispute, the **evidence** required to convince adherents of an established position to reject it in favor of an alternative view. When one presents a compelling **argument** in support of one's position, the burden of **proof** shifts to one's opponent; that person must now present new evidence to overcome the support offered for one's own view. When one of these competing views fits well with common sense, the opposing view is generally held to have the initial burden of proof. *See also* DEFEATER; OVERRIDER.

– C –

CALIBRATION OF CONFIDENCE. *See* CONFIDENCE.

CAMBRIDGE PLATONISTS. A loosely knit group of philosophers and theologians at the University of Cambridge in the seventeenth century, including Benjamin Whichcote (1609–1683), Ralph Cudworth (1617–1688), Henry More (1614–1687), and John Smith (1616–1652). Defending Anglican Christianity against Calvinism, Puritanism, and atheism, they emphasize the role of reason in religion. The faculty of reason is also seen as the source or foundation for fundamental principles of religion and ethics. Although one may not be able to defend one's **beliefs** in ways that would satisfy the **Pyrrhonian skeptic**, these beliefs qualify as **knowledge** nonetheless. *See also* NEOPLATONISM; PLATO; RELIGIOUS KNOWLEDGE.

CARNAP, RUDOLF (1891–1970). German-born philosopher who later moved to the United States. Carnap was a member of the **Vienna Circle** for a time and endorsed **logical empiricism**. His *Der Logische Aufbau der Welt* (*The Logical Structure of the World*, 1928), a project influenced by **Bertrand Russell** and **Ernst Mach**, seeks to uncover the logical structure of **experience**. An **empiricist**, Carnap endorses the verifiability criterion of meaning, the view that the meaning of a sentence is determined by the conditions in which it would be verified. Because strict confirmability is too demanding for many scientific **propositions**, he acknowledges that we cannot be **certain** our scientific **beliefs** are true.

Carnap describes the degree of **confirmation** (a form of **probability** similar to **credibility**) as a relationship between **evidence** and a **hypothesis**; this is part of an attempt to clarify the nature of confirmation in **science**. Ultimately, the basis for the fundamental **principles** of **induction** rests on **intuition**. *See also* PRINCIPLE OF VERIFIABILITY; REDUCTION SENTENCE; SCIENCE; VERIFICATIONISM.

CARTESIAN CIRCLE. René Descartes's argument for the existence of **God**, presented in the third of his *Meditations on First Philosophy* (1641), was criticized by **Marin Mersenne** and **Antoine Arnauld** as being circular. Descartes appeals to God's existence and perfection in arguing that **clear and distinct ideas** must be true, but his argument for God's existence seems to depend on the assumption that clear and distinct ideas are true, making this argument logically circular. Descartes's response is that some **propositions** can be seen to be true even without relying on God to guarantee the **truth** of clear and distinct ideas, although most critics do not find this satisfactory. *See also* CIRCULAR REASONING.

CARTESIAN SKEPTICISM. *See* SKEPTICISM.

CARTESIANISM. A philosophical school of thought founded by **René Descartes**, from "Cartesius," the Latin form of his name. Central elements include the **indubitability** criterion of **truth** (a **proposition** will be accepted as true only if it cannot be **doubted**), substance dualism, and a **theory** of **clear and distinct ideas**. *See also* PROBLEM OF THE CRITERION; SKEPTICISM.

CĀRVĀKA. A materialist school of thought in Indian philosophy. Some forms regard only **sense perception** to be a **reliable** source of **knowledge**, although **inferences** about states of affairs that can be perceptually confirmed are often included.

CASSIRER, ERNST (1874–1945). German philosopher and historian. He argues that our **knowledge** arises from our capacity to use symbolism to form **experience** and that the forms of human experience are linked to the forms of human culture, such as religion, myth, art, **science**, language, and history. He concludes that culture is the proper subject matter of philosophy.

CAUSAL THEORIES OF KNOWLEDGE AND JUSTIFICATION. A family of **theories** that claim that epistemic evaluation should focus on the causal history of the **beliefs** being evaluated. In his *Belief, Truth and Knowledge* (1973), **David Armstrong** presents a causal theory of **knowledge** such that one's belief that *p* qualifies as knowledge only if the **fact** that p contributed to causing this belief and that this causal connection between the fact and the belief is reliable. In other words, if p had not been true, then I would not have believed that p. **Fred Dretske**, in his *Knowledge and the Flow of Information* (1981), presents his causal account in terms of signals and **information theory**: My belief that p qualifies as knowledge only if that belief was caused by my receiving a signal conveying the information that p. **Alvin Goldman**'s *Epistemology and Cognition* (1986) presents a reliability theory of knowledge according to which one's belief that p is **justified** only if it results from a **belief-forming process** that is generally reliable and that would have generated true beliefs in relevant **counterfactual** situations in which p is false. The latter condition prevents beliefs that are accidentally true from qualifying as knowledge but invokes a notion of **relevant alternatives** that is not clearly delineated.

The two most prominent criticisms of causal theories of knowledge such as those of Armstrong, Dretske, and Goldman are that they fail to explain our knowledge of **facts** that cannot enter into causal relations (e.g., our knowledge of arithmetic cannot result from our causal interaction with numbers) and that there are cases in which the causal condition is met but the belief in question is not justified and so cannot qualify as knowledge.

Reliabilism, the dominant causal theory of **epistemic justification**, claims that a belief is justified only if it is produced by a reliable belief-forming process. Theorists who regard epistemic justification as being a matter of degree generally add that the degree to which a belief is justified is linked to the degree to which the belief-forming process is reliable. If the belief-forming process is reliable to degree 0.8, then the resulting belief might be justified to degree 0.8 (where 0 is complete lack of justification and 1 is complete justification).

Critics point out that reliabilists have not yet offered a clear and complete **explanation** of how the belief-forming process is to be identified or individuated. One difficulty is that descriptions of these processes must be neither too wide nor too narrow. Suppose that in very dim light I think I see a raccoon in my yard and form the belief that this is so. The appropriate belief-forming process cannot be simply vision. That description is too broad to take into account the poor viewing conditions. In addition, this would lead to all my visually formed beliefs being justified to the same degree, and this seems highly implausible. If the description of the belief-forming process is so narrow that it specifies a great deal about the circumstances and the content of the belief, then it risks yielding the result that my beliefs are perfectly justified when they are true and completely unjustified when they are false. A further criticism is that no clear account of reliability has been provided. Determining the reliability of a system involves examining how it functions in other actual and possible situations, but which of these are relevant to this determination? If my vision would generate false beliefs in very odd situations (e.g., in an atmosphere with only 5 percent oxygen or when I approach the surface of the sun), does this count against its reliability in the current (normal) situation? Addressing this issue often involves invoking a rather vague notion of relevant alternatives.

A more fundamental criticism of causal theories of epistemic evaluation is that they fit best with **externalism**, the view that these evaluations should be carried out not from the subject's point of view but from the viewpoint of an omniscient observer. Critics point out that internalism, the view that epistemic evaluation should be carried out from the subject's point of view, is more plausible. *See also* CAUSATION; IDEAL OBSERVER.

CAUSATION. The relationship between cause and effect, involving events, states, or objects. This **concept** plays a central role in our understanding of our world and of ourselves and is particularly prominent in **explanation**. **Beliefs** about causal connections pose special epistemological difficulties. **David Hume** famously argues in his *Treatise of Human Nature* (1739–1740) that although we repeatedly observe event a followed by event b and form a "habit of mind" that leads us to anticipate b when we observe a, this is not sufficient to **justify** our belief that a causes b. Causation, he says, involves a necessary connection between cause and effect, and we have no **evidence** about whether a is necessarily followed by b. Our beliefs about causal connections are founded on an unjustified **belief** that nature is uniform (i.e., that the future will be like the past and that unobserved events are like those we observe). *See also* CONTINGENCY; EXPLANATION; INDUCTION, PROBLEM OF; NECESSITY; UNIFORMITY OF NATURE.

CERTAINTY. Either the **psychological** state of being convinced of a **proposition**'s **truth** or any of several epistemic statuses or degrees of **epistemic warrant** a proposition can have, such as logical certainty, metaphysical certainty, or moral certainty. I am psychologically certain that a proposition is true if I have no **doubt** whatsoever that it is true. **Peter Unger**, a defender of **skepticism**, argues that psychological certainty is necessary for **knowledge** and that because this certainty is rarely found, we have little or no knowledge. This view has not found wide support, and most epistemologists regard psychological certainty as having relatively little significance.

Discussions of certainty sometimes arise in the context of setting forth conditions of knowledge: If certainty is a necessary or sufficient condition for knowing something, how should this certainty be understood? **Roderick Chisholm** argues that a proposition is epistemically certain only if there is no other proposition that is more warranted than it. Drawing on **René Descartes**'s work, some philosophers define a proposition as having **Cartesian** certainty if there are no grounds for doubting it; this is sometimes put in terms of ruling out **skeptical alternatives**.

Even though it is possible that a proposition is false, I may be morally certain that it is true, provided that my **evidence** supporting this proposition is so strong that I could not reasonably be blamed if I am mistaken. A proposition that is demonstrably true in every **possible world** is logically certain. Such a demonstration of its truth would typically take the form of deriving it from fundamental truths of **logic**. A proposition is metaphysically certain if it would have to be true in other possible worlds, not because it is a truth of logic but because of other features every possible world must have. To use an example from Peter van Inwagen, it may be metaphysically certain that a functioning passenger jet cannot be constructed solely of Jell-O and whipped cream.

Ludwig Wittgenstein argues that a belief's certainty results from the role it plays in a system of beliefs: A belief is certain if it can be appealed to in defense of other beliefs but cannot itself be reasonably challenged. Thus, our linguistic and social practices will indicate which of our beliefs are certain. For instance, we are certain that the world has been in existence for a very long time. Skeptics respond that showing that we *do* accept these beliefs as true is insufficient; what is needed is a demonstration that our evidence *entitles* us to accept them.

Certainty is often discussed in the context of skepticism. Skeptics sometimes argue that certainty of some sort is necessary for knowledge, that this certainly is lacking in our beliefs, and thus that our beliefs do not qualify as knowledge. Counterarguments deny either that knowledge requires certainty or that certainty is more readily available than the skeptics claim. **G. E. Moore**, in his *Philosophical Papers* (1959), and Peter Klein, in his *Certainty: A Refutation of Skepticism* (1981), take the latter approach. *See also* BASIC BELIEF; ERROR; INFALLIBILITY; MORAL EPISTEMOLOGY; REASONS FOR BELIEF; RELIABILISM.

CHANG, HSÜEH-CH'ENG (1738–1801). Chinese philosopher and historian. He claims that all **beliefs**, practices, and institutions in society arise to meet natural necessities. This is part of a dialectical theory of civilization.

CHARRON, PIERRE (1541–1603). French theologian. Following **Michel de Montaigne**, he defends Catholicism in *The Three Truths* (1595), presenting skeptical challenges against atheism and other religions. Our limited minds cannot grasp **God**'s nature, and we have no epistemic ground for rejecting Catholicism, so we should accept it on **faith**. In *On Wisdom* (1603), Charron argues that we can know only what God reveals to us. *See also* RELIGIOUS KNOWLEDGE; REVELATION.

CH'ENG. Chinese term meaning "sincerity." **Confucius** explains in the *Doctrine of the Mean* that *ch'eng* is real, **true**, and incapable of **illusion** or **error**. It is central to the Way of Heaven.

CHIH. Chinese term meaning "**knowledge**." (It has a homophone translated as "will.") Used as a noun, "*chih*" may refer to one's cognitive capacity to know or to one's actual attainment of knowledge or wisdom. Used as a verb, it refers to one's understanding or realization of a **truth**, typically regarding ethics.

CHIH-HSING HO-I. Chinese term meaning the unity of **knowledge** and action; this is a central issue in Confucian ethics. It deals with the relationships among will, desire, and practicality. *See also* CONFUCIUS.

CHISHOLM, RODERICK (1916–1999). American philosopher and professor at Brown University. He takes a notion of **epistemic justification** to be basic and employs it in defining other **epistemological** terms. For example, in his *Theory of Knowledge* (3rd ed., 1989), he explicates "**proposition** *p* is beyond reasonable **doubt** for an individual *S*," as "*S* is more justified in believing *p* than in withholding **judgment** on *p*." Epistemic justification, he argues, comes from **sense perception**, **memory**, positive coherence among beliefs, and the self-presenting nature of certain mental states. Beginning with the **analysis** of what he takes to be clear, uncontroversial instances of justified **belief**, Chisholm proposes **epistemic principles** describing the circumstances in which justification arises from each of these sources. These principles also indicate our epistemological duties; we ought to reflect critically on our beliefs, improving the epistemic status of our beliefs or eliminating them, as appropriate.

Chisholm's theory of justification is a form of **foundationalism**, although it has elements of **coherentism** as well. Coherence can increase the justification of beliefs that have other epistemic factors in their favor, but coherence alone cannot generate justification. His theory is also a form of epistemic **internalism**; he takes our capacity to reflect on and epistemically improve our beliefs to be central to understanding epistemic evaluation. *See also* BASIC BELIEF; EXTERNALISM/INTERNALISM; PROBLEM OF THE CRITERION.

CHUANG TZU (fourth century B.C.). Also called Chuang Chou, he was a Chinese Taoist philosopher. The text *Chuang Tzu* points out that there can be no neutral perspective from which to decide between opposing views expressed from different perspectives. This realization should lead us to regard these views as less important and to place less emphasis on whether a **judgment** is **true** or false.

CHURCHLAND, PATRICIA (1943–). American philosopher; professor at the University of California, San Diego, and a founder of neurophilosophy. In her *Neurophilosophy: Toward a Unified Science of the Mind/Brain* (1986) and *Brain-Wise: Studies in Neurophilosophy* (2002), she argues that traditional epistemological **theories** are flawed because of their failure to learn from **empirical** neuroscience. As a result, epistemological theories make false assumptions about **propositional attitudes**, the nature of mental representations, and the ways in which information is gathered and manipulated. Correcting these **errors** will require modifying or perhaps abandoning our understanding of **beliefs**. *See also* ELIMINATIVE MATERIALISM; NATURALIZED EPISTEMOLOGY.

CHURCHLAND, PAUL (1942–). American philosopher who was educated at the University of Pittsburgh. He has taught at the University of Manitoba and is now a professor at the University of California, San Diego. His *Scientific Realism and the Plasticity of Mind* (1979) is an important defense of **scientific realism**, and his *A Neurocomputational Perspective: The Nature of Mind and the Structure of Science* (1989), a contribution to the growing field of neurophilosophy, argues against **folk psychology** and in defense of **eliminative materialism**. *See also* NATURALIZED EPISTEMOLOGY.

CHURCH'S THESIS. Alonzo Church's thesis, stated in 1935, that an effectively calculable function (i.e., **algorithm**) of positive integers is a recursive function. It was given its current name by Stephen Kleene in his *Introduction to Mathematics* (1952). This fundamental notion of mathematical **logic** plays an important role in understanding **Kurt Gödel**'s incompleteness theorems, computer science, artificial intelligence, and other areas of investigation. *See also* MATHEMATICAL KNOWLEDGE.

CICERO, MARCUS TULLIUS (106–43 B.C.). Roman statesman and essayist. Although he did not formulate any original philosophical positions, he is notable for his introduction of Greek philosophy into Roman culture. He notes that our **impressions** of the world may be mistaken but does not believe this leads to **skepticism**. Some of our impressions are more "persuasive" than others and can appropriately be used in guiding action. *See also* APPEARANCE/ REALITY.

CIRCULAR REASONING. Exemplified by any **argument** in which the relationships of support or **evidence**, when diagrammed, would form a circle. Arguments should support their conclusions by presenting premises that are well established and whose **truth** makes the truth of the conclusion more likely. Circular reasoning employs one's acceptance of the conclusion to support the premises. Also known as "begging the question," or "*petitio principii*," circular reasoning is generally fallacious. However, some forms of reasoning involving feedback are nonfallaciously circular. *See also* CARTESIAN CIRCLE; EPISTEMIC CIRCULARITY; INFORMAL FALLACIES.

CLARKE, SAMUEL (1675–1729). English philosopher and theologian; a noted correspondent of **Gottfried Leibniz**. A **rationalist**, he argues that we can be certain of **God**'s existence, some points of theology, and ethical principles. His apparent neglect of the role of divine **revelation** drew considerable criticism. *See also* CERTAINTY; RATIONALISM.

CLEAR AND DISTINCT IDEA. For **René Descartes**, an **idea** whose **truth** is guaranteed by its nature. A clear and distinct idea is one that can be grasped entirely by the mind without having to rely on **memory**, one in which nothing is hidden or unclear, and of whose truth **God** would not allow one to be mistaken. The "**light of reason**" enables one's faculty of **judgment** to "see" the truth of clear and distinct ideas. *See also* A PRIORI/A POSTERIORI KNOWLEDGE; CERTAINTY; INTUITION; RATIONALISM.

CLEMENT OF ALEXANDRIA (A.D. ca. 150–ca. 215). Theologian of the early Christian church. Influenced by Greek philosophy and gnosticism, he taught that we can rise from our imperfect **knowledge** to the hidden knowledge (*gnosis*) revealed in Christ, who was reason (*logos*) incarnate. *See also* FAITH; RELIGIOUS KNOWLEDGE; REVELATION.

CLIFFORD, WILLIAM KINGDON (1845–1879). English mathematician and philosopher. He argues that one has a moral obligation to investigate each **belief** to determine what **evidence** we have for or against it and no moral entitlement to hold a belief if one possesses insufficient evidence supporting it. This approach led to his eventual rejection of Catholicism. *See also* ETHICS OF BELIEF; EVIDENTIALISM; MORAL EPISTEMOLOGY.

CLOSURE PRINCIPLE. Also known as the principle of deductive closure, this is the **epistemic principle** that if one knows that p, then one also knows all **propositions** trivially entailed by p. For example, if one is justified in believing propositions p and q, then one is justified in believing their conjunction, p *and* q. This principle is central to the **lottery paradox** and as a result is regarded by some epistemologists as false.

Although the closure principle is intuitively plausible, it is often exploited by skeptics who argue that ordinary **beliefs** about the **external world** entail the falsehood of **skeptical alternatives** such as that one is a **brain in a vat**; because one's **evidence** is insufficient to rule out the possibility that one *is* a brain in a vat (and other skeptical alternatives), one's beliefs about the world do not qualify as **knowledge**. This strategy is challenged by **Fred Dretske** ("Epistemic Operators" [1970] and "The Pragmatic Dimension of Knowledge" [1981]) and others (e.g., G. Stine, "Scepticism, Relevant Alternatives, and Deductive Closure" [1976]). *See also* DEDUCTION; INTUITION; KK THESIS; LOGIC; PROBLEM OF THE CRITERION; RELEVANT ALTERNATIVES; SKEPTICISM.

COGITO ERGO SUM. Latin: "I think, therefore I am." In his *Discourse on Method* (1637), **René Descartes** argues that this **proposition** is **indubitable** and thus that we can be **certain** that it is true. In *Meditations on First Philosophy* (1641), he makes this the foundation of his structure of **knowledge**. The term "*cogito*" is commonly used to refer both to this proposition and to the method by which Descartes establishes our knowledge. *See also* FOUNDATIONALISM; RATIONALISM; SCIENTIFIC METHOD; SELF-EVIDENCE.

COGNITIVE DISSONANCE. A mental phenomenon postulated by Leon Festinger in his *Cognitive Dissonance* (1957). This is mental stress or discomfort experienced when one's **beliefs** or attitudes conflict with one another. When one retains a belief despite compelling **evidence** that it is false, this may result from the fact that rejecting this belief and adopting the corresponding true one would result in unacceptably high cognitive dissonance. *See also* COHERENTISM; CREDULITY; FAITH; RATIONALITY.

COHERENCE THEORY OF TRUTH. *See* TRUTH.

COHERENTISM. The view that **beliefs** are justified or qualify as **knowledge** in virtue of being members of a coherent system of beliefs. Perhaps the clearest presentation of this **theory** is **Laurence BonJour**'s *The Structure of Empirical Knowledge* (1985). Contrary to **foundationalism**, coherentism understands **epistemic justification** to be primarily a feature of entire sets of beliefs and only secondarily of individual beliefs. Coherentist theories of knowledge and justification are typically internalist and add the requirement that the subject must be aware of or have introspective **access** to the system's coherence. The coherentist's response to the **epistemic regress argument** is that it is unnecessary to find a noninferentially justified **basic belief**; instead, a belief's justification arises from the other beliefs to which it is connected by coherence-making relationships (such as logical **consistency** and explanatory relationships).

Because the **truth** of a **belief** is generally taken to be a necessary condition for its qualifying as knowledge, coherentism fits naturally with the **coherence theory of truth**, although a coherentist could hold some other theory of truth instead. Holding some other theory of truth (e.g., the **correspondence theory of truth**) exposes coherentism to a serious objection: It has difficulty ruling out the possibility that a set of beliefs could be highly coherent and that most or all of them could be false. This is a serious problem because truth is necessary for knowledge, and justification should be truth conducive. *See also* EXTERNALISM/INTERNALISM; INFERENTIAL BELIEF; INTROSPECTION.

COLLECTIVE BELIEF. An attribution of a **belief** to a group of people. This may simply be that most or all of the members of the group hold this belief, or it may be that members of a group recognize that they are jointly committed to upholding this belief, even when this differs from their individual beliefs. A central issue is thus whether collective beliefs can be reduced to sets of individual beliefs. *See also* SOCIAL EPISTEMOLOGY; SOCIOLOGY OF KNOWLEDGE.

COMMONSENSISM. The view, defended by **Thomas Reid** and **G. E. Moore**, that "common sense" is generally a **reliable** guide to **truth** and **knowledge**. A central implication of this approach is that we know most or all of the things we generally think we know. For instance, we know that there is a world of physical objects and that this world has existed for a very long time. Commonsensism does relatively little in explaining how we come to know these things; it relies on **confidence** in our sensory systems and the **fact** that our commonsense **beliefs** have survived considerable **experience**. Any **theory** of knowledge that sets a standard so demanding that we have little or no knowledge would be rejected. It is more reasonable for us to accept our confidently held beliefs than to accept a theory that implies that we do not know these things. This view precludes many forms of **skepticism**. Reid postulates that a belief is known in this commonsense way if (1) this belief is universally accepted, (2) all languages reflect this common acceptance, (3) negating this belief yields an absurdity, and (4) in our ordinary, practical affairs, we cannot help but believe it. *See also* INTUITION; PROBLEM OF THE CRITERION.

COMMUNICATION THEORY. *See* INFORMATION THEORY.

COMMUNICATIVE RATIONALITY. In the work of **Jürgen Habermas**, communicative rationality refers to people's capacity to engage in discourse about disputed issues in such a way as to arrive at objectively correct results. This involves assessing "validity claims" (of **truth**, rightness, or sincerity) so as to arrive at consensus. Habermas argues that democratic social structures are preferable because they alone allow for this sort of uninhibited discourse. *See also* SOCIOLOGY OF KNOWLEDGE; TESTIMONY.

COMPETENCE KNOWLEDGE. *See* PROCEDURAL KNOWLEDGE.

COMTE, AUGUSTE (1798–1857). French philosopher and sociologist. The founder of **positivism**, Comte argues that our **knowledge** of the world is based on **observation** but that knowledge of unobservable physical objects is impossible. Positivism, which is applied primarily to the **sciences**, is an approach that restricts all theorizing to the observable. Scientific **predictions** and **explanations** involve laws of succession, not causal laws; causes are unknowable. *See also* CAUSATION; EMPIRICISM; NATURAL SCIENCE.

CONCEIVABILITY. The capacity to be conceived or grasped by the mind. This need not involve mental images; a chiliagon (a regular one-thousand-sided polygon) is conceivable, although one cannot form a mental image of it. Conceivability is sometimes used as a test of logical possibility, but this is unreliable. Similarly, inconceivability is often interpreted to indicate more than our inability to grasp something; it has sometimes been taken to indicate logical impossibility. *See also* CONTINGENCY; IMAGINATION; POSSIBLE WORLDS.

CONCEPT. The content of an **idea** (or a constituent of it) or a principle for determining membership in a particular class. One possesses a concept when one is able to apply it correctly. It may be that one cannot possess one concept without possessing other related concepts as well. **Hilary Putnam** argues that one cannot possess certain concepts unless one has had **experience** of the **external world**.

CONCLUSIVE EVIDENCE. *See* EVIDENCE.

CONDILLAC, ÉTIENNE BONNOT de (1714–1780). French philosopher; a leading figure in the French Enlightenment. An **empiricist**, his *Traité des Sensations* (*Treatise on Sense Perception*, 1754) examines how **sense perception** contributes to understanding by considering a statue whose sensory systems are activated one by one. His position, which is strongly influenced by **John Locke**'s, also examines the role of language in contributing to **knowledge**. *See also* EMPIRICISM; EXPERIENCE.

CONDITIONAL PROOF. An **argument** of the form, "*q* follows from *p*; therefore, if *p* then *q*." Alternatively, the rule of **inference** that allows one to infer the conditional, "If p then q" when q can be derived, given the assumption that p. *See also* LOGIC; PROOF.

CONDITIONAL PROPOSITION. A **proposition** of the form "if p, then q." This is usually symbolized $p \supset q$ and is logically equivalent to the proposition that "either *not-p* or q" (symbolized $\sim p \vee q$). Propositions of this form are true unless the antecedent (p) is true and the consequent (q) is false. *See also* LOGIC.

CONFIDENCE. The degree to which one accepts a **belief** or one's level of **certainty** that a belief is true. This is typically a psychological description and may be independent of the degree of support one's **evidence** provides for that belief.

In empirical **psychology**, one's confidence is said to be well calibrated when one's confidence in one's beliefs is strongly correlated with the frequency of the **truth** of those beliefs. One's confidence is poorly calibrated when the degree of confidence is only weakly correlated with the frequency of the truth of one's beliefs. Studies show that most people are overconfident about the truth of their beliefs when those beliefs concern complex or difficult matters. *See also* EXTERNALISM/INTERNALISM; FAITH.

CONFIDENCE INTERVAL. In the statistical **analysis** of data, a **confidence** interval indicates the statistical range within which a statistical **hypothesis** has a specified likelihood of being true. For instance, if half of the one hundred marbles one examines are white and half are black, there is a 95 percent confidence interval that half the marbles in the entire collection are white, with a margin of error of ± 0.10. This sample also yields a 99 percent confidence interval that half the marbles in the entire collection are white with a margin of error of ± 0.12, or a 90 percent confidence interval with a margin of error of ± 0.08. *See also* PROBABILITY.

CONFIRMATION. The relationship between **evidence** and the **belief** or **hypothesis** it supports. Confirmation increases the epistemic status of the belief or hypothesis, either by only a small increment or by making it (nearly) **certain**. *Qualitative* confirmation increases epistemic status but does so in a way that does not lend itself to quantification. *Quantitative* confirmation increases epistemic status by a quantifiable amount, typically expressed in terms of **probabilities**. This is studied chiefly by **Bayesians**. *Comparative* confirmation weighs and compares the epistemic support provided by different pieces of evidence (or the differences in support provided by a piece of evidence to two or more beliefs or hypotheses).

The **paradox of the ravens** poses a puzzle for confirmation. Finding particular black ravens provides confirmation for the hypothesis that all ravens are black. Because "All ravens are black" is logically equivalent to "All nonblack things are nonravens," finding a non-black nonraven (e.g., a brown bandicoot) should also provide confirmation for the hypothesis that all ravens are black. This, however, is counterintuitive. *See also* BAYESIANISM; PROBABILITY; VERIFICATIONISM.

CONFUCIUS (sixth to fifth century B.C.). Also known as K'ung Ch'iu, K'ung Tzu, or Kung Fu-Tzu; a Chinese philosopher and founder of the Confucian school of thought. His teachings, collected in the *Lun Yü* (*Analects*), present *jen*, the ethical ideal, and discuss the observance of rites (*li*), and *ch'eng*, sincerity or **truth**.

CONNECTIONISM. A model of cognitive systems in which the representation and processing of information is distributed throughout the system. This approach to cognitive modeling is also known as "neural networking" or "parallel distributed processing." Based on **observations** of the architecture of the brain, connectionist systems comprise many simple processing units linked together as a network. There are different types of connectionist systems, but generally each unit has a numerical value that changes as it interacts with surrounding units or is stimulated by input to the system.

Rather than being programmed, these systems learn through training. This takes place as the connections between processing units are given different weights, changing the capacity of connected units to excite or inhibit one another. The strengths and weaknesses of connectionist systems mirror those of human cognition; they are better suited for tasks such as pattern recognition than for complex mathematics, and damaging them results in slower, more mistake-prone functioning rather than abrupt failure. Connectionist systems also use generalizations to respond appropriately to novel inputs and perform well on tasks that require satisfying many constraints at once.

Patricia and **Paul Churchland** point out that connectionist systems do not have states with discrete propositional content and use this in their **argument** that **propositional attitudes** such as **beliefs** are part of a **folk psychology** that should be abandoned. *See also* EXPERIENCE; NATURALIZED EPISTEMOLOGY; PSYCHOLOGY.

CONSCIOUSNESS. *Phenomenal* consciousness is outwardly directed; it is one's **experience** or awareness of one's body or environment. *Introspective* consciousness is inwardly directed; it is one's experience or awareness of one's mental contents and perhaps of the mind itself. A state or event is said to be in one's consciousness if there is some way it seems to the individual to have or experience it. The **act/object analysis** of consciousness claims that each conscious state has an object (e.g., a tickle, **memory**, red patch) that is the subject of that state, but the **adverbial theory of perception** rejects this and argues that these states are best described as ways of being conscious. There is ongoing debate among philosophers of mind about whether conscious experiences are reducible to or explicable in terms of purely physical (probably neurological) states and events.

Introspective consciousness is our principal source of information about minds, but empirical **psychology** shows that **introspection** provides neither complete nor **infallible access** to mental states and activities. **David Hume** points out that although introspection reveals the present contents of the mind, it does not reveal the mind itself. *See also* APPERCEPTION; EXTERNALISM/INTERNALISM; GIVEN, THE; OBJECTIVE/SUBJECTIVE; PRIVACY OF MENTAL STATES.

CONSISTENCY. A property of a set of **propositions** such that the set is free from contradictions. A set of propositions is consistent if there is an interpretation under which they can all be true at once. Alternatively, it is a property of a set of propositions such that no proposition of the form "*p* and *not-p*" can be derived from the members of that set. *See also* LOGIC.

CONTEXTUALISM. The view that **beliefs** are inferentially justified by their connections with other beliefs in a given context. Versions of this view are defended by **John Dewey**, **John L. Austin**, and **Ludwig Wittgenstein**. Justifying a belief does not require ruling out all **skeptical alternatives**; only **relevant alternatives** need to be ruled out, and this can be done by appealing to other beliefs in the set or context. This can resemble **foundationalism** in that the **epistemic justification** of a belief involves showing that it is based on other beliefs that are contextually basic; however, it differs from foundationalism in that these contextually **basic beliefs** have no intrinsic justification. A belief that is contextually basic in one setting will be inferentially justified in some other setting, drawing its justification from its connections to other beliefs that are (in that setting) contextually basic. *See also* COHERENTISM; INFERENCE.

CONTINENTAL EPISTEMOLOGY. A set of epistemological issues and approaches that developed in continental Europe (particularly in France and Germany) beginning in the nineteenth century. Although continental **epistemology** is not a unified body of **theories**, issues, or methods, some prominent components can be identified. **Knowledge** is understood as having an essentially subjective component, linked to one's embeddedness in a historical context. **Truth** is not absolute but relative to a historical and cultural context. **Beliefs** and their formation are examined at the level of entire cultures, not merely at the level of the individual. The context and interrelationships among beliefs are of more importance than their propositional content. Instead of attempting to respond to **skepticism**, continental epistemology is more interested in examining how and whether our culturally and historically limited perspective plays a role in gaining knowledge. Instead of trying to gain epistemic **access** to a mind-independent **reality**, the focus is on a "lived world," or a reality constructed by our **experience**s, languages, and cultures.

 G. W. F. Hegel, Karl Marx, and **Friedrich Nietzsche** examine the movement of history and the nature of our historically embedded perspective as well as the implications this has for the nature of truth, belief, and knowledge. **Phenomenology** rejects the subject/object division assumed in Anglo-American epistemology, replacing it with one's experience of the object, the "thing-for-me." **Hermeneutics** examines the ways in which our experience and knowledge is formed by our historical setting and other factors and dissolves the distinction between the subject and object or between the reader and the text. **Jürgen Habermas** regards inquiry not as yielding knowledge but rather an agreement among researchers. Inquiry is also influenced by the power structure in which it takes place: Inequalities of power will yield skewed results. The methods used in research are not independent of the values and goals of the researchers, but these values and goals can still be rationally evaluated.

Ferdinand de Saussure and Claude Lévi-Strauss, working against the background of **phenomenalism**, examine what conditions must be met for experience to be possible; this became known as the structuralist movement. The poststructuralist reaction against this rejects the view that experience can be understood in ways that ignore the cultural and historical context in which experience occurs. Nietzsche's influence is evident here in the claims that understanding knowledge systems involves understanding the desires and political relationships among those involved and that truth is grounded in how language is used (rather than in, say, correspondence between **facts** and **propositions**).

Traditional analytic epistemology is criticized by **Jacques Derrida** for its failure to understand the nature of language. Language does not make clear or stable reference to the world, and its elements are interconnected in complex and changing ways. This makes the task of pinning down a belief's **justification** impossible. This shifting web of linguistic components is expanded by **Michel Foucault** to include objects, behaviors, and other cultural features.

Continental epistemology also includes **feminist epistemology**, particularly as feminism has developed in France. One aspect of feminist epistemology is the view that the traditional analytic desire for objective knowledge and justification is an outgrowth of masculine thinking and that it masks a desire to dominate and control. This is evident also in the linear reasoning used in theorizing. *See also* ANALYCITY; BELIEF-FORMING PROCESS; CONNECTIONISM; CONTEXTUALISM; OBJECTIVE/SUBJECTIVE; SCIENTIFIC METHOD; SOCIOLOGY OF KNOWLEDGE.

CONTINGENCY. A property of a **proposition** such that it is possibly true but not necessarily true; that is, the proposition is true in at least one—but not all—**possible worlds. Empiricists** believe that contingent truths can be known only by means of **experience**, but this is disputed by **rationalists**. *See also* NECESSITY.

CONVENTION. A way in which a word can be given meaning. A word has meaning by convention if its meaning lies in a set of rules about how this word is to be used in relation to others in the language. This contrasts with words that are given meaning by ostension, that is, assigning an object, property, mental state, and so on as the word's meaning. **Propositions** expressed using these terms with conventional meaning are often said to be true by convention. *See also* CONVENTIONALISM; GRAMMAR; TRUTH.

CONVENTIONALISM. The view that the **truth** of logical and mathematical **propositions** is something we decide, not something determined by the world. Our linguistic conventions establish definitions of the central terms in **logic** and mathematics and also establish axioms and rules of **inference**. *See also* GRAMMAR; MATHEMATICAL KNOWLEDGE.

CONVERGENCE. A situation in which **evidence** of different types or from different sources all support the same **belief** or **theory**. For instance, evidence from eyewitnesses, electronic surveillance equipment, footprints, and the medical examiner's report may all support the conclusion that Jones murdered Smith. Convergence is epistemically important because it contributes to the coherence and explanatory value of evidence and helps rule out **errors** and **skeptical alternatives**. *See also* COHERENTISM; REFLECTIVE EQUILIBRIUM.

CONVERSATIONAL IMPLICATURE. First clearly described and analyzed by **H. Paul Grice**, this is an examination of how remarks made in conversation imply more than can be logically inferred from what is said. For example, if I say that I am out of milk and you reply that there is a store around the corner, you are conversationally implying that the store sells milk, that it is now open, and perhaps that I should now go there to purchase milk.

Grice identifies several rules of conversational implicature, such as the rule of relevance, which states that remarks made in conversation should be relevant to the topic, and the maxim of quantity, which states that one should state as much relevant information as one believes. *See also* GRAMMAR; TESTIMONY.

COPERNICAN REVOLUTION. Nicolaus Copernicus (1473–1543) challenged the **theories** of Ptolemy (ca. 100–178) by explaining the movement of the stars and planets in terms of the motion of the earth and an earthbound observer instead of by attributing motion solely to the heavenly bodies around a stationary earth. Metaphorically, any new approach to a subject matter that is radically different from accepted approaches, especially when the new approach attributes events or properties to changes in the observer. *See also* KANT, IMMANUEL; KUHN, THOMAS.

CORDEMOY, GÉRAUD de (1626–1684). French philosopher. He defends and expands on many of **René Descartes**'s views and defends him against charges that his natural philosophy is incompatible with orthodox **belief**. He differs from Descartes in endorsing atomism and the possibility of the void. *See also* RATIONALISM.

CORRESPONDENCE THEORY OF TRUTH. *See* TRUTH.

COUNTERFACTUALS. A subjunctive or contrary-to-**fact** conditional whose antecedent is admittedly false. A conditional, or hypothetical, statement has the form "If p, then q," where p is the antecedent and q is the consequent. A counterfactual condition is one in which a **proposition** known to be false is used as the antecedent. For example, "If the polar icecaps had melted, Vancouver would be underwater." Unlike other conditionals, the **truth** or falsity of a counterfactual is not straightforwardly determined by the truth or falsehood of its components (antecedent and consequent). *See also* LOGIC; POSSIBLE WORLDS.

COURNOT, ANTOINE-AUGUSTINE (1801–1877). French mathematician and economist. He argues that **science** is logically organized **knowledge** and explains knowledge and **justification** in terms of **probabilities**.

COVERING LAW MODEL OF EXPLANATION. A view of scientific **explanation** originating with **Aristotle** that takes it to be a variety of deductive **argument** that includes a universal law among its premises. Universal laws are taken to express constant conjunctions of properties. The deductive-nomological explanations described by **Carl Hempel** and Carl Oppenheim fall under this heading. This model of explanation can be expanded to include statistical or probabilistic laws. *See also* DEDUCTION; PROBABILITY; SCIENCE.

CREDIBILITY. The credibility of a source is the reliability with which it presents us with **truths** or the degree to which information from that source should be accepted as true. The credibility of a **proposition** is the degree to which it should be accepted as true, given the **evidence** in the subject's possession. *See also* AUTHORITY; BELIEF; EXTERNALISM/INTERNALISM; FALLIBILISM; SOCIAL EPISTEMOLOGY; TRUTH.

CREDULITY. The willingness to believe, even in the absence of adequate **evidence**. Incredulity is the unwillingness to believe, even in the face of compelling evidence. Neither is generally regarded as a desirable characteristic. *See also* BELIEF; FAITH.

CRITICAL COGNITIVISM. The view, described by **Roderick Chisholm**, that particular instances of **knowledge** can be identified and that examination of these cases will allow one to formulate a general account of the nature of knowledge. Like **commonsensism**, this view begins with the assumption that global forms of **skepticism** are false and that we have at least some knowledge. As presented by Chisholm, critical cognitivism goes beyond commonsensism by proposing standards for knowledge. All our knowledge is rooted in **sense perception**, **introspection**, **memory**, and reasoning. *See also* PROBLEM OF THE CRITERION; REID, THOMAS; SKEPTICISM.

CRITICAL REALISM. Like **direct realism**, it claims that observers are directly aware of objects in a mind-independent **external world** but also states that what is immediately present to **consciousness** is a mental state. This mediating function of mental states allows critical realism to overcome the difficulties direct realism has in explaining **illusions** and hallucinations. It attempts to avoid the difficulties facing **John Locke**'s **representative realism** by distinguishing between the object known and the mental state by which it is known. *See also* IMMEDIACY; REALISM/ANTIREALISM; SELLARS, WILFRID.

CRITICAL SKEPTICISM. *See* SKEPTICISM.

CRITICAL THEORY. Any of various social **theories** (including the **Frankfurt School**, feminism, and liberation theology) that explore the causes of oppression using empirical **evidence** and current social and economic theories. Critical theory rejects **positivism**, **empiricism**, cultural relativism, and a **fact**/value distinction. It seeks not only to explain oppression but also to offer to the oppressed practical steps toward emancipation. *See also* CONTINENTAL EPISTEMOLOGY; EPISTEMIC RELATIVITY; FEMINIST EPISTEMOLOGY; MARXISM; SOCIOLOGY OF KNOWLEDGE.

CRUCIAL EXPERIMENT. An experiment that simultaneously tests two competing **theories** or **explanations**, supporting one and disconfirming the other. For example, Antoine Lavoisier burned mercury in an enclosed space to test the phlogiston theory and what would later become the oxygen theory. These theories generated incompatible **predictions**, and **observation** allowed one to decide between them. **Pierre Duhem** argues that crucial experiments are impossible because one cannot enumerate all the possible theories that could explain the phenomena at issue. *See also* CONFIRMATION; HYPOTHETICO-DEDUCTIVE METHOD; SCIENCE.

CZOLBE, HEINRICH (1819–1873). German philosopher. He argues that **sensation** is the root of **knowledge** and that knowledge involves a spatial copy of what is known. He also claims that **ideas** have spatial properties.

– D –

d'AILLY, PIERRE (1350–1420). French philosopher and prelate. He distinguishes between the "**natural light**" of **indubitable knowledge** and reason. He also argues that **experience** and experiment cannot yield **certainty** and that the classical "**proofs**" of **God**'s existence yield only **probability** and not certainty.

DAVIDSON, DONALD (1917–2003). American philosopher who was educated at Harvard University; he was a professor at Stanford University. In his *Inquiries into Truth and Interpretation* (1984), he uses his **theory** of radical interpretation to argue that if a subject has many coherent **beliefs**, then many of those beliefs are true. Given information about the subject's circumstances and the sentences the subject takes to be true in those circumstances, a radical interpreter would be obligated by the **principle of charity** to interpret these beliefs in such a way that most of them are true. *See also* COHERENTISM; GIVEN, THE; INDETERMINACY OF TRANSLATION; TRUTH.

DEATH OF EPISTEMOLOGY. A loosely knit collection of criticisms of **epistemology** as it is traditionally pursued, particularly within **analytic** philosophy. These **arguments** typically target the theoretical **presuppositions** that give rise to epistemological issues and take the central concern to be showing that global **skepticism** (the claim that none of our **beliefs** has any measure of **epistemic justification**) is false.

   Richard Rorty argues that the challenge of global skepticism depends on the assumption that **knowledge** requires establishing a correspondence between mental representations and mind-independent **reality** and that this skeptical challenge dissolves when we adopt a **pragmatic** or behaviorist understanding of beliefs. Another line of argument takes **foundationalism** as the root of radical skepticism and points out that **coherentism** or some other view of justification and **knowledge** could circumvent this. **Naturalized epistemology** also plays a part in the "death of epistemology" movement. By turning to empirical **psychology** or some other branch of **natural science** to describe and evaluate our beliefs (or other states that supplant beliefs), the skeptical challenge will be avoided. *See also* ADORNO, THEODOR; QUINE, W. V. O.

DECISION THEORY. The study of making choices rationally. When this study includes the ways in which one person's choices affect and are affected by the choices of others, it is called **game theory**. *See also* RATIONALITY.

DECONSTRUCTION. A form of criticism in which **concepts** and principles whose use is established by a philosophical position are used against that position. Texts are subjected to a very close reading with a view to identifying tensions or contradictions within a position. This term was introduced by **Jacques Derrida**, who uses this strategy in arguing against views of language and meaning that are assumed in much Western philosophy. *See also* HEGEL, G. W. F.; GRAMMAR.

DEDUCTION. Any **argument** or logical process that guarantees the **truth** of the conclusion provided that the premises are true. **René Descartes** and others have argued that **knowledge** can be established only by utilizing **indubitable** premises and deduction. *See also* ARGUMENT; INDUCTION; INTUITION; LOGIC.

DEDUCTIVE CLOSURE PRINCIPLE. *See* CLOSURE PRINCIPLE.

DEFEASIBILITY. The property of statements, **arguments**, principles, and **epistemic warrant** that they can be defeated by some competitor. In **epistemology**, a **belief**'s warrant or **justification** is defeasible if adding further **evidence** would decrease this justification. A piece of evidence capable of thus decreasing a belief's justification is sometimes called a **defeater** before it is added to the subject's stock of evidence and an **overrider** when the subject is in possession of that piece of evidence. *See also* GETTIER CASES; *PRIMA FACIE* REASONS.

DEFEATER. A **fact** or piece of **evidence** not yet in the subject's possession but that would, if added to the subject's set of evidence, defeat or **override** the subject's **epistemic justification** for a **belief**. For example, suppose that while in a friend's home I look at the clock and form the belief that it is nearly time for lunch. Although I am unaware of this, the clock I have observed is broken; it always indicates 10 minutes before 12 o'clock. This piece of evidence, not yet in my possession, is a defeater; if added to my set of evidence, it would decrease the justification of my belief. Thus, the justification for this belief is **defeasible**. When the piece of evidence is in my cognitive possession, it is called an overrider. *See also* EXTERNALISM/INTERNALISM; GETTIER CASES; *PRIMA FACIE* REASONS.

DENNETT, DANIEL (1942–). American philosopher; he was a student of **Gilbert Ryle** at Oxford University and is now a professor at Tufts University. He has made important contributions to the philosophy of mind, philosophy of **science, naturalized epistemology**, and the free will debate. In his *The Intentional Stance* (1987), he defends an **instrumentalist** view of mental states, arguing that an individual or system has **beliefs**, desires, and other mental states provided that one gains an **explanatory** advantage by thinking of it in those terms; this is what he calls adopting the "**intentional stance**." *See also* BELIEF.

DEONTOLOGISM. *See* EPISTEMIC DEONTOLOGISM.

DERRIDA, JACQUES (1930–2004). French philosopher, born in Algiers. He attempts to resist, disrupt, and subvert much of traditional Western philosophy, including any epistemological attempts to establish secure foundations or **certainty** for our beliefs. His **deconstruction** of philosophical **theories** led to his rejection of essentialism, **foundationalism**, and the traditional understanding of meaning. *See also* CONTINENTAL EPISTEMOLOGY; DEATH OF EPISTEMOLOGY.

DESCARTES, RÉNE (1596–1650). French philosopher and mathematician. Known as the founder of the "modern" era in philosophy, Descartes made important contributions in many areas of philosophy. His rationalist **epistemology** begins with the **method of doubt**, presented in his *Meditations on First Philosophy* (1641; 2nd ed., 1647). Descartes notes that even our ordinary commonsense **beliefs** may be mistaken and uses the **indubitability** criterion of **truth** to establish which beliefs are true and can function as a foundation for other beliefs. The "*cogito ergo sum*" ("I think, therefore I exist") **argument** presents such a foundational belief: The belief that I exist must be true whenever I consider it. From this starting point of self-awareness, he reestablishes his **knowledge** of other things, including the **external world**. An important step in this process is establishing **God**'s existence. Descartes argues that his **idea** of God could have been **caused** only by God, although this argument is widely criticized. God's perfection is then used to establish the truth of beliefs about the external world; a perfect being would not engage in systematic deception. *See also* BASIC BELIEF; CARTESIAN CIRCLE; CARTESIANISM.

DEWEY, JOHN (1859–1952). American philosopher and education theorist. A founder of **instrumentalism** (a form of **pragmatism**), he criticizes traditional **epistemology** for isolating its concerns from a much broader examination of thought and learning, a **theory** of inquiry. He rejects what he called the spectator theory of **knowledge**, a passive view of the knowing subject, and argues that the focus should be on the "situation" in which the process of inquiry takes place. Instead of attempting to **analyze** a mental act of knowing, an account is given of the process of learning and the abilities and dispositions that result; the end result is, he argues, a superior understanding of epistemological issues. *See also* BELIEF-FORMING PROCESS.

DHARMAKĪRTI (seventh century A.D.). Indian **Buddhist** philosopher. His *Pramānavārttika* (*Explanation of the Touchstones*) is an important work on **epistemology** and **logic**. He defends a form of **idealism**, arguing that there are no objects with mind-independent existence; they exist only in perception. His *Santānāntara-siddhi* (*Establishment of the Existence of Other Minds*) includes a defense of his use of the **argument from analogy** in inferring the existence of minds from his **observation** of intelligent behavior. *See also* OTHER MINDS, PROBLEM OF.

DIALECTIC. For **Plato**, dialectic is a type of conversation or collaborative argument that seeks answers to philosophical questions. **Hypotheses** and definitions are examined and rejected if flaws are discovered, and by repeating this process, one's innate **knowledge** of the **Forms** may eventually be recollected.

For **G. W. F. Hegel**, "dialectic" has several uses. The content and application of **concepts** can be discovered through dialectical **analysis**, a process of examining, criticizing, and refining concepts, moving from simple, general concepts to a network of more complex concepts. Dialectical **arguments** begin by examining and criticizing a simple principle within a given domain. The flaws discovered at this stage lead to presenting a more complex and promising principle that then becomes the subject of further criticism. The end result is an acceptable principle, and the preceding dialectical argument supports it. The relations among objects or concepts are called dialectical when they seem to be independent but are in fact interdependent. *See also* BELIEF-FORMING PROCESS; LINEAR JUSTIFICATION.

DIALLELUS. From the Greek *di allēlon*, "through one another." A circular **argument**. *See also* CIRCULAR REASONING.

DIANOIA. Greek: the human mental faculty of formulating **arguments** and drawing conclusions from them. *See also* PLATO; RATIONALITY.

DIRECT REALISM. Sometimes called "naïve realism," it is the **theory** that mind-independent objects in the **external world** are the direct objects of **sense perception**. This contrasts with indirect or **representative realism**, which states that the perception of external objects is mediated by one's awareness of mental representations of those objects. Although one's perception of an object may be **caused** by that object, this perception may nevertheless be epistemically direct (although it is causally mediated).

Critics argue that direct realism is unable to account satisfactorily for **illusions** and hallucinations, which may be experientially indistinguishable from veridical (i.e., accurate, truthful) perception. If these are cases in which the direct object of perception is a mental state, why does veridical perception not also have a mental state as its direct object? And if hallucinations do not have mental states as their objects, it seems that the direct realist must either find some external object of which the subject is directly aware or explain why hallucinations are unlike perception. *See also* CAUSATION; IDEA; LOCKE, JOHN; OBJECTIVE/SUBJECTIVE; REALISM/ANTIREALISM.

DISCOVERY, LOGIC OF. *See* LOGIC OF DISCOVERY.

DISPOSITION. The property of an object such that it responds in a characteristic way to particular situations or stimulations. For example, solubility is a dispositional property: A soluble object is one that will dissolve when in contact with an appropriate liquid. Dispositions are typically expressed in **counterfactual** conditionals and are contrasted with occurrent or categorical properties.

In *The Concept of Mind* (1949), **Gilbert Ryle** argues that a mental state such as **belief** is best understood as the disposition to behave in characteristic ways under certain circumstances. As long as the relevant counterfactual conditionals are true, Ryle says that it does not matter which processes or states are involved in producing those behaviors. This view of belief separates it from **introspection** and consciously entertaining **propositions**. *See also* BEHAVIORISM; DENNETT, DANIEL.

DIVIDED LINE ANALOGY. In his *Republic* (509d–511e), **Plato** uses the analogy of a divided line to illustrate the various objects of **knowledge** or opinion and the sources of **evidence** or forms of cognition associated with them. Beginning with a vertical line, Plato describes it as being divided unequally so that the top portion is larger than the bottom. The top portion represents the realm of genuine knowledge, and this is shown to be more real and important than the bottom, which represents mere opinion. Each of these portions of the line is then subdivided so that their top and bottom sections preserve this same ratio. The topmost of the four resulting sections represents knowledge (*noesis*) and involves one's grasp of the **forms**. Beneath this is a smaller line segment representing reasoning (*dianoia*) and involves one's grasp of mathematics and other forms of abstractions. The next two line segments are below the major division, indicating that they have to do with the world of appearances (rather than the world of the forms). The higher of these represents belief (*pistis*) and involves one's acceptance of the world as it presents itself to one's senses. The bottom line segment represents imagination (*eikasia*) and involves the lowest form of cognition: supposition. Higher segments of the divided line represent epistemic success, and lower segments represent epistemic shortcomings or failures.

DIVINE FOREKNOWLEDGE. God's **knowledge** of the future, particularly of human actions; a consequence of God's omniscience and required by most orthodox theology. Some argue that God is outside of time or that all moments of time are present for God.

It has been argued, notably by Boethius, that divine foreknowledge of one's actions is inconsistent with one's freedom to act as one chooses. Critics respond that this confuses "If God knows that I will do x, then I will do x" (which is compatible with my freely deciding to do x) with "If God knows that I will do x, then I must do x" (which yields incompatibility with free will but is not implied by divine fore-knowledge). Others argue that there are no **truths** about the future or that truths about future free actions are not knowable (so that God's omniscience should be interpreted as knowledge of all knowable truths). **Luis de Molina** contends that God possesses "**middle knowledge**" of our future actions that is compatible with our free will.

DOGMATISM. The characteristic of clinging to views despite com-pelling **evidence** to the contrary or of being more confident of one's views than one's evidence warrants. The **Pyrrhonian skeptics** regard dogmatism as the mental disorder of rashly forming **beliefs** about matters that are not evident and then being anxious about whether these beliefs are true. They recommend **skepticism** and the tranquil-lity of suspending **judgment** as a cure for this illness. *See also* CER-TAINTY; CREDULITY; FAITH.

DOUBT. The **propositional attitude** of failing to believe, typically aris-ing in response to one's realization of the possibility of **error**. **C. S. Peirce** regards doubt as an unsatisfactory mental state, as opposed to **belief**, that we seek to remove by means of learning. Doubt and the dif-ficulty of overcoming it are at the root of **skepticism**. **René Descartes's method of doubt**, employed in his *Meditations on First Philosophy* (1641, 1647), is used to identify beliefs that are **indubitable** and thus suitable for forming the foundation of one's **knowledge**.

DOXASTIC. From the Greek *doxa* ("belief"), pertaining to **belief**. Dox-astic mental states are or incorporate beliefs and are contrasted with nondoxastic states, such as emotions and desires. A doxastic principle is a principle governing beliefs, and doxastic practices (discussed by **William Alston**) are the ways in which we form, modify, criticize, and defend beliefs. *See also* BELIEF-FORMING PROCESS; NATU-RALIZED EPISTEMOLOGY; PSYCHOLOGY.

DOXASTIC LOGIC. *See* EPISTEMIC LOGIC.

DRETSKE, FRED (1932–). An American philosopher, Dretske was trained at the University of Minnesota and has taught at Duke University, Stanford University, and other institutions. He has contributed to numerous issues in philosophy, particularly those involving visual perception and the nature of **consciousness**. In particular, he is noted for his application of **information theory** to the **analysis** of **knowledge**. His works include *Seeing and Knowing* (1969), *Knowledge and the Flow of Information* (1981), *Explaining Behavior* (1988), and *Naturalizing the Mind* (1995). *See also* PROBLEM OF THE CRITERION.

DUCASSE, CURT JOHN (1881–1969). An American philosopher born in France. Although he wrote on many topics, in **epistemology** he rejects **sense data** and defends the **adverbial theory of perception**, arguing that the sensory qualities of objects are ways of perceiving rather than objects of **perception**.

DUHEM, PIERRE-MAURICE-MARIE (1861–1916). French physicist and historian of the philosophy of **science**. He holds an **instrumentalist** view of physical **theories**, arguing that although theoretical **propositions** may be useful or not useful, they are neither true nor false. The Duhem Thesis states that physical experiments involve **observations** combined with interpretations so that experiments do not test a single **hypothesis** but entire groups of them; thus, experimental **evidence** cannot conclusively falsify an hypothesis. *See also* NEURATH, OTTO; QUINE, W. V. O.; SCIENTIFIC METHOD; TRUTH.

DUNS SCOTUS, JOHN (1266–1308). Scottish Franciscan philosopher and theologian. He argues that **God** created each creature with a unique haecceity, an individual essence not shared by any other object. Haecceities are objectively real and potentially universal and are the basis of scientific **knowledge**. Scotus argues that **Augustine**'s account of illumination as the source of **certainty** was untenable and would lead instead to **skepticism**. He also produces an **argument** for the existence of God that united various traditional lines of argument.

See also OBJECTIVE/SUBJECTIVE; RELIGIOUS KNOWL-
EDGE.

DUTCH BOOK. A combination of bets that would result in a net loss
for the bettor regardless of the outcome. The Dutch book **argument**
concludes that a rational person's degrees of **belief** must be guided by
probability calculus in order to avoid losses in a Dutch book situation. *See also* BAYESIANISM; RATIONALITY.

DUTY. *See* EPISTEMIC DEONTOLOGISM.

– E –

EDUCTION. The process of clarifying an **argument**, **experience**, text,
or phenomenon prior to logically analyzing it. This may involve
drawing out features that are implicit or hidden. *See also* ANALY-
SIS; HERMENEUTICS; LOGIC.

EFFECTIVE PROCEDURE. A finite step-by-step procedure for
computing the values of a function. Each step is "mechanical" in the
sense of not requiring any understanding or insight. An effective procedure is also known as an **algorithm**. A function is computable if
there is an effective procedure for determining its values.

EGOCENTRIC PREDICAMENT. An apparent epistemic problem
each person faces in trying to gain empirical **knowledge** of the **external world**. One's **experience** seems to provide **evidence** only about
how the world appears and not about how it actually is. Furthermore,
because experience is private, there seems to be no way to learn about
the experiences of others. Thus, one can learn about oneself but
not about others or the external world. *See also* APPEARANCE/
REALITY; DESCARTES, RENÉ; OTHER MINDS, PROBLEM
OF; PRIVACY OF MENTAL STATES.

ELENCHUS. A conversation or cross-examination in which one's
claim to **knowledge** is refuted by showing that it is inconsistent with
one's other **beliefs**. As used by the Sophists, refutation is its sole pur-

pose. As used by **Socrates**, this refutation is followed by further investigation that may ultimately result in one's recollection of knowledge of the **Forms**. *See also* APORIA; DECONSTRUCTION.

ELIMINATIVE MATERIALISM. The view that the **folk psychology** understanding of the mind is fundamentally mistaken and should be rejected in favor of a materialist view in which such **concepts** as **belief** and desire will be replaced with concepts from an acceptable **science** of the mind/brain. *See also* CHURCHLAND, PAUL; NATURALIZED EPISTEMOLOGY.

EMPIRICISM. From the Greek *empeiria* ("experience"), empiricism is a broad school of thought according to which **experience** is crucial for **knowledge** or **justified true belief**, particularly about the **external world**. This school of thought is opposed to **rationalism** and generally includes a **skeptical** attitude toward a faculty of **intuition** by which **truths** might be known. Empiricism can also be formulated as an account of the origins of **ideas** or **concepts**, stating that these are acquired by means of the senses. In this sense, empiricism is opposed to the doctrine of **innate ideas**.

One of the major challenges empiricists face is to explain how **inferential** knowledge can be rooted in experience without making unacceptable assumptions about the world. Empiricists differ with regard to the nature of experience and about experience's relationship to concepts and **beliefs**.

According to some empiricists, the content of all concepts is ultimately derived from experience, although defenders of **rationalism** argue that attempts to connect experience with concepts are inadequate. *See also A PRIORI/A POSTERIORI* KNOWLEDGE; NATURAL SCIENCE; OBSERVATION; SENSE PERCEPTION.

ENCYCLOPEDIA. French title: *Encyclopédie*; full English title: *Encyclopedia, or a Descriptive Dictionary of the Sciences, Arts and Trades*. Begun by the French publisher Le Breton, the seventeen-volume work was released progressively from 1751 until 1772 and was accompanied by eleven volumes of plates. It collected the **knowledge** of the time, particularly secularist and **rationalist** views of the French Enlightenment.

ENTHYMEME. A syllogism or **argument** presented in such a way that a premise or even the conclusion is not explicitly stated. The unstated premise is commonly one that the reader is understood to accept and supply to complete the argument. *See also* CONVERSATIONAL IMPLICATURE.

ENUMERATIVE INDUCTION. *See* INDUCTION.

EPAPOGĒ. Greek term meaning **induction**, as opposed to reasoning by syllogism. **Aristotle** describes it as the **inferential** move from particulars to the universal. This term is also applied to **arguments** intended to trap an opponent.

EPICUREANISM. A philosophical school of thought within Hellenistic philosophy, founded by **Epicurus** (ca. 341–271 B.C.) and his colleagues. Epicureanism includes an atomistic view of the world, the claim that **sensations** are all true, and a hedonistic ethic. Epicurean communities separated themselves from surrounding society and endeavored to live by their founders' principles.

EPICURUS (ca. 341–271 B.C.). A Greek philosopher who argues that only **sensation** provides an **indubitable** foundation for **knowledge**. His view is a form of **empiricism**, although he does not focus on **inferences** from **experience** to claims about external objects. He argues that all sensations are true because the senses function mechanistically, adding no interpretation to the information they pass along. *See also* HOBBES, THOMAS; SENSE PERCEPTION; SEXTUS EMPIRICUS.

EPIPHANY. An event, usually sudden, by means of which a divine being reveals itself or imparts other **knowledge**. This event typically results in the recipient of this knowledge experiencing a feeling of **certainty** of its **truth**. The divine origin of beliefs is regarded in religious circles as justifying them fully; no further **evidence** or other epistemic defense of them is necessary. *See also* FAITH; RELIGIOUS KNOWLEDGE.

EPISTEMIC CIRCULARITY. First clearly identified by **William P. Alston** ("Epistemic Circularity," reprinted in his *Epistemic Justifica-*

tion, 1989), this is the circularity involved when one seeks to defend or demonstrate the **reliability** of a source of **belief** in ways that require relying on beliefs generated by that source. For instance, one might argue that vision is reliable by listing the visually formed beliefs that have been accurate. Doing so would involve using vision to assess these beliefs, and this introduces epistemic circularity. Alston contends that epistemic circularity is importantly different from **circular reasoning** and that epistemically circular arguments are not viciously circular; that is, they are still capable of providing compelling **evidence** for their conclusions.

EPISTEMIC DEONTOLOGISM. The view that **epistemic justification** should be understood in terms of duty. A **belief** is justified if the believer has not violated any epistemic obligations (or if holding this belief is permissible for this believer). This implies that our beliefs are under our **voluntary** control and that we have **introspective access** to our beliefs, to **belief-forming processes**, and to the standards or obligations that ought to be followed. In other words, epistemic deontologism implies **internalism** and voluntarism. Critics, including **William Alston**, argue that our beliefs are largely involuntary and thus that epistemic deontologism is founded on a false assumption. *See also* CHISHOLM, RODERICK; EXTERNALISM/ INTERNALISM.

EPISTEMIC DEPENDENCE. A proposition *a* is epistemically dependent on *b* if one cannot know (or be **epistemically justified** in believing) *a* unless *b* is one's **evidence** for *a*. For example, **knowledge** of physical objects may be epistemically dependent on **sensory experience**. If *a* is epistemically dependent on *b* but *b* is not epistemically dependent on *a*, then *b* is epistemically prior to *a*. *See also* EPISTEMIC PRIORITY; FOUNDATIONALISM; LINEAR JUSTIFICATION.

EPISTEMIC JUSTIFICATION. The positive, normative state of doing (or being likely to do) well with respect to epistemic goals or standards. Also, a defense of **beliefs** that provides compelling **evidence** for the conclusion that they are justified. The most common epistemic goal is having beliefs that are nonaccidentally true and are formed on some satisfactory basis. Justification is widely regarded as a **necessary** condition for **knowledge**, and so the study of justification is one of **epistemology**'s central tasks.

Theorists disagree about whether justification attaches primarily to the belief itself or to the believing subject. In addition, as **William Alston** points out in his *Epistemic Justification* (1989), there is a difference between the activity of justification and the state of being justified, and one may be in the state of being justified without ever participating successfully in the activity of justification. *See also* PROBLEM OF THE CRITERION.

EPISTEMIC LEVELS. As described by **William Alston** in "Level Confusions in Epistemology" (in his *Epistemic Justification*, 1989), the epistemic level of **beliefs**, **propositions**, and states of affairs is determined by the presence or absence of **epistemic operators** such as "believes that," "knows that," "is justified in believing that," and so on. A belief, proposition, or state of affairs is moved to a higher epistemic level with each addition or iteration of such operators. Carelessness and confusion about epistemic levels results in **error** and unnecessary difficulty and often contributes to **arguments** in support of **skepticism**. *See also* EPISTEMIC JUSTIFICATION.

EPISTEMIC LOGIC. Also known as **doxastic** logic, it is the **logic** of **belief**. Beginning with Georg Henrik von Wright in the 1950s, it has been generally regarded as a branch of **modal logic**. He notes the similarities between **necessity**, **contingency**, and impossibility on the one hand and **falsification**, undecidability, and **verification** on the other. **Jaakko Hintikka** develops epistemic logic in his *Knowledge and Belief* (1962), analyzing **knowledge** and other central epistemic **concepts** in terms of **possible worlds**.

EPISTEMIC OPERATOR. An expression that can be prefixed to a sentence to generate a new sentence such that the resulting sentence is at a different **epistemic level** or concerns a different epistemic property. The following are **examples** of epistemic operators: "It is plausible that . . . ," "I know that . . . ," "I have **evidence** that . . . ," "I **doubt** that . . . ," "It is **indubitable** that . . . " *See also* ALSTON, WILLIAM P.

EPISTEMIC PERCEPTION. *See* SENSE PERCEPTION.

EPISTEMIC POSSIBILITY. According to **Jaakko Hintikka**'s *Knowledge and Belief* (1962), a **proposition** is epistemically possible for a subject, *S*, at a particular time if it is logically consistent with what *S* knows at that time. Epistemic possibility can also be defined in terms of *S*'s **evidence**, *S*'s **beliefs**, or *S*'s **justified** beliefs instead of *S*'s **knowledge**. *See also* EPISTEMIC LOGIC.

EPISTEMIC PRINCIPLE. A principle that relates epistemic **concepts** (e.g., **knowledge, epistemic justification,** or **evidence**) to one another or that relates epistemic concepts to nonepistemic ones. Epistemic principles may state how the **rationality** or epistemic status of a **belief** or belief system should be evaluated or how beliefs should be maintained or revised. There is some dispute about the epistemic status of epistemic principles, including disagreement about whether epistemic principles are **necessarily** or **contingently** true, whether we know that these principles are true, and what evidence we have for their **truth**.

EPISTEMIC PRIORITY. A **proposition**, *a*, is epistemically prior to *b* if *b* is **epistemically dependent** on *a* but *a* is not epistemically dependent on *b*. Foundationalists argue that **basic beliefs** are epistemically prior to **inferential beliefs**. *See also* EPISTEMIC DEPENDENCE; EVIDENCE; FOUNDATIONALISM.

EPISTEMIC PRIVACY. A **proposition**, *p*, is epistemically private for a subject, *S*, only if *S* has noninferential **knowledge** (or **justified true belief**) that *p* but no other subject could have noninferential knowledge (or justified belief) that *p*. For example, it may be that one has epistemic privacy with respect to propositions about one's **introspectively** available mental states. Others can know about these mental states only indirectly (e.g., by means of **testimony** or **inferences** from behavior or physical states). *See also* CONSCIOUSNESS; GIVEN, THE; INTROSPECTION; OTHER MINDS, PROBLEM OF; PRIVACY OF MENTAL STATES; PRIVILEGED ACCESS.

EPISTEMIC PROBABILITY. The likelihood that a **belief** is true, given a specified set of **evidence**. The epistemic **probability** of a

proposition, p, given a body of evidence, e, is often linked to the degree to which a rational subject would believe that p when in possession of e. *See also* BAYESIANISM; DEFEASIBILITY; DEFEATER.

EPISTEMIC REGRESS ARGUMENT. An **argument**, typically used in support of **foundationalism** (and some forms of **skepticism**), for the conclusion that a **belief** can be inferentially **justified** only if it is linked appropriately to a belief that is noninferentially justified. If my belief that p is justified because it is based on another belief, q, that serves as **evidence** for p, then my belief that q must also be justified. If my belief that q is not justified, then it cannot provide adequate evidence for my belief that p. My belief that q must be justified either by its own nature or because it is based on a further belief, r, that is my evidence for q. If my belief that q is justified because it is based on my belief that r, then the same question arises for r: Is it justified by its own nature or because it is based on some further belief, s? Thus, examining the justification for my initial belief gives rise to a regress of justification questions.

The evidential chains that emerge as this regress continues must fall into one of these four patterns: 1) the evidential chain continues without end, 2) the evidential chain forms a loop or circle, 3) the evidential chain terminates in an unjustified belief, or 4) the evidential chain terminates in a justified belief whose justification does not depend on relationships to other beliefs. Pattern 1 cannot provide a satisfactory account of one's justification in believing that p because an unending chain of beliefs would have no justification to transmit from stage to stage. Pattern 2 faces a similar objection; rather than transmitting justification, it seems guilty of **circular reasoning**. (Important aspects of this claim are challenged by **coherentism**.) Pattern 3 also has no justification to transmit. Only pattern 4 can provide the belief that p with **epistemic justification**.

Pattern 4 implies the division of justified beliefs into those that are inferentially justified and those whose justification does not depend on relationships with other beliefs. The latter are known as **basic beliefs**. Foundationalism adopts this division and claims that to be inferentially justified, a belief must be linked in appropriate ways to basic beliefs. **Pyrrhonian skepticism** argues that any attempt to defend one's beliefs will result in pattern 1, 2, or 3 and thus that none of one's beliefs are justified or qualify as **knowledge**. *See also* BELIEF-FORMING PROCESS; INFERENTIAL BELIEF; LINEAR JUSTI-FICATION.

EPISTEMIC RELATIVISM. The view that **knowledge**, **epistemic justification**, or **truth** is relative to a **theory**, conceptual framework, social or historical context, or individual standpoint. Defenders point to the difficulty in developing nonrelative accounts of these **concepts**, while critics argue that one cannot defend epistemic relativism without illegitimate reliance on nonrelative standards for truth or knowledge. *See also* CONTINENTAL EPISTEMOLOGY; CON-TEXTUALISM; DEATH OF ESPISTEMOLOGY; PRAGMATISM; PROBLEM OF THE CRITERION; RELEVANT ALTERNATIVES; SOCIOLOGY OF KNOWLEDGE.

EPISTEMIC VAGUENESS. *See* VAGUENESS.

EPISTEMIC VIRTUE. Intellectual virtues that lead one to attain the epistemic goals of having nonaccidentally true **beliefs** that cover a wide range of subject matter. These include a desire for true beliefs, a willingness and ability to gather and evaluate **evidence**, and a willingness to submit strongly held beliefs to critical examination. Secondarily, epistemic virtue may describe a belief that an epistemically virtuous subject would hold. *See also* IDEAL OBSERVER; VIRTUE EPISTEMOLOGY; VOLUNTARISM.

EPISTEMIC WARRANT. The property (whatever it turns out to be) that, when combined with **truth**, makes the difference between **knowledge** and mere true **belief**. This is examined by **Alvin Plantinga** in his *Warrant: The Current Debate* (1993) and *Warrant and Proper Function* (1993). *See also* PROBLEM OF THE CRITE-RION.

EPISTEMOLOGY. From the Greek *epistêmê* ("**knowledge**") and *logos* ("**explanation**"), the core area of philosophy that studies the nature of knowledge, **justification**, **evidence**, and related **concepts**. The central questions addressed by epistemology are: What is the nature of knowledge and justification? What **necessary** and sufficient conditions must be met for a **belief** to be justified or qualify as knowledge? What are the limits of knowledge and justified belief?

Historically, the answers to these questions have been sought in normative **theories** that examine the nature of one's reasons for holding a belief. **Foundationalism** and **coherentism** exemplify this approach. More recently, naturalistic approaches to these issues have been explored; these determine a belief's epistemic status by examining the mechanisms or conditions involved in their formation and maintenance. **Reliabilism** exemplifies this approach. *See also* BELIEF-FORMING PROCESS; EXTERNALISM/INTERNALISM; METAEPISTEMOLOGY; NATURALIZED EPISTEMOLOGY; PROBLEM OF THE CRITERION; REASONS FOR BELIEF; SKEPTICISM; and the Introduction.

EPOCHÉ. For **Edmund Husserl**, the basic method of **phenomenology**. It is the study of one's own **consciousness** of other objects or properties, examining what makes it consciousness *of* those objects. These properties of consciousness are transcendental in that they are **necessary** for any **appearance** of a world, and the process of reflection in which one's attention is shifted from the objects of consciousness to consciousness itself is called transcendental reduction. *See also* INTROSPECTION; OBJECTIVE/SUBJECTIVE.

EQUIPOLLENCE. The view, described by **Sextus Empiricus**, that for any issue whatever, the **arguments** on each side will be equally compelling. The reasonable response is to suspend **judgment** on all issues; this results in **skepticism**. *See also* ANTINOMY; APORIA.

EQUIVALENCE. Statements are logically equivalent if each can be derived from the other, materially equivalent if they have the same **truth** value, and equivalent in meaning if each could be substituted for the other in any context without any change in truth or meaning. *See also* CLOSURE PRINCIPLE; GRAMMAR; LOGIC.

EQUIVALENCE CONDITION. The claim that whatever confirms the statement that p also confirms any statement logically **equivalent** to p. This plays an important role in the **raven paradox**: "All ravens are black" is logically equivalent to "All nonblack things are non-ravens," so observing a red car should provide **confirmation** for "All ravens are black." This, however, is highly counterintuitive. *See also* CLOSURE PRINCIPLE.

EQUIVOCATION. Using an expression in two or more senses within a single context. For **example**, in "Nothing is better than heaven, and a ham sandwich is better than nothing, so a ham sandwich is better than heaven," the word "nothing" is used in two different senses. Similarly, the word "law" is used in different senses in "All laws are framed by a law-maker, so a lawmaker must have framed the laws of nature." When equivocation occurs in an **argument**, the fallacy of equivocation may be committed. *See also* INFORMAL FALLACIES.

ERISTIC ARGUMENTATION. Developed by the Sophists, the art of persuasion in the context of controversy, including the use of fallacious reasoning. *See also* ARGUMENT; INFORMAL FALLACIES.

ERROR. Believing what is false or believing something true but believing it to a degree that does not accord with the strength of one's **evidence**. In addition to error in what one believes to the degree to which one believes it, error also describes flaws in the means by which **beliefs** are formed or maintained. Thus, for instance, there are calculation errors and **perceptual** errors. According to **René Descartes**, error results from exercising one's will beyond the limits of one's understanding; this can lead to believing falsehoods. The frequency of error and the difficulty in identifying and correcting error are often cited in **arguments** for **skepticism**. In the experimental **sciences**, the range of **probable** error in measurements indicates the statistical likelihood that other attempts to measure the same thing will yield values that fall within the indicated range. When statistically evaluating parameters, a type 1 error is to reject a true null **hypothesis**, and a type 2 error is to accept a false null hypothesis. *See also* BELIEF-FORMING PROCESS; SCIENTIFIC METHOD.

ETHICS AND EPISTEMOLOGY. These two branches of philosophy have interesting structural similarities: Both seek to formulate normative principles and apply them to aspects of human life. Some disputes within **epistemology** resemble those within ethics: What is the role of the **concept** of blameworthiness? Should evaluations be undertaken from the subject's point of view, or should it include information not available to the subject? One important difference is that ethics deals with actions freely performed by agents, but the beliefs examined by epistemologists are unlikely to be under one's voluntary control. *See also* ETHICS OF BELIEF; EXTERNALISM/INTERNALISM; OBJECTIVE/SUBJECTIVE; VOLUNTARISM.

ETHICS OF BELIEF. The view that **knowledge** and **epistemic justification** are best understood in terms of ethical or quasi-ethical **duties** and rights. **W. K. Clifford** defends this view in his "The Ethics of Belief," arguing, "It is wrong always, everywhere, and for anyone, to believe anything on insufficient **evidence**." One has a right to believe that *p* only if one is in possession of evidence that substantially supports *p*; one also has an obligation to examine that evidence. This approach tends to assume epistemic internalism and **voluntarism**. *See also* EPISTEMIC VIRTUE; EXTERNALISM/INTERNALISM.

EVIDENCE. Information or **experience** that bears on the **truth** or falsehood of a **belief** or **proposition**. Evidence plays a prominent role in many **theories** of **knowledge**, **epistemic justification**, and **rationality**. **Sense perception**, the **testimony** of others, **memory**, **knowledge**, justified beliefs, and processes of **induction** or **deduction** are common sources of evidence. Evidence in support of *p* is said to be conclusive when it guarantees the truth of *p* and rules out the possibility of *not-p*. Inconclusive evidence makes it **probable** that *p* but leaves open the possibility that *not-p*. *Prima facie* reasons support *p* but may be **overridden** or **defeated** when more evidence is gathered. Skeptics often argue that knowledge requires conclusive evidence and that this is not available.

There is no generally accepted account of how evidence provides support for a proposition. For **example**, one can have the experience of seeing fifty-seven pebbles without this providing evidence for the proposition that there are fifty-seven pebbles here; one's experience does not readily extract this information. It is also unclear what conditions must be met for one to be in possession of evidence.

Some argue that because experiences do not have propositional content and are not themselves epistemically justified, they cannot transmit justification to beliefs; thus, experiences would not qualify as evidence. Others argue that although experiences may not be justified (and so cannot transmit justification), they are capable of generating justification. Thus, a **basic belief** might be justified because of its relationship to an experience. *See also* DEFEATER; EVIDENTIALISM; PROBLEM OF THE CRITERION; SELF-EVIDENCE; SKEPTICISM.

EVIDENCE OF THE SENSES. **Evidence** provided by **sense perception**. This form of evidence is important for **foundationalism**, as it can be a source of **basic beliefs**.

There is disagreement about whether the **experience** itself is the evidence. Some argue that because experiences have no propositional content and are not themselves justified, they cannot transmit **epistemic justification** to **beliefs**. Others argue that experiences can generate justification for beliefs without being justified themselves. It may also be that it is not the experience itself that provides the evidence but one's beliefs *about* that experience. My belief that I am now having experience *e* may be justified by my current awareness of that experience, but it may be that it is the belief rather than the experience that provides evidence for other propositions. *See also* EMPIRICISM.

EVIDENTIALISM. The **theory** that one's **belief** that *p* is **epistemically justified** only if one's **evidence** supports *p*. This is often accompanied by the claim that one's degree of belief should correspond to the degree of support provided by the evidence. Evidentialism is contrasted with causal theories of **epistemic justification**, for example, that focus on the causal chain leading up to the formation of the belief rather than on the subject's evidence.

In philosophy of religion, evidentialism is the view that religious beliefs are justified or can be rationally accepted only if they are supported by one's total evidence (all of one's **knowledge** and justified beliefs). This is often used in attacking religious beliefs. *See also* BELIEF-FORMING PROCESS; CAUSATION; COHERENTISM; PARTIAL BELIEF.

EVOLUTIONARY EPISTEMOLOGY. The view that human **knowledge**, and particularly scientific knowledge, develops by means of a process analogous to the evolution of biological organisms. Scientific **theories** are said to vary and adapt in response to the pressures exerted by **observations** and explanatory demands. Some take a more literal view of evolution, arguing that our ways of thinking, forming **beliefs**, and evaluating **evidence** have evolved in such a way as to help us adapt to our environment. Evolutionary **epistemology** is a form of **naturalized epistemology**.

An objection to the analogical version of evolutionary epistemology is that the random variations in biological organisms are not analogous to new **hypotheses** proposed in **science**. In addition, biological variation and evolution are not goal directed, but the growth of human knowledge seems to be.

A continental version of evolutionary epistemology sees it as an extension of **Immanuel Kant**'s philosophy, providing a biological **explanation** of how the mind forms and transforms **experience**. *See also* BELIEF-FORMING PROCESS; CONTINENTAL EPISTEMOLOGY; GENETIC EPISTEMOLOGY.

EXAMPLES/COUNTEREXAMPLES. An example is an object, event, or state of affairs presented by ostention or description. Examples are typically used as **evidence** in support of existentially quantified claims or to clarify or lend plausibility to universally quantified claims. For instance, in arguing that all members of category A have feature f, one may present examples of As that are f. This is typically accompanied by an **argument from analogy** for the conclusion that the unexamined As will also be f. In some fields of study, particular examples have attained the status of important test cases; any theory or generalization must provide the accepted results in these cases in order to be worthy of further examination.

Although examples are often used in defending **theories**, this approach depends on the assumption that our pretheoretic views of these cases are correct. Questioning this assumption is often met with considerable resistance and considerably complicates the process of evaluating theories. For instance, the debate about **epistemic internalism and externalism** includes disputes about which of our pretheoretic **judgments** about particular cases should be accepted.

Internalists tend to accept the common view that the **beliefs** held by a deceived **brain in a vat** are **epistemically justified**, but externalists reject this judgment as an **error**.

Counterexamples are an important component of **arguments** against theories or other generalizations; a single confirmed case suffices to demonstrate that a universally quantified statement is false. For instance, the **Gettier cases** showed the flaws in the **JTB theory of knowledge**. Responses to counterexamples tend to focus on whether the case exists or is possible, whether the judgments made about it are correct, and whether the theory or statement being challenged can account for it. *See also* LAKATOS, IMRE.

EXPERIENCE. A mental state or event with a felt character; it may also have representational content (e.g., **sense perception**). There is disagreement about the relationship between the properties an experience possesses and those it represents, although in many cases representational content is linked to the **cause** of the experience. For example, the auditory experience of hearing glass break represents breaking glass because it is generally caused by glass breaking.

The **act/object analysis** of experience states that there is an object of each experience, although this may not be a material object. This act/object structure is reflected in the ways in which we describe experiences. The objects of experience are sometimes said to be **sense data**, mental entities that actually possess the characteristics represented by the experience. The **adverbial theory of perception** rejects this act/object distinction and replaces it with a description of the way in which the subject is experiencing.

Experience plays a central role in **foundationalism** by generating **justification** for many (but not all) **basic beliefs**. *See also* CONSCIOUSNESS; EMPIRICISM; MERLEAU-PONTY, MAURICE.

EXPERIMENT. *See* CRUCIAL EXPERIMENT; HYPOTHETICO-DEDUCTIVE METHOD; SCIENTIFIC METHOD.

EXPLANATION. Explanations aid our understanding of situations, objects, **concepts**, or events by answering our what, why, and how questions. The explanandum is that which is being explained, and the explanans does the explaining.

Events generally prompt **causal** explanations, and a given event can be explained in various ways and at various levels. For example, I tripped because the sidewalk is uneven, because I was not paying attention to where I was going, because I was in a hurry, and so forth. The **covering law model of explanation** attempts to subsume the event being explained under a general law. If the law is deterministic, the result is a deductive-nomological explanation. If the law is probabilistic, the result is an inductive-statistical explanation.

Human actions are generally explained by reference to **beliefs**, desires, attitudes, and so forth. These are often teleological explanations in that they center on the agent's goals. Functional explanations are common in the biological sciences; for example, the rabbit kept very still in order to avoid being detected by predators. *See also* DEDUCTION; HEMPEL, CARL GUSTAV; INDUCTION; INFERENCE TO THE BEST EXPLANATION; MECHANISTIC EXPLANATION; PROBABILITY; SCIENCE.

EXTERNAL WORLD. All objects and events that are external to the observer, usually regarded as existing independently of the mind. Epistemic questions arise about whether an external world exists and, if it does, whether it is independent of the mind and whether it is possible for one to know what that world is like.

Direct realism states that a mind-independent world exists and that observers know about it by means of direct epistemic or perceptual **access** to external objects and events. Direct access to the world, it is argued, provides an adequate basis for **knowledge** of that world, but critics respond that this view is unworkable. **Illusion** and hallucination do not seem to be easily explained by this view, nor does it fit well with what we know about how our sensory systems function. **Representative realism** also begins with the claim that a mind-independent world exists but states that observers are aware of it indirectly by means of being aware of mental representations of that world. However, **propositions** about **appearances** do not seem to entail any propositions about the external world, so our indirect awareness seems incapable of providing **certainty** about the external world. Skeptics have seized on this as supporting their claim that we have no knowledge of that world. One response has been that an **inference to the best explanation** supports our **beliefs** about the external world and that this suffices for knowledge.

See also IDEA; IDEALISM; OBJECTIVE/SUBJECTIVE; SENSE PERCEPTION.

EXTERNALISM/INTERNALISM. A **theory** of **epistemic justification** or **knowledge** is internalist if the evaluation of **beliefs** is conducted from the subject's own point of view and externalist if it is conducted from the point of view of an **omniscient observer**. Internalist theories require that the subject have introspective **access** to some or all of the factors that make a belief justified (e.g., **experience**, **evidence**, or cognitive processes). Externalist theories do not require that the subject have any introspective access to these factors. For example, an internalist version of **foundationalism** might require that in order for an **inferential belief** to be justified, the subject must be able to identify introspectively the **basic beliefs** from which it gains its support. An externalist version would require only that an inferential belief be linked in the right ways to basic beliefs, regardless of whether the subject has or could have any cognitive access to this. Strong versions of internalism require that the subject actually be aware of all factors that make a belief justified, and weak versions require only that the subject *could* have introspective access to these factors under the proper circumstances. Internalist theories have been criticized as being **psychologically** unrealistic, and externalist theories have been criticized for being strongly counterintuitive.

There is also an externalist/internalist distinction drawn among views of how beliefs and other mental states gain their content. Internalists in this sense claim that the content of mental states is determined solely by properties internal to the subject's mind or brain, while externalists claim that content is determined at least in part by factors external to the subject. *See also* CONSCIOUSNESS; INTROSPECTION; NATURALIZED EPISTEMOLOGY; OBJECTIVE/SUBJECTIVE; VOLUNTARISM.

EXTRASENSORY PERCEPTION. *See* PARAPSYCHOLOGY.

– F –

FACT. Although there is ongoing disagreement about the nature of facts, a common **realist** view takes them to be states of affairs that are the case regardless of whether anyone is aware of them or knows about them. According to the **correspondence theory of truth**, correspondence with facts makes **propositions** true.

FAITH. A commitment of **belief** or trust, generally on religious matters, particularly when the commitment is independent of **evidence**. To believe something on faith is to accept it deliberately and **voluntarily**, perhaps guided by the character or commands of **God**. The nature and role of faith is disputed, as is its relationship with **rationality**. **Thomas Aquinas** in his *Summa Theologica* argues that faith and reason are suitable for different matters and that which one believes on faith ranks below **knowledge** (*scientia*) because one is unable to provide a demonstration of its **truth**.

George Santayana describes what he called "animal faith," which is our commitment to the existence of the **external world** as illustrated by our actions. This variety of faith, which might be called common sense, is proposed as a more suitable foundation for philosophy than **René Descartes**'s method of **doubt**. *See also* CREDULITY; ETHICS OF BELIEF; RELIGIOUS KNOWLEDGE; VOLUNTARISM.

FALLACY. *See* INFORMAL FALLACY.

FALLIBILISM. The view that we cannot be **certain** of the **truth** of some specified body of our **beliefs** (and perhaps all of them); these beliefs could be false. **C. S. Peirce** defends fallibilism with respect to scientific **theories**, pointing out that they are always vulnerable to contrary **evidence**. Fallibilism is widely rejected for beliefs about simple logical and arithmetic **propositions** and perhaps for propositions about one's current conscious states.

Fallibilism is also the view that beliefs formed by means that are subject to **error** can still qualify as **knowledge**. *See also* CERTAINTY; SKEPTICISM.

FALSIFIABILITY. *See* CRUCIAL EXPERIMENT; LOGICAL POSITIVISM; TESTABILITY.

FALSIFICATION. *See* POPPER, KARL; VERIFICATION.

FELDMAN, RICHARD (1948–). American philosopher who was trained at Cornell University and teaches at the University of Rochester (Rochester, New York). Professor Feldman's contributions in **epistemology** span a wide variety of issues, from attempts to modify the understanding of **knowledge** in light of the **Gettier cases** to **naturalized epistemology**, the nature of **evidence**, and the **externalist/ internalist** debate. He is noted as a defender of **evidentialism**.

FEMINIST EPISTEMOLOGY. A family of related criticisms of traditional **epistemology** and theoretical proposals. Feminist criticisms of traditional epistemology argue that the dominance of white middle-class men has led to skewed **theories** that do not represent the **experiences** of other classes. Epistemology's pretence of being **objective** and value free conceals the vested interests of those in social and political power and serves to perpetuate the oppression of women and other groups. The passive, idealized knower assumed by much of traditional epistemology distracts us from real people, their sociopolitical circumstances, and their actual practices in gaining **knowledge**. Thus, a central question in feminist epistemology is, *Whose* knowledge are we studying?

Some feminist epistemologies challenge **science**'s claim that it is objective and value free, arguing that all empirical investigations are influenced by race, gender, class, and other factors. Instead of striving to eliminate these factors from science, we should recognize them and design our inquiries so that we employ values and standpoints that do not perpetuate oppression.

Feminist criticisms also target the traditional assumption that all people know in the same ways. There are, feminist epistemology claims, many different ways of knowing, and none of these can be given privileged status. Furthermore, contrary to the assumptions of traditional epistemology, knowing is a cooperative, social activity, not one involving a single, isolated individual. *See also* COLLECTIVE BELIEF; CONTINENTAL EPISTEMOLOGY; IDEAL OBSERVER; MARXISM; SOCIAL EPISTEMOLOGY; SOCIOLOGY OF KNOWLEDGE.

FEYERABEND, PAUL (1924–1994). Austrian-born philosopher, he studied **science** at the University of Vienna and became widely known as a philosopher of science. He spent much of his career in the United States. He argues that there is no **scientific method** and advocates "epistemological anarchism," according to which any approach may be used in furthering science. The scientific outlook on the world is not inherently superior to other viewpoints. *See also* KUHN, THOMAS.

FIGURE-GROUND DISCRIMINATION. The visual discrimination between the object and the background, with the resulting impression of depth. This can be seen in **ambiguous** figures such as the Necker cube and the work of Edgar Rubin (1886–1951). This is often used in defending the claim that interpretation plays a large role in **sense perception**. *See also* THEORY LADEN.

FIRST PHILOSOPHY. For **Aristotle**, the study of metaphysics, the study of being *qua* being. For **René Descartes**, an investigation that is epistemically prior to more specific philosophical or scientific investigations. *See also* EPISTEMIC PRIORITY; FOUNDATIONALISM.

FIRTH, RODERICK (1917–1987). American philosopher. He defends **foundationalism**, arguing that **sense perception** could provide **basic beliefs** and that only inductive **inferences** were required to link these to our **inferential beliefs** about the **external world**. He also defends **phenomenalism**. *See also* INDUCTION.

FOLK PSYCHOLOGY. A set of **commonsense** principles about human mentality and behavior. These principles posit the existence of **propositional attitudes** such as **beliefs** and are sometimes known as "belief-desire **psychology**." Some claim that these principles together amount to an empirically **testable** psychological theory. **Paul Churchland** and other eliminativists argue that folk psychology makes false empirical **presuppositions** (e.g., the structure of mental representations is like that of language) and that it cannot be connected adequately with other scientific work regarding the brain; therefore, they say, folk psychology should be abandoned. Some defenders of folk psychology deny that it is a **theory** (and thus that it is immune from theoretical evaluation), while others acknowledge that it is a theory and argue that it is an adequate one. *See also* ELIMI-NATIVE MATERIALISM; EMPIRICISM; NATURALIZED EPIS-TEMOLOGY.

FORM. In the middle works of **Plato**, a Form (*eide*) is an abstract object, somewhat like a universal. Forms are eternal, perfect, and unchanging; the properties and classifications of physical objects are explained in terms of their participation in Forms. Only the Forms can be the objects of genuine **knowledge**, and this knowledge is attained through recollection (*anamnesis*).

Aristotle criticizes Plato's **theory** of Forms and distinguishes instead between the form (or essence) and matter of physical objects. *See also* ABSTRACT ENTITY.

FOUCAULT, MICHEL (1926–1984). French philosopher and historian. He developed the "archeology of **knowledge**," an approach to the history of thought that examines entire systems independent of any representations or intentions of individuals. This was followed by a genealogical account that explains how social power structures bring about changes in these discursive structures. Power and knowledge are inextricably linked, and power is always exercised through knowledge. *See also* CONTINENTAL EPISTEMOLOGY; FEMINIST EPISTEMOLOGY; MARXISM; SOCIAL EPISTEMOLOGY; SOCIOLOGY OF KNOWLEDGE.

FOUNDATIONALISM. The view that **knowledge** and **epistemic justification** have a two-tiered structure, with **inferential beliefs** supported by **basic beliefs**. Basic beliefs are **immediately** justified; they do not depend for their justification on any other **beliefs**. Instead, they are justified by their own nature or by their connections with **introspective** or **perceptual** states. Inferential beliefs are mediately justified because they depend for their justification on connections with other justified beliefs. In tracing the source of justification of an inferential belief, eventually it will end in one or more basic beliefs. The roots of foundationalism can be found in **Aristotle**'s *Posterior Analytics* and **René Descartes**'s *Meditations on First Philosophy*.

The dominant motivating force behind foundationalism is the **epistemic regress argument**. This states that in explaining why a belief is justified, one must trace the source of that justification. The chain of justificatory links will 1) continue without end; 2) loop back on itself, forming a circle; 3) terminate in an unjustified belief; or 4) terminate in a justified belief whose justification does not rely on its connections to other beliefs (i.e., a basic belief). Alternatives 1, 2, and 3 are rejected as unable to provide any justification for the beliefs they support, and alternative 4, the only acceptable one, describes the foundationalist structure.

Strong foundationalism requires that basic beliefs be maximally justified and thus that there is no possibility that such a belief could be false. Moderate foundationalism requires only that basic beliefs have some substantial level of justification, leaving open the possibility that a basic belief could be false. Foundationalists also disagree about what sorts of connections between basic and inferential beliefs are capable of transferring epistemic justification.

Critics have attacked the beliefs identified by foundationalists as basic, arguing that such beliefs are psychologically improbable or epistemically suspect. Critics also point out that many of our justified beliefs do not seem to be connected in the required ways to basic beliefs; thus, foundationalism seems to be unable to account for the epistemic status of many of our beliefs. *See also* GIVEN, THE; LINEAR JUSTIFICATION; SELF-EVIDENCE.

FRANKFURT SCHOOL. A group of philosophers, social scientists, and cultural critics at the Institute for Social Research (Frankfurt, founded in 1929). **Theodor Adorno** (1903–1969), Max Horkheimer (1895–1973), and Herbert Marcuse (1898–1979) were among its prominent early members. This group developed and applied **critical theory**, combining philosophy and the social sciences to identify and change the oppression found in each culture. Epistemically, the Frankfurt School defends the view that there is no absolute **truth**; instead, it is relative to historical settings and practical concerns. *See also* CONTINENTAL EPISTEMOLOGY; DEATH OF EPISTEMOLOGY; EPISTEMIC RELATIVITY; FEMINIST EPISTEMOLOGY; SOCIOLOGY OF KNOWLEDGE.

FREGE, GOTTLOB (1848–1925). German mathematician and philosopher. He made important contributions to many areas of philosophy and is sometimes called "the father of **analytic** philosophy." In **epistemology**, he discusses **mathematical knowledge**, arguing that the objects of this **knowledge** are grasped immediately by reason and that the central step in knowing an **abstract entity** is to understand its identity conditions.

FREUD, SIGMUND (1856–1939). Austrian psychologist, founder of psychoanalysis. He theorizes that only a part of our mental contents are readily available to **consciousness** and that this conscious portion is based on and shaped by unconscious drives and motives, developed in infancy and having to do with bodily functions. Our dreams, apparently meaningless actions, and apparently accidental utterances are the result of these unconscious states and processes. *See also* INTROSPECTION; PSYCHOLOGY.

FUNCTIONALISM. A theory of mind according to which a mental state is that which causally connects specified inputs to outputs. A system or individual has a **belief**, for instance, if and only if the right functional roles are played. Mental states are multiply realizable: Many different physical systems could play the functional role of connecting these inputs to these outputs. The nature of the physical system is irrelevant to the content of the mental state.

Critics argue that functionalism is unable to distinguish between mental and nonmental states and that it is unable to distinguish among different kinds of mental states. *See also* CAUSATION; CONNECTIONISM.

– G –

GADAMER, HANS-GEORG (1900–2002). A German philosopher who studied with **Martin Heidegger**, Gadamer developed **hermeneutics** into a general account of interpretation that applies to all cases of understanding. One's horizon (the set of **beliefs**, expectations, point of view, and so on) allows one to make interpretations and have **knowledge** but also places limits on that knowledge. Gadamer rejects what he calls the **Cartesian**, objectivist understanding of **truth**, **rationality**, and knowledge and argues that **truth** and rationality are relative to a context of language and culture. His most noted work is *Wahrheit und Methode* (*Truth and Method*, 1960). *See also* CONTINENTAL EPISTEMOLOGY; EPISTEMIC RELATIVISM; SOCIOLOGY OF KNOWLEDGE.

GAME THEORY. The study of making choices rationally in situations in which what one chooses affects and is affected by the choices of others. Work in this area may shed light on the nature of **rationality**, how **beliefs** are influenced by communities of believers, and what to believe in situations of uncertainty. *See also* DECISION THEORY; RATIONALITY.

GASSENDI, PIERRE (1592–1655). French philosopher and scientist, and author of the fifth set of objections to **René Descartes's** *Meditations on First Philosophy* (1641). Gassendi developed an account of scientific **knowledge** based on the **hypothetico-deductive method**. This is a **science** of **appearances**, focusing on how the world seems to us. Although **certainty** is unattainable, **skepticism** can still be avoided.

GENERALIZATION. *See* INDUCTION.

GENETIC EPISTEMOLOGY. The study of how **knowledge** develops over time. This study includes how a particular individual's knowledge develops, how it develops in a community of believers, and how it develops within a species. This is closely related to **evolutionary epistemology** and the history of **science**. *See also* PIAGET, JEAN; SOCIAL EPISTEMOLOGY.

GENETIC FALLACY. *See* INFORMAL FALLACIES.

GETTIER CASES. The traditional view of **propositional knowledge**, originating with **Plato**, is that a justified true **belief** qualifies as **knowledge**; this is known as the tripartite or **JTB theory of knowledge**. In his 1963 article "Is Justified True Belief Knowledge?" Edmund Gettier (1927–) presents two **counterexamples** to this, showing that these criteria are not sufficient for knowledge.

In one example, Smith and Jones apply for a job, and Smith's **evidence** indicates that Jones will get it and that Jones has 10 coins in his pocket. From this, he infers that the person who will get the job has 10 coins in his pocket. In fact, Smith will get the job, and he, too, has 10 coins in his pocket. Although Smith's belief was true and justified, it was only accidentally true, so it does not qualify as knowledge.

In the other example, Smith's evidence supports his belief that Jones owns a Ford, although this is actually false. From this belief, Smith infers that either Jones owns a Ford or Brown is in Barcelona. Although Smith does not realize it, Brown actually is in Barcelona, so this disjunctive belief is true. Again, Smith's belief is true and justified, but it is not knowledge.

These Gettier cases give rise to the Gettier problem: How should the JTB theory of knowledge be modified to avoid these and similar counterexamples? Some philosophers have defended the JTB theory and criticized Gettier's counterexamples, but the abundance of Gettier-style cases has led most either to modify the existing criteria or to find a fourth criterion that would properly capture the nature of knowledge. Although a number of solutions have been proposed, none has yet gained wide support. *See also* PROBLEM OF THE CRITERION.

GIVEN, THE. The contents of one's current **sense experience**, to which one has immediate **access**. One's **beliefs** about these sense experiences are traditionally said to be justified independently of any belief or **evidence** apart from the **experience** itself. Beliefs about these experiences are carefully distinguished from beliefs about the **external world** or perceived objects.

Because one's awareness of the given does not involve **inferences** or external **causal** processes, it has been claimed that beliefs about the given are **infallible, incorrigible**, or **indubitable**. Some **foundationalists** claim that beliefs about the given are basic and can serve as the epistemic foundation for other beliefs. Critics argue that the given is **psychologically** implausible, and few current **theories** of **knowledge** or **epistemic justification** include it. *See also* BASIC BELIEF; IMMEDIACY; INTROSPECTION; INTUITION; PERCEPTION; SELF-EVIDENCE; SENSE DATA.

GLANVILL, JOSEPH (1636–1680). English philosopher and Anglican minister. He argues that although **certainty** is possible for mathematics and theology, human corruption makes it unattainable for all other subject matters. *See also* FALLIBILISM; MATHEMATICAL KNOWLEDGE; SKEPTICISM.

GOD. Conceptions of God differ considerably among cultures and religions, but God is often regarded as an ultimate reality, a perfect and powerful being worthy of worship. Because God is often seen as separate or different from the natural, material world, special epistemic challenges arise: If God is not known through **sense perception** or reason, how do these **beliefs** arise and do they qualify as **knowledge**? Answers vary considerably, with common appeals to **faith** and **revelation**.

The question of God's existence is a vexed one. Theists have proposed a number of **arguments** for the conclusion that God exists, but these have many critics. A number of social and psychological **explanations** have been offered for our persistent religious beliefs. *See also* DIVINE FOREKNOWLEDGE; IDEAL OBSERVER; RELIGIOUS KNOWLEDGE.

GÖDEL, KURT (1906–1978). Austrian logician and mathematician. In 1931, he proved the incompleteness of certain formal systems. One of his two incompleteness theorems shows that a formal system of this sort cannot include **proofs** of all the true sentences that can be formulated in it. The other incompleteness theorem shows that these formal systems cannot prove their own **consistency**. *See also* CHURCH'S THESIS; MATHEMATICAL KNOWLEDGE.

GOLDMAN, ALVIN IRA (1938–). American philosopher; he has taught at Rutgers University and the University of Arizona. His work in **epistemology** includes contributions to understanding **relevant alternatives** and the **externalism/internalism** debate. His *Epistemology and Cognition* (1986) is an important development and defense of **reliabilism**, and his *Knowledge in a Social World* (1999) advances work in **social epistemology**. His *Liasons: Philosophy Meets the Cognitive and Social Sciences* (1992) includes work on **naturalized epistemology**.

GOODMAN, NELSON (1906–1998). American philosopher; he held faculty positions at the University of Pennsylvania, Brandeis University, and Harvard University. His *Ways of Worldmaking* (1978) expanded the understanding of **epistemology** to include areas of understanding not included by the traditional view (e.g., aesthetics, **projectability** of predicates). Rejecting the notions of **necessity** and **analyticity**, Goodman argues that systems of thought are built around **propositions** that are initially **credible** but that may later be rejected if doing so will result in a more credible system. Rightness replaces **truth** as the central epistemic desideratum; a proposition is right if it is part of a maximally credible system, and it may have this property even if it is not true.

Our classifications are also an epistemic issue. In his *Fact, Fiction and Forecast* (1955), Goodman defines a projectible property as one that can transfer credibility from known cases to unknown ones and thus can play a role in **induction**. Predicates are projectible if they are entrenched, embedded in our current systems and practices. A predicate such as "grue," the property of being examined before future time t and found to be green or not examined before t and being blue, could not be entrenched because it could not transfer credibility from known to unknown cases.

Because the arts can enhance our understanding, Goodman argues that aesthetics is a branch of epistemology. The arts involve systems of symbols, and these can help us understand the world. The arts can also function as samples, literal or metaphorical, of aspects of the world and so allow us to draw conclusions about unobserved parts of the world. *See also* COHERENTISM; GRUE PARADOX.

GRAMMAR. A system of rules establishing the structure of a language, including the language's syntax, the rules governing the construction of sentences in that language. Noam Chomsky (1928–) and others have proposed that a grammar is also a **theory** of a language and shows what is known by a competent speaker about that language. Chomsky proposes that there is a universal grammar, a structure shared by all natural languages, actual or possible, and that human **knowledge** of this grammar is innate. *See also* INNATE IDEA.

GRICE, H. PAUL (1913–1988). British philosopher. In defending **causal theories** of **sense perception**, he argues against what would later come to be known as **naturalized epistemology**. An epistemic account of **perception**, he claims, should be broad enough as to be **consistent** with whatever **science** discovers about our sensory systems. He also defends **sense-data** theories, arguing that they could be described in ways that are ontologically neutral. Grice also proposes a theory of **conversational implicature**, showing how our ordinary remarks imply information that cannot be logically derived from what we say. For example, suppose I say that I am out of milk and you reply that there is a store around the corner. Your remarks conversationally imply that the store is open, that it sells milk, and that I ought to go there and buy some. *See also* SOCIAL EPISTEMOLOGY; TESTIMONY.

GROUNDS. The basis or **evidence**, **judgments**, **experiences**, and so forth on which a **belief** depends for its **epistemic justification**. The *genetic* grounds of a belief comprise the evidence and so forth that actually played a role in forming, revising, or maintaining that belief, regardless of whether the believer is aware of them or recognizes their epistemic role. The *nongenetic* grounds of a belief comprise the evidence and so forth that the believer would present in defense of that belief, regardless of whether these factors actually played a role in the formation, revision, or maintenance of that belief. Internalist epistemic theories tend to focus on nongenetic grounds, and externalist theories tend to focus on genetic grounds. *See also* EXTERNALISM/INTERNALISM; FOUNDATIONALISM.

GRUE PARADOX. A **paradox** of **induction** proposed by **Nelson Goodman** in his *Fact, Fiction and Forecast* (1955). For every inductive **argument** we regard as acceptable, we can generate analogous arguments that are not acceptable. Consider this inductive argument: All emeralds that have been examined are green; therefore, all emeralds are green. This seems acceptable, but it is analogous to this: All emeralds that have been examined are grue; therefore, all emeralds are grue. Grueness is the property of being examined before some future time *t* and being found to be green or not being examined before *t* and being blue. The first argument indicates that emeralds examined after *t* will be green, while the second indicates that they will be blue.

It cannot be that both arguments are correct, but there seems to be no nonarbitrary basis for rejecting one argument and not the other.

Goodman's solution is to distinguish between **projectible** and nonprojectible **hypotheses** or predicates. The first argument is acceptable because the property of greenness is entrenched in our language and is projectible; that is, it can transfer **credibility** from observed cases to unobserved ones. The second argument is unacceptable because grueness is neither entrenched nor projectible. Thus, he argues, inductive arguments can be saved from the grue paradox. *See also* INDUCTION, PROBLEM OF.

– H –

HABERMAS, JÜRGEN (1929–). German philosopher and sociologist. A member of the **Frankfurt School**, he is a leading proponent of **critical theory**. Critical theory, which is closely linked to **Marxism**, seeks to explain the development of capitalist societies, point out the domination and exploitation inherent in them, and propose ways in which people can be released from these forms of oppression. In *Knowledge and Human Interests* (1968), Habermas argues that the various **sciences** and other areas of investigation (including critical **theory**) each has its own orientation and interests and that the **empirical** statements generated by each form of inquiry is true only within the structure that inquiry creates. The **correspondence theory of truth** is rejected in favor of a consensus theory: A statement is true only if it would be accepted only within an imagined situation of ideal discourse, one in which all participants are equal and seek answers through reasoning and without coercion. *See also* CONTINENTAL EPISTEMOLOGY; EPISTEMIC RELATIVISM; FEMINIST EPISTEMOLOGY; SOCIOLOGY OF KNOWLEDGE.

HAMILTON, WILLIAM (1788–1856). Scottish philosopher and professor at the University of Edinburgh (1821–1856). He endorses a form of **commonsensism** but holds that our **experiences** of the world are always relative to our own perspective; the world as it is in itself is unknowable. *See also* EGOCENTRIC PREDICAMENT; EPISTEMIC RELATIVISM; EXPERIENCE; SKEPTICISM.

HARTMANN, NICOLAI (1882–1950). German philosopher, born in Latvia, who worked on issues in **epistemology**, metaphysics, ethics, and the history of philosophy. He defends a realist view according to which we apprehend both physical objects and Platonic **Forms**; the latter include moral values and mathematical objects. Our apprehension of moral values takes place by means of emotion. *See also* ABSTRACT ENTITY; MORAL EPISTEMOLOGY; REALISM/ANTIREALISM.

HASTY GENERALIZATION. *See* INFORMAL FALLACIES.

HEGEL, GEORG WILHELM FRIEDRICH (1770–1831). German idealist philosopher. Rejecting the traditional epistemological ideal of **certainty**, Hegel defends a **fallibilist** account of **epistemic justification**. Justification results primarily from the deliberate, reflective process of developing one's **beliefs** and **experiences** into a systematic conceptual scheme. We have **knowledge** of particulars by means of the application of these **concepts**. Even so, this knowledge arises in a particular historical context, and the conceptual system we apply may one day be replaced with a superior alternative. When criticizing other epistemological views, Hegel generally proceeds by internal means, using that view's own claims against it. This is part of a wider philosophical strategy of self-examination and criticism.

Instead of regarding objects as the causes of experience while remaining themselves unsensed and unknowable (a widely held view, found in **John Locke** and **Immanuel Kant**, among others), Hegel endorses a **holistic** ontology that understands objects in terms of their causal interactions with one another. **Laws of nature** are then seen as relationships among **observations** or observable phenomena.

Much of Hegel's **epistemology** is presented in his *Verhältnis des Skeptizismus zur Philosophie* (*The Relationship of Skepticism to Philosophy*, 1802) and *Phänomenologie des Geistes* (*Phenomenology of Spirit*, 1807). His three-volume *Wissenschaft der Logik* (*Science of Logic*, 1812, 1813, 1816) examines the nature of **arguments** and **explanations** and considers the nature and role of such categories as experience, being, essence, and **appearance**. It is through these and related concepts that our knowledge of the world is possible. *See also* CAUSATION; CONTINENTAL EPISTEMOLOGY; EPISTEMIC RELATIVISM; IDEALISM.

HEIDEGGER, MARTIN (1889–1976). German philosopher and a major contributor to **phenomenology** and existentialism. Controversy continues regarding his membership in and apparent complicity with the Nazi Party. Ontology is a central concern for Heidegger, and his early work endorses a view of objects that draws on their context, significance, and meaning. His monumental *Sein und Zeit* (*Being and Time*, 1927) begins with an **analysis** of *Dasein* (human existence or being-in-the-world) and the ways in which its structures make human **knowledge** possible. By examining the phenomenology of our "average everydayness," he hopes to overcome the assumptions made in traditional metaphysics and uncover the significance of our interactions with things. *See also* CONTINENTAL EPISTEMOLOGY; EPISTEMIC RELATIVISM.

HELVÉTIUS, CLAUDE ADRIEN (1715–1771). French philosopher, a significant influence on eighteenth-century **empiricism** and materialism. His books *De l'esprit* (*The Spirit*) (1758) and *De l'homme* (*The Person*) (published posthumously) present and defend a materialist view of mind according to which all **knowledge** is rooted in **sense perception**. Like **Thomas Hobbes**, he argues that all our actions are motivated by self-interest and that this egoistic nature guides our search for knowledge.

HEMPEL, CARL GUSTAV (1905–1997). Born and educated in Germany, Hempel emigrated in 1937 to the United States, where he taught mathematics and physics at Yale, Princeton, and Pittsburgh universities. He defends a form of **logical positivism**, arguing that **science** is the only true form of **knowledge**. Instead of focusing on the meaning or verifiability of individual **propositions** (as other positivists tended to do), he claims that an entire scientific **theory** is the fundamental unit of cognitive significance and that the interpretation of theories must involve both **observational** and theoretical terms. His **raven paradox** challenges our traditional understanding of supporting **evidence** by pointing out that, logically (albeit counterintuitively), observing nonblack items that are not ravens (e.g., a green bush) is evidence supporting the proposition that all ravens are black.

Hempel's work on the nature of scientific **explanation** has been very influential. He argues that events are explained by subsuming them under a general "covering" law. Deductive-nomological explanations arise when the covering law is deterministic. Nondeterministic or statistical laws generate statistical explanations. In either case, the role of the explanation is to provide premises that show that the explained event could reasonably be expected in the circumstances at issue. *See also* COVERING LAW MODEL OF EXPLANATION; INDUCTION, PROBLEM OF; PRINCIPLE OF VERIFIABILITY.

HERMENEUTIC CIRCLE. First made clear by Friedrich Schleiermacher (1768–1834), this is an **observation** about the nature of the interpretation of a text. One version of the circle points out that the interpretation of the parts of a text depends on the interpretation of the whole but that the interpretation of the whole depends on the interpretation of its parts. Another, more profound version points out that every interpretation is itself based on other interpretations. This circle of interpretation is not generally regarded as vicious. *See also* CIRCULAR REASONING; EPISTEMIC DEPENDENCE; HERMENEUTICS.

HERMENEUTICS. The **theory** or art of interpretation. From its origins in the study and interpretation of sacred texts, hermeneutics has become an investigation of the ontology of understanding, interpreting entities that are constituted through their continual interpretation of their world. **Martin Heidegger**, for instance, regards interpretation as an interaction between an interpreter and a text that transforms each of them. Hermeneutics is opposed to **foundationalism** in that it views **science** and all other ways of knowing as inescapably embedded in and influenced by culture. *See also* CONTINENTAL EPISTEMOLOGY; EPISTEMIC RELATIVISM.

HEURISTICS. Cognitive procedures (typically unconscious) that enable the subject to substitute complex **judgment** tasks with simple tasks that can be performed quickly, although with a higher incidence of **error**. Heuristics are evolutionarily valuable because they speed up responses to environmental stimuli but are an important source of bias and confusion. For instance, common human heuristics vitiate our estimates of **probability**, frequency, and **causality**. *See also* NATURALIZED EPISTEMOLOGY.

HILBERT, DAVID (1862–1943). German mathematician and philosopher of mathematics; he taught at Königsberg (where he was born) and at Göttingen universities. He applies **Immanuel Kant**'s understanding of **knowledge** to geometry, defending Kant's claim that continuity is an **idea** of pure reason and attempting to provide a foundation for geometry that does not rely on any principle of continuity. Hilbert also draws a distinction between real and ideal mathematics: Real mathematics consists of true mathematical **propositions** and their **proofs**, and ideal mathematics consists of sentences that do not express genuine propositions but play a valuable role in our procedures for identifying true mathematical propositions. His work **presupposes** that human thought is (or ought to be) patterned on classical **logic**. *See also* MATHEMATICAL KNOWLEDGE.

HINTIKKA, JAAKKO (1929–). Finnish philosopher, trained in Helsinki. He has taught at Helsinki University, Stanford University, Florida State University, and Boston University. His *Knowledge and Belief* (1962) presents the modal **logic** of **knowledge** and **belief** and applies this to such **epistemological** issues as the **KK thesis**. This book also initiated work in **epistemic logic**.

HISTORICAL KNOWLEDGE. Knowledge of the past based on present **evidence**. This is problematic because, as **Bertrand Russell** points out in his *The Analysis of Mind* (1912), it is possible that there is no past for us to know about. None of our evidence can rule out the possibility that the universe is only a few minutes old, having sprung into existence complete with history books, fossils, and apparent memories. Skeptics draw on this and the unreliability of **memory** to argue that we have no knowledge of history and perhaps not even **justified true beliefs** about it. Our historical knowledge is also undermined by our reliance on people's descriptions, recollections, and other statements. Such evidence is tainted by the beliefs, attitudes, and choices of the speakers or authors. *See also* EPISTEMIC RELATIVISM; HISTORICISM; SKEPTICISM; SOCIAL EPISTEMOLOGY; TESTIMONY.

HISTORICISM. The view that there can be no ahistorical standpoint for our **knowledge** of human actions, events, or societies. This is sometimes extended to the claim that *any* phenomenon can be understood only by examining its historical development. The methodology of historians should be applied to all the human sciences (e.g., politics, economics, law, ethics). "Historicism" has also been used to refer to the view that history proceeds according to historical laws or that history has a *telos* toward which it progresses in an orderly, predictable way. *See also* HISTORICAL KNOWLEDGE; NATURAL LAW.

HOBBES, THOMAS (1588–1679). English philosopher and political theorist. He tutored the young Charles II and wrote the third set of objections to **René Descartes**'s *Meditations on First Philosophy* (1641). In his *Elements of Law* (1650) and *Leviathan* (1651), Hobbes develops a form of **empiricism** that distinguishes between original **knowledge** (or knowledge of **fact**) and scientific knowledge (or knowledge of consequence). Original knowledge results from **sense perception** and has as its content the **observation** of properties of particular objects. Scientific knowledge, which is much more valuable, has as its content **necessary** connections among events or **ideas**. In addition, scientific knowledge is propositional; it uses names and symbols to represent the objects of past **sensations** and **logic** to determine the relationships among **propositions**. It allows us to go beyond our sensations of pleasure or pain in determining something's value; scientific knowledge enables us to examine consequences and connections that go beneath our prescientific valuations *See also* SCIENCE.

HOLISM. The view that whether a **belief** is **justified** depends on the entire system of belief in which it is embedded. A central consequence of this is that the fundamental unit of **confirmation** in **science** is an entire **theory** rather than a single **hypothesis** or **proposition**. When a prediction is false, the theory that generated it need not be rejected. The theory can be maintained, and the background beliefs may be revised. This view has been held by **Pierre Duhem**, **Rudolf Carnap**, and **W. V. O. Quine**, among others. *See also* COHERENTISM; LINEAR JUSTIFICATION.

HSIN. Chinese term meaning "honesty" or "**faith**." (It has a homonym that means "heart" or "feeling.") In the Confucian tradition, *hsin* is a cardinal virtue and consists in being true to one's word. *Hsin* can also mean religious faith.

HUAI NAN TZU. An ancient Chinese compendium of **knowledge**, compiled by a group of scholars and presented to Emperor Wu, around 140 B.C. It comprises twenty essays on a wide range of topics.

HUME, DAVID (1711–1776). Scottish philosopher, born and educated in Edinburgh. An **empiricist**, Hume holds that all the contents of the mind originate in **sense experience**; thus, his position is a form of empiricism. In sense **experience**, the mental object is an **impression**; in other forms of thought, the mental object is an **idea** (which is like an impression but "strikes upon the mind" with less "force and liveliness"). All our thoughts are about either matters of **fact** (which are true or false contingently) or relations of ideas (which are true or false necessarily). The negation of a true relation of ideas is self-contradictory. Relations of ideas can be known by "the operation of pure thought," but thought alone cannot yield **knowledge** of matters of fact.

Hume carefully investigates **beliefs** regarding matters of fact that are not currently present to our senses. In such cases, he concludes, our beliefs are based in part on a relation of cause and effect, and this in turn relies on an assumption that nature is uniform and that the future will fall into the same patterns as the past. These claims, however, cannot be supported by either reason or experience. It is not reason but what Hume calls "**imagination**" that accounts for our ways of thinking about **causation** and future or unobserved events. From an epistemic point of view, this leaves many of our beliefs about matters of fact without a satisfactory basis; these beliefs do not qualify as **knowledge**. *See also* CLEAR AND DISTINCT IDEA; CONTINGENCY; IDEA; IMMEDIACY; MEMORY; NECESSITY; SKEPTICISM; TABULA RASA; UNIFORMITY OF NATURE.

HUMEAN SKEPTICISM. *See* SKEPTICISM.

HUSSERL, EDMUND (1859–1938). German philosopher and mathematician. After receiving his Ph.D. in mathematics, Husserl began working on philosophical issues. Influenced by **Franz Brentano**'s work on **intentionality**, Husserl created **phenomenology**, which is a philosophical study of our **consciousness** of objects. This first appears in his *Logishe Untersuchungen* (*Logical Investigations*, 1900–1901) and is developed in new ways in *Ideen* (*Ideas*, 1913). In the latter he distinguishes between the *natural attitude*, which we adopt when dealing with the objects and events around us, and the *transcendental attitude*, which involves distancing oneself from the natural attitude and reflecting on one's own conscious experience.

The **epoché** or **transcendental reduction** involves reflecting on those aspects of one's consciousness that make it consciousness *of* particular objects; these characteristics are the *noemata*, or the object described phenomenologically. The corresponding mental activity is *noesis*. Each *noema* has an object meaning that combines the various parts of our **experience** into the experience of a single object and a thetic component that distinguishes between perceiving an object, remembering it, and so forth. These *noemata* are very complex and heavily influenced by culture and one's past experience.

We can work out the essences or *eidos* of objects by trying in the **imagination** to remove features from those objects. Some of these removals would leave the imagined object intact, but others would result in the loss of that object. In the latter sort of case, one recognizes by means of eidetic **intuition** that the feature in question is part of the object's essence. This process can be used not only on the objects around us but on **perception**, **memory**, and other intentional states as well. The eidetic **analysis** of intentional states leads one to the recognition of certain necessary **truths**; for example, any material object has parts and properties in addition to those currently presented to one's consciousness. *See also* ACT/OBJECT ANALYSIS; CONTINENTAL EPISTEMOLOGY; EPISTEMIC RELATIVISM; INTROSPECTION; NOETIC.

HUTCHESON, FRANCIS (1694–1746). Scottish philosopher and Presbyterian minister, born in Drumalig, Ireland; he received theological training at the University of Glasgow. In *An Essay on the Nature and Conduct of the Passions and Affections with Illustrations on the Moral Sense* (1728), he argues that people have internal senses that enable them to perceive instances of moral and aesthetic properties. These senses generate pleasure or approval when presented with beautiful objects or benevolent actions. The fact that we have these positive responses to actions that are indifferent to or in conflict with our own interests is taken as **evidence** that these responses are not based on egocentric reasoning. *See also* MORAL EPISTEMOLOGY.

HYPOTHESIS. A claim (typically scientific) deemed plausible and tentatively proposed for testing. Hypotheses that are **confirmed** or supported by the **evidence** may then become **theories** (or components of theories). *See also* ABDUCTION; FALSIFIABILITY; HYPOTHETICO-DEDUCTIVE METHOD; SCIENCE; TESTABILITY.

HYPOTHETICO-DEDUCTIVE METHOD. A method of testing a **hypothesis** by conjoining it with a description of initial conditions and examining the logical **implications** of this conjunction. These implications serve as **predictions** that are then tested by **observation**. Repeated true predictions offer inconclusive support for the **truth** of the hypothesis, but false predictions demonstrate that either the hypothesis, the statement of initial conditions, or both are false. *See also* ABDUCTION; DUHEM, PIERRE-MAURICE-MARIE; HUME, DAVID; INDUCTIVISM; POPPER, KARL; SCIENCE; TESTABILITY.

– I –

IDEA. For **Plato**, ideas are **Forms**, abstract ideals in which material objects participate. In the seventeenth and eighteenth centuries, beginning with **René Descartes**, ideas are the contents of the mind, the objects of **consciousness**. **John Locke**, **George Berkeley**, **Nicolas Malebranche**, **Antoine Arnauld**, **Gottfried Wilhelm Leibniz**, and others disagree about the origins, nature, and role of ideas. The central issues are whether ideas are representational or nonrepresentational, whether representational ideas are acts or objects, and whether ideas can be **innate**.

An innate idea is one that is possessed from birth and may be either a **concept** or a universal **truth** (such as an elementary truth of logic or **arithmetic**). For Descartes, innate ideas seem to be inborn mental capacities. Locke argues that we have no innate ideas. *See also* CLEAR AND DISTINCT IDEA; DIRECT REALISM; REPRESENTATIVE REALISM.

IDEALISM. The view that the world and its objects are somehow dependent on the mind, either because objects simply are **ideas** or because the world we **experience** is shaped by the structure of the mind. For **George Berkeley**, for instance, physical objects are a certain sort of cluster of ideas in a mind. Note that idealism does not deny the existence of physical objects but denies that they are mind-independent material entities. Being physical on this view amounts to being observable (at least in principle). *See also* ABSTRACT ENTITY; EXTERNAL WORLD; PHENOMENALISM; REALISM/ANTIREALISM.

IDEAL OBSERVER. A hypothetical, omniscient being whose **beliefs**, attitudes, and responses are appealed to in various philosophical **theories**. The ideal observer may also be described as being omniscient, disinterested in what is observed, perfectly rational, and morally virtuous.

Adam Smith's moral theory states that a moral **judgment** is true only if an ideal observer would also arrive at that judgment (*A Theory of Moral Sentiments*, 1759). **Roderick Firth** ("Ethical Absolutism and the Ideal Observer," 1952) appeals to an ideal observer to determine the content of moral judgments: Statements about something's being morally good or bad *mean* that an ideal observer would respond to that thing with moral approval or disapproval. *See also* MORAL EPISTEMOLOGY; OBSERVATION.

IDEAL PROPOSITION. In the work of **David Hilbert**, a sentence in ideal mathematics, playing a metatheoretic function and typically used in an **argument** that does not provide genuine **proof** or **justification** for its conclusion. Ideal propositions play a regulative role in guiding what Hilbert calls "real mathematics." *See also* MATHEMATICAL KNOWLEDGE.

IDEOLOGY. For Destutt de Tracy (1754–1836), ideology is the attempt to provide a scientific, naturalistic **explanation** of **ideas** and thought processes. He hoped that this would lead to the discovery and elimination of **error** and ultimately to the development of a utopian society. For Karl Marx (1818–1883), ideology is the set of historical, religious, political, and related ideas that purport to justify a particular socioeconomic system and to misrepresent that system to the people involved in it. Ideologies can be exposed and corrected only by changing the social and economic factors that give rise to them. The term "ideology" is now also used pejoratively to describe political views with which one disagrees. *See also* EPISTEMIC RELATIVISM; MARXISM; SOCIAL EPISTEMOLOGY.

IGNORATIO ELENCHI. See INFORMAL FALLACIES.

ILLATIVE SENSE. A cognitive ability posited by **John Henry Newman** that enables one to identify with **certainty** the **truth** of a **judgment** about concrete or historical matters. This ability is developed by means of education and **experience**; an individual's illative sense is generally limited to a particular subject area. *See also* HISTORICAL KNOWLEDGE.

ILLUSION. A perceptual state that is inaccurate or misleading. The moon illusion, for instance, is the **appearance** that the moon is much larger when near the horizon than when high overhead. Because illusions can be phenomenally indistinguishable from veridical **perception**, they have figured largely in **skeptical alternatives** and **arguments** for **skepticism**. *See also* ARGUMENT FROM ILLUSION; ERROR; FALLIBILITY; SENSE PERCEPTION.

IMAGINATION. The mental capacity to think, often in a quasi-perceptual way, about that which is novel, contrary to fact, or not currently perceived. **George Berkeley** and others use this term to refer to thinking by means of the manipulation of mental images. Imagination has puzzled some because it appears to be intentional or to be about something, but there may be nothing in existence for it to be about (as when one imagines a unicorn or a golden mountain). There are also unresolved questions about the relationship between imagination and **sense perception**. *See also* INTENTIONALITY.

IMMEDIACY. Also known as "presence," it is the property of being present to the mind without any intermediaries. Our own mental states are commonly said to be known immediately, in contrast with our **knowledge** of the **external world** (which is mediated by **perception** or **sensation**) or our knowledge of others' mental states (which is inferred from their behavior and hence mediated by our perceptions). **Bertrand Russell** says that we know **sense data** and universals "by acquaintance," reflecting his **belief** that we are immediately acquainted with these objects. This immediate acquaintance is said to confer an epistemic advantage over that knowledge that is gained via mediated means: The mediation may involve **errors** or distortions that are thought to be absent in the case of immediacy.

Immediacy is also used to refer to causal immediacy, the situation in which there is no causal intermediate between the object itself and our awareness of it. This seems to apply to our own mental states, but **William Alston** points out that we generally do not know the causal chain leading to our mental states, and so this immediacy may be lacking. *See also* EGOCENTRIC PREDICAMENT; GIVEN, THE; INFERENCE; INTROSPECTION; KNOWLEDGE BY ACQUAINTANCE; OBJECTIVE/SUBJECTIVE; PRIVACY OF MENTAL STATES.

IMPLICATION. A relationship among **propositions** such that the **truth** of one guarantees the truth of another; in such cases, the latter is said to be implied by the former. An **argument** is said to be deductively valid when its premises deductively imply its conclusion. Material implication is the logical **inference** from a **conditional proposition** and its antecedent of its consequent: If p then q; p; therefore, q. *See also* CONVERSATIONAL IMPLICATURE; DEDUCTION; LOGIC.

IMPLICATURE. *See* CONVERSATIONAL IMPLICATURE; GRICE, H. PAUL; IMPLICATION.

IMPRESSION. For **David Hume** in his *A Treatise of Human Nature* (3 vols., 1739–1740), a type of **perception** and therefore immediately present to the mind. Impressions of **sensation** are more forceful or vivacious than impressions of **reflection**. Hume, an **empiricist**, argues that the content of all impressions originates in the operation of the senses. *See also* GIVEN, THE; IMMEDIACY; INTROSPECTION; SENSE PERCEPTION.

INCOMMENSURABILITY. In the philosophy of **science**, the property of two scientific **theories** when their terms cannot refer to any single set of theory-neutral **observations**. *See also* FEYERABEND, PAUL; KUHN, THOMAS.

INCORRIGIBILITY. The property of a **belief** such that it is impossible for there to be compelling **evidence** that this belief is incorrect. **A. J. Ayer** and others hold that one's beliefs about one's own mental states are incorrigible, although experimental **psychology** has since shown that our **introspective** access to our mental states is not as unproblematic as was once thought. *See also* CERTAINTY; FREUD, SIGMUND; INDUBITABILITY; NATURALIZED EPISTEMOLOGY.

INDETERMINACY. *See* INDETERMINACY OF REFERENCE; INDETERMINACY OF TRANSLATION; VAGUENESS.

INDETERMINACY OF REFERENCE. The claim, defended by **W. V. O. Quine**, that there can be no **fact** of the matter about what the terms in a language refer to. Any of our **observations** of the users of a language will be consistent with many different **hypotheses** regarding the referents of referring terms. *See also* AMBIGUITY; INDETERMINACY OF TRANSLATION; VAGUENESS.

INDETERMINACY OF TRANSLATION. The claim, defended by **W. V. O. Quine**, that there is no one, uniquely correct translation of statements in one language into another language. Any translation must be guided by the stimulus conditions under which a competent speaker of the language will accept that statement as true. However, Quine argues that there will always be several mutually incompatible translations that meet this requirement. This was part of Quine's **argument** against the **analytic/synthetic distinction**. *See also* AMBIGUITY; ANALYTICITY; GRAMMAR; INDETERMINACY OF REFERENCE; VAGUENESS.

INDIAN EPISTEMOLOGY. Epistemology in India has been concerned primarily with the distinction between true and false thought, often in the context of addressing **skeptical** concerns. A number of similarities can be found between this tradition and work done in the West. For instance, both examine cases in which **beliefs** are true but unwarranted, such as those that are accidentally true (e.g., a gambler's accidentally true **prediction** or true conclusions derived from false premises).

One issue on which Indian epistemologists have disagreed is akin to the **KK thesis**: Can one know that *p* without knowing that one knows that *p*? The **Buddhists**, Vedāntins, and others defend the KK thesis, arguing that each thought or cognition is automatically known by the subject. The **Nyāya** disagree, claiming that one's **knowledge** that *p* and one's recognition of that mental state are separate events, occurring at different times.

Indian epistemologists have also examined carefully situations in which one's knowledge arises from hearing or reading what is said by honest experts. This includes knowledge of history originating in reading accounts written by **reliable** historical figures and knowledge of ethical standards originating in reading holy writ. This variety of knowledge involves linguistic competence and a general grasp of the content. *See also* AUTHORITY; *PRAMĀ*; *PRĀMĀṆYA*; *PRATYAKṢA*.

INDIRECT KNOWLEDGE. *See* FOUNDATIONALISM; INFERENTIAL BELIEFS.

INDIRECT PROOF. A form of deductive **argument** in which one assumes the negation of the **proposition** one wishes to prove, derives a contradiction from this (typically along with other premises), and concludes that the proposition in question must be **true**. *See also* DEDUCTION; LOGIC; PROOF.

INDUBITABILITY. The property of a **belief** or **proposition** of being incapable of being **doubted**. **William Alston** (*Epistemic Justification*, 1989) points out that this may be interpreted as a **psychological** inability to doubt the **truth** of a belief, the logical impossibility of doubting it, or the logical impossibility of there being good **evidence**

against that belief. Although each of these has been presented at one time or another as an epistemic desideratum, the third is widely regarded as being the most significant. *See also* CERTAINTY; INCORRIGIBILITY; REASONS FOR BELIEF.

INDUCTION. Any nondemonstrative **inference** in which the conclusion goes beyond the content of the premises. This is known as an **ampliative inference** and includes **probability** theory, statistical reasoning, and computability **theory**.

Induction can take many forms. Enumerative or instantial induction is a generalization drawn from a collection of specific instances. For example, I have observed one hundred black crows, so I infer that all crows are black. A hypothetical **deduction** is the inference that a particular **hypothesis** is the best **explanation** of a certain body of **observational** data or other **evidence**. W. D. Ross describes a process of **intuitive** induction in which one observes that a particular factor is morally significant in a particular instance and infers from this that that sort of factor would be morally significant in all other instances.

Mathematical induction differs from the other forms in that it guarantees the **truth** of its conclusion. It proceeds as follows: A particular claim is shown to be true of zero; it is also shown that for any natural number x, if this claim is true for all natural numbers less than x, it is true of x as well; the conclusion is that this claim is true for all natural numbers. *See also* INDUCTION, PROBLEM OF; INFERENCE TO THE BEST EXPLANATION; LOGIC; PROJECTIBILITY.

INDUCTION, NEW RIDDLE OF. Nelson Goodman (*Fact, Fiction and Forecast*, 1955) presents what he calls the "new riddle of **induction**" and illustrates it using the property of being "grue" (green if examined before time t or not examined before t and being blue). If we examine many emeralds before time t and find that all are green, we might use standard **enumerative induction** to draw the conclusion that all emeralds are green. However, we could also use those **observations** to support the conclusion that all emeralds are grue. The puzzle arises from the fact that these conclusions are incompatible with one another (the first suggests that additional emeralds observed after t will be green and the latter that they will be blue), but the **evidence** seems to support each one equally.

Goodman's solution to this puzzle is to divide the terms used in inductive **arguments** into those that are projectible and those that are not. A projectible term is one that has been used frequently in such **inferences** and is entrenched in our language. Only inductive arguments using entrenched, projectible terms can confer support on their conclusions. *See also* GRUE PARADOX; INDUCTION, PROBLEM OF; PROJECTIBILITY.

INDUCTION, PRINCIPLE OF. The claim that the future will be like the past, that nature is uniform, or that unobserved cases resemble observed ones. This principle is assumed in inductive arguments, although **David Hume** argues that we have no reason for thinking that it is true. *See also* INDUCTION; INDUCTION, PROBLEM OF; UNIFORMITY OF NATURE.

INDUCTION, PROBLEM OF. Although **ampliative inferences**, particularly **inductions** whose premises are about a sample of observed cases and whose conclusions are about unobserved cases, are generally regarded as providing substantial (albeit inconclusive) support for those conclusions, the problem of induction is that such **inferences** seem to rely on assumptions for which we have no **evidence**. **David Hume** points out that we often assume that nature is uniform, that the future will be like the past, or, more generally, that unobserved cases will be like observed ones. (This is sometimes referred to as the **principle of induction**.) We have no logical or *a priori* reasons for thinking these assumptions are true; there is nothing inconsistent about their negations. Hume argues that much of our reasoning depends on our understanding of **causation**, but this may be nothing more than the constant conjunction of **experiences** combined with a "habit of mind." Thus, if we really do have good inductive **reasons for believing** that the sun will rise tomorrow morning, the inductive process seems to be unable to account for them.

Another aspect of the problem emerges for hypothetical induction, taking a body of **evidence** as supporting a **hypothesis** that is taken to explain it best. The problem is that for any given body of evidence, there will be two or more explanatory hypotheses that are compatible with the evidence but incompatible with each other. The problem is that there does not seem to be any way of nonarbitrarily selecting one as the best of these **explanations**; thus, how can the evidence be said to support *this* hypothesis?

Hans Reichenbach (*Experience and Prediction*, 1938) responds to the problem of induction by agreeing with Hume that we have no good reason for accepting the principle of induction and by defending induction not as a form of logical **argument** but as a **pragmatically** valuable method for developing "posits." A posit is not a **belief** (which would involve regarding it as true) but rather a sort of wager one makes about future observations; it must be continually adjusted in light of what is actually observed. Critics of this approach point out that this does not overcome the fundamental problem that there is no nonarbitrary way of choosing an explanation or posit.

Peter F. Strawson (*Introduction to Logical Theory*, 1952) uses **ordinary language philosophy** in his response to the problem of induction. He argues that the problem arises only if one tries to hold induction to the standards of deductive **logic** (i.e., requiring that it be impossible for the conclusion to be false if the premises are true). Unfortunately, Strawson simply claims that it is **analytic** that the cases appealed to in the premises of an enumerative induction provide good evidence for the argument's conclusion; he takes this to be established by how we ordinarily talk about such evidence. This dependence on ordinary language philosophy exposes Strawson's response to all its flaws. *See also* CONSISTENCY; GRUE PARADOX; INFERENCE TO THE BEST EXPLANATION; REASONS FOR BELIEF; UNIFORMITY OF NATURE.

INDUCTIVE EXPLANATION. *See* COVERING LAW MODEL OF EXPLANATION.

INDUCTIVE LOGIC. The branch of **logic** that evaluates **ampliative inferences** (inferences whose conclusions go beyond the information contained in their premises). *See also* INDUCTION; INDUCTION, PROBLEM OF; INFERENCE.

INDUCTIVISM. The view that scientific **hypotheses** receive **confirmation** or evidential support from predictive successes. A hypothesis that, along with various background statements, successfully predicts an **observation** is, according to inductivism, thereby made more

credible. This view is subject to **David Hume**'s criticism that it assumes that future and unobserved instances will be like observed instances. *See also* GRUE PARADOX; HEMPEL, CARL; INDUCTION, PROBLEM OF; SCIENCE; UNIFORMITY OF NATURE.

INFALLIBILITY. The impossibility of one's being mistaken about a particular **belief**. For **example**, it is sometimes claimed that people's beliefs about their own current mental states are infallible (i.e., it is impossible for us to be mistaken about which mental states we currently are in). *See also* CERTAINTY; GIVEN, THE; INCORRIGIBILITY; INDUBITABILITY; INTROSPECTION.

INFERENCE. The process of drawing a conclusion from **evidence**, premises, or assumptions; also, the conclusion thus drawn. There is typically a **psychological** requirement: As a result of *believing* the evidence, one must come to *believe* the conclusion. This sets inferences apart from **arguments** that may never influence anyone's **beliefs**. The difficulties involved in working out a more complete definition of inference are explored by **Ludwig Wittgenstein** (*Remarks on the Foundations of Mathematics*, 1956). *See also* DEDUCTION; LOGIC.

INFERENCE TO THE BEST EXPLANATION. A nondeductive form of **argument** in which **observations** or states of affairs are taken to be **evidence** supporting an **explanation** that would account for them. The form of such an argument is this: 1) A particular state of affairs S obtains. (This may be put in terms of observations.) 2) If explanation E were **true**, then we would expect S. Therefore, it is likely that 3) E is true. **Inferences** of this sort are fundamental to **science**.

Because any given state of affairs could be explained in two or more ways, this argument form must be supplemented with some means of determining which of the available explanations is best. In general, an explanation is preferred if it is simple, capable of explaining a broad range of phenomena, and calls on the same sorts of entities or regularities that we commonly employ in other explanations.

Obviously, an explanation could meet all these criteria without being true, and critics point out that the criteria themselves employ undefended—and perhaps indefensible—assumptions about the nature of our world. *See also* ABDUCTION; HUME, DAVID; OCKHAM, WILLIAM OF; UNIFORMITY OF NATURE.

INFERENTIAL BELIEF. A **belief** that is epistemically justified because of its relationships with other beliefs. **Foundationalism** is a **theory** of **knowledge** and **epistemic justification** that divides all beliefs into basic and inferential and says that **basic beliefs** are justified by their own nature. Inferential beliefs are justified only to the extent that they are properly based on these basic beliefs. *See also* INFERENCE; LINEAR JUSTIFICATION.

INFINITE REGRESS ARGUMENT. A form of **argument** that purports to show that one is not justified in believing a **proposition** because the **justification** would result in an infinite regress and that either there could not be such a regress or the existence of such a regress would entail that the **belief** at issue is unjustified. A regress is a sequence of objects, events, arguments, or states of affairs such that each arises from or depends on the item that precedes it in that sequence.

In **foundationalism**, an infinite regress argument is used to support the claim that some beliefs (**basic beliefs**) must be **epistemically justified** by their own nature. To defend the claim that a belief is epistemically justified, it is common to show how that belief is based on or related to certain other beliefs. This raises new questions about the epistemic status of these other beliefs, and one may defend these by showing that their justification arises from their relationships with some additional set of beliefs. The foundationalists point out that if this process (of defending one belief by introducing more beliefs that, in turn, are defended by introducing still more beliefs) goes on infinitely, none of these beliefs will have been shown to be justified. The process generates a series of material conditionals: If a is justified, then b is justified; if b is justified, then c is justified; and so forth. These conditionals are logically compatible with the claim that *none* of these beliefs are justified. (The material conditional "If p, then q" is true whenever p is false.) The foundationalists argue that because some of our beliefs are clearly justified, some of these justificatory chains of reasoning must eventually come to a stop with a belief that is justified and whose justification does not depend on its connections with any other beliefs. Such a sequence-ending belief is called a basic belief and is taken to be justified by its own nature.

This line of argument assumes that justification is linear rather than holistic. That is, a belief's justification is seen as being transferred or generated by its connections with other beliefs. However, if some form of **holism** is true and beliefs are justified by their role in an entire system of belief, then the regress described by the foundationalists will never get started. *See also* COHERENTISM; CONDITIONAL PROOF; CONDITIONAL PROPOSITION; EPISTEMIC DEPENDENCE; LINEAR JUSTIFICATION.

INFORMAL FALLACIES. Errors in reasoning or tactics used in **arguments** to persuade someone that a position is correct although those tactics fall short of providing compelling **evidence**. A fallacy is said to be informal when the error or tactic has to do with a flawed strategy or misuse of argument (rather than with the formal structure of the argument). For example, a fallacy may use the emotions or prejudices of the audience to sway opinion or play on **ambiguity**.

Argumentum ad baculum, or "argument to the club," involves persuading others to agree with one's conclusion not because one has provided evidence of its **truth** but because one has threatened those who disagree. For example: Those who disagree with my proposal will be fired; therefore, I am sure you agree with my proposal.

Argumentum ad hominem is a personal attack. This may be either an attack on the moral character or truthfulness of one's opponent or pointing out that the opponent's position is internally inconsistent. The latter form can be a reasonable and appropriate form of argument.

Argumentum ad ignorantiam, or "argument to ignorance," takes the absence of evidence for a **proposition**'s truth to be an indication that this proposition is false (or it may take the absence of evidence that a proposition is false as indicating that this proposition is true). For example: No one has proven that fish are incapable of experiencing pain; therefore, fish are capable of experiencing pain.

Argumentum ad populum, or "argument to the people," defends a conclusion by pointing out that it is widely accepted and assuming that any view held by the majority will always be true. For example: 85 percent of Americans believe that **God** exists; therefore, God exists.

Argumentum ad misericordiam, or "argument to pity," appeals to the audience's sympathies to gain support for one's position. For example, someone trying to convince a loan officer that a loan would be repaid promptly might point out how much the children would suffer if the loan were not approved.

Argumentum ad verecundiam, or "appeal to authority," involves citing an **authority** as backing for a claim. This can be a reasonable means of providing support for a conclusion, but it can be used fallaciously as well. The **error** lies in appealing to someone who is not actually an authority on the matter at issue, misinterpreting what an authority has said, or turning the argument into a personal attack on one's opponent by claiming that she or he does not have proper respect for the authority. (The last of these is a species of *ad hominem* argument.)

Circular argument is a form of *begging the question* and involves simply assuming that the conclusion of one's argument is true rather than providing independent **reasons for believing** it. This is also known as *petitio principii*. For example: I believe that everything printed in the local newspaper is accurate; my evidence for this is that the local newspaper says that it is always accurate and that it is never mistaken. Not all circular arguments are fallacious, however. According to **holism**, beliefs may be justified by their role in a larger system of belief. In such cases, an argument defending a particular belief may cite many related propositions and eventually return to its starting point. To avoid vicious or fallacious circularity, this circle must include enough additional material to present a large and **coherent** system.

Composition is the fallacy of **inferring** that the properties of the whole will be possessed by the parts. For example: The dogs in this competition are from all over the world; Lulu is a dog in this competition; therefore, Lulu is from all over the world. This fallacy should not be confused with **inductive** argument to a generalization.

Denying the antecedent involves the misuse of negations in **conditional propositions**. For example: If there is someone outside, then the dog will bark; it is not the case that there is someone outside; therefore, it is not the case that the dog will bark. This is often confused with the

deductively valid argument form known as *modus tollens*: If there is someone outside, then the dog will bark; it is not the case that the dog is barking; therefore, it is not the case that there is someone outside. *Equivocation* involves using an **ambiguous** term in two or more senses within an argument, relying on this shift in meaning to support the conclusion. For example: **John Stuart Mill** (*Utilitarianism*, 1861) argues that the only evidence that something is desirable is that people actually desire it; people desire pleasure; therefore, pleasure is desirable. "Desirable" is sometimes used to mean "worthy of being desired" and sometimes to mean "capable of being desired." (This is an example of the reasonable and appropriate form of an *ad hominem* argument, that is, attacking the internal inconsistencies within someone's reasoning.)

The *fallacy of hasty generalization* involves reasoning from one or a few particular cases to a general conclusion. For instance: The Ford car I own is unreliable; therefore, all Fords are unreliable. Such generalizations can be supported only by a large sample of representative cases.

The *fallacy of many questions*, also known as the *complex question fallacy*, is illustrated by the question, "When did you stop beating your spouse?" Such questions make **presuppositions** (in this case, that the person being questioned has beaten his or her spouse), and this is fallacious when these presuppositions are not well founded.

The *genetic fallacy* involves attributing something undesirable about the origins or associations of a proposition to the proposition itself. It is a sort of "guilt by association" maneuver. For example, one might try to discredit an opponent's view by saying, "Isn't that just what the Nazis said?" This is closely related to the *argumentum ad hominem*.

Ignoratio elenchi, or "ignorance of refutation," is the failure to stick to the point in an argument.

Poisoning the well is similar to the *argumentum ad hominem* in that it attempts to persuade the audience to reject a claim by discrediting the speaker rather than examining the evidence for the claims in question. For example, one might say, "Janet's claim that she is innocent must be false because she would say she is innocent even if she were guilty."

Post hoc, ergo propter hoc, or "after this, therefore because of this," arguments infer that because event or state of affairs *a* was followed by *b*, then *a* must have caused *b*. For example: After I washed my car, it began to rain; therefore, washing the car caused it to rain. This fallacy also leads us to interpret correlations as **causal** relationships. For example, the correlation between cancer cases and living in the proximity of a particular factory may be interpreted as indicating that something at the factory is causing cancer. *Post hoc, ergo propter hoc* reasoning also underlies many superstitions. For instance, "Wild Bill" Hickok was shot to death just after he had been dealt a pair of aces and a pair of eights in a poker game. Some inferred that this poker hand somehow contributed to his death, and "aces and eights" is now known as the "dead man's hand;" those who hold such a hand may feel that they are in danger of dying.

Slippery slope arguments are often used in ethical debates and invoke the harmful consequences of allowing any instances of a particular type of action to support the conclusion that no instances of that type of action should be permitted. This need not be fallacious, for the consequences of an action are often quite relevant to one's decisions and evaluations. However, slippery slope arguments can go awry when there is no evidence to support these predictions of harmful consequences or when it is incorrectly assumed that one's audience is unwilling to take any risks. *See also* CIRCULAR REASONING.

INFORMAL LOGIC. The branch of **logic** that studies and evaluates **arguments** as they arise in ordinary situations and circumstances. This involves looking beyond the logical form of the argument to its use in a particular context. *See also* INFORMAL FALLACIES.

INFORMATION THEORY. Also known as communication **theory**, information theory is the mathematical study of information and communication. The central question has been how a message that originates at one point can be reproduced accurately at some other point. Information exists independently of anyone who communicates or interprets messages; in fact, information does not depend on minds at all. Information is generated by events or states of affairs and transmitted by signals regardless of whether anyone understands or even notices them. The mathematics of information theory deals with the measurement and transmission of information, not with its interpretation. An event or state of affairs generates information by reducing uncertainty or ruling out possibilities.

Philosophers, notably **Fred Dretske** (*Knowledge and the Flow of Information*, 1981), have employed information theory in developing theories of **knowledge**. The **objective** nature of information and its connection with events or states of affairs "out there in the world" make it suitable as a basis for knowledge, particularly in externalist theories. *See also* CONNECTIONISM; EXTERNAL WORLD.

INNATE IDEA. Ideas are said to be innate when they cannot be accounted for by **experience**. Such ideas are either inborn or created in us by **God**. The innateness of ideas has often been taken as **evidence** of their **truth**; particularly if these ideas are created in us by God, it has been argued, they could not be false.

Plato maintained that our understanding of **arithmetic** and geometry could be explained only by saying that we already possess these ideas and that our process of "learning" is actually recollection (**anamnesis**). Innate ideas were appealed to commonly in philosophy until **John Locke** (*An Essay Concerning Human Understanding*, 1690) proposed that the ideas in question could be explained better by **empirical** means. In the twentieth century, Noam Chomsky suggested that the fundamental structure of human language is innate, although this understanding of innateness is sufficiently different from its ancestors that it need not conflict with the empirical arguments against innate ideas. *See also A PRIORI/A POSTERIORI* KNOWLEDGE; GRAMMAR.

INSCRUTABILITY OF REFERENCE. *See* INDETERMINACY OF REFERENCE; QUINE, W. V. O.

INSTRUMENTALISM. In the philosophy of **science**, instrumentalism is the view that a scientific **theory** is a system for using a set of **observations** to generate a set of **predictions**. The statements that make up the theory have no reference or **propositional** content and thus do not imply the existence of any sort of objects; thus, instrumentalism is a form of antirealism.

In the philosophy of **John Dewey**, instrumentalism is the view that the status of **concepts** and the **rationality** of actions are to be understood in terms of how they allow us to predict, control, and explain our **experiences** of the world. *See also* REALISM/ANTIREALISM.

INTENTIONAL STANCE. *See* DENNETT, DANIEL.

INTENTIONALITY. Something's intentionality is its "aboutness," its reference to or content regarding something beyond itself. **Beliefs**, like many other mental states, are intentional; they point beyond themselves to something else. **Franz Brentano** (*Psychologie vom empirischen Standpunkt* [*Psychology from an Empirical Standpoint*], 1874) argues that intentionality is the dividing line between the mental and the physical: The mental is intentional, but the physical is not. Disagreements about the nature and role of intentionality continue in philosophy, and the intentionality of mental states is seen as a central issue in the philosophy of mind. *See also* INDETERMINACY OF TRANSLATION.

INTERNALISM. *See* EXTERNALISM/INTERNALISM.

INTROSPECTION. The conscious mental process of attending to one's own mind and its states or events. Introspection has often been regarded as an **infallible** source of **knowledge** regarding one's own mind and mental states, and **foundationalists** have often regarded the **beliefs** formed through introspection as basic. However, recent work in experimental **psychology** indicates that introspection is prone to **error**. Introspection differs from other senses such as vision: While the things I sense using vision, touch, and so on could (at least in principle) be perceived by others, only I can introspectively observe my own mental states.

Although some philosophers assume that all mental states can be introspectively observed, **Sigmund Freud** and others argue that some mental states or processes are not available to this inner sense. Furthermore, **David Hume** argues that although introspection may reveal mental states or processes to us, it does not reveal the mind or self. *See also* APPERCEPTION; BASIC BELIEF; CERTAINTY; CONSCIOUSNESS; GIVEN, THE; INDUBITABILITY; OBJECTIVE/SUBJECTIVE; PRIVACY OF MENTAL STATES.

INTUITION. A source of **knowledge** that does not involve the senses or any process of **inference**. **Propositions** known in this way may include simple **truths** of **arithmetic** or geometry, simple truths of **logic**, or moral truths; these are also known as **self-evident** propositions. **John Locke** (*An Essay Concerning Human Understanding*, 1690) claims that intuition plays a role in **deduction** by showing one the "connexion of ideas" or that the inferential steps involved are truth preserving. Some mystics claim that there can be an intuitive grasp or apprehension of **God**. For **Immanuel Kant**, intuition is a sort of mental visualization by which we can learn what is implied by **concepts**. *See also* DEDUCTION; GIVEN, THE; MYSTICISM.

ISOCRATES (436–338 B.C.). Greek philosopher, student of **Socrates**, and rival of **Plato**. He argued against teaching theoretical philosophy and warned of the dangers of misused rhetoric. *See also* INFORMAL FALLACIES.

ISOSTHENEIA. Often translated, "**equipollence**," a term used by **Sextus Empiricus** and other ancient Greek philosophers in discussions of **skepticism**. It means that the available **evidence** provides equal support to both sides of an issue. *See also* APORIA.

– J –

JACOBI, FRIEDRICH HEINRICH (1743–1819). German novelist and essayist. In his *David Hume über den Glauben, oder Idealismus und Realismus* (*David Hume on Belief, or Idealism and Realism*, 1787), he critiqued **Immanuel Kant**'s transcendental philosophy, particularly the account of things-in-themselves. **David Hume**'s skeptical arguments led Jacobi to adopt a form of **direct realism**, not because it was supported by compelling **evidence** but because he made a "**leap of faith**." He claimed that because of skeptical arguments and the general failure of philosophy, such leaps were required not only in religion and morality but in all areas of life as well. *See also* FAITH; SKEPTICISM.

JAMES, WILLIAM (1842–1910). American philosopher. As a Harvard University student, he studied science and then taught physiology, psychology, and finally philosophy at that institution. Influenced by **Charles Peirce**, he played a central role in the development of **pragmatism**, a philosophical movement that stresses the relationship between **theory** and praxis. Thought is evaluated by determining whether it assists in satisfying our interests; thus, a true **belief** is one that fits well with our existing beliefs and improves our interaction with the world. James defended a version of **empiricism** according to which temporal, **causal**, and other relationships in the world are affectively experienced and that we have a direct acquaintance with them.

In *The Will to Believe and Other Essays* (1897), James argued that one cannot properly believe a religious or moral claim unless one has explored all the alternatives to that position. This exploration involves working to look beyond one's current views and be "willing to believe" in new things. The uncertainty and tentativeness that result are, he said, desirable.

His epistemology is most fully developed in his *Pragmatism* (1907), in which he argues that **truth** or falsehood of theories and **propositions** cannot be determined apart from their consequences and role in **experience**. Beliefs and other mental states are redescribed as functional processes. *See also* BELIEF-FORMING PROCESS; COHERENTISM; FALLIBILITY; SKEPTICAL ALTERNATIVES.

JASPERS, KARL THEODOR (1883–1969). German philosopher and psychologist and a member of the existentialist movement. In his *Philosophie* (1931, 1956) and *Von der Wahrheit* (*On Truth*, 1947), Jaspers contrasts scientific **knowledge** with the ways in which subjectivity and **objectivity** are interrelated in our **experience** of ourselves, our freedom, and other aspects of the human condition. *See also* CONSCIOUSNESS; SCIENCE; SENSE PERCEPTION.

JEVONS, WILLIAM STANLEY (1835–1882). British economist and philosopher. Noted for his introduction into formal **logic** of the inclusive "or," he also used subjective **probability** to evaluate competing hypotheses. Jevons also argued that **science** can yield only approximations of **truth**. *See also* OBJECTIVE/SUBJECTIVE.

JHĀNA. A term used in Theravada **Buddhism** meaning "contemplation" or "meditation." It denotes a sequence of four (or sometimes five) states of **consciousness** involving the gradual elimination of affective **experience**.

JOHNSON, WILLIAM ERNEST (1858–1931). English philosopher and logician, lecturer at Cambridge University, and father of John Maynard Keynes. He studied deductive and inductive **inference** and developed an adverbial account of **experience**. *See also* ADVERBIAL THEORY OF PERCEPTION; DEDUCTION; INDUCTION.

JTB THEORY OF KNOWLEDGE. The justified true belief (JTB) **theory** of knowledge is the view that a **belief** qualifies as **knowledge** if and only if it is both true and justified. No specific accounts of **epistemic justification** or **truth** are specified by the JTB theory of knowledge, but it is typically associated with internalist accounts whereby the justification is linked to the subject's ability to defend the belief in question against skeptical challenges. The JTB theory of knowledge is often said to have its origins in **Plato** (*Theaetetus* 200–210; although Plato considers this view, he does not accept it), and is widely held to have been refuted by Edmund Gettier's **counterexamples**. *See also* EXTERNALISM AND INTERNALISM; GETTIER CASES; PROBLEM OF THE CRITERION; SKEPTICISM.

JUDGMENT. Either the act of judging, the mental faculty responsible for performing such actions, or the result of such a mental act. **Aristotle** claimed that all judgments fit one of these **logical** forms (or perhaps some combination of them): All S are P, Some S are P, No S are P, and Some S are not-P. For **Immanuel Kant**, the act of arriving at judgments involves the application of **concepts**.

JUSTIFICATION. *See* EPISTEMIC JUSTIFICATION.

JUSTIFIED TRUE BELIEF. *See* JTB THEORY OF KNOWLEDGE.

– K –

KANT, IMMANUEL (1724–1804). German philosopher; a leading figure in modern philosophy. He was a professor at the University of Königsberg from 1770 until his death. His most important **epistemological** and metaphysical work is presented in his *Critique of Pure Reason* (1781; 2nd ed., 1787). Also noteworthy are his *Critique of Practical Reason* (1788), which presents his ethical theory, and *Critique of Judgment* (1790), which deals with aesthetics.

The *Critique of Pure Reason* examines the issue of *a priori* **knowledge**. In it, Kant seeks to separate genuine *a priori* **knowledge**, which he defends against skeptical attacks, from false claims of such knowledge. He begins by setting forth the distinctions between *a priori* and empirical knowledge, necessary and contingent **propositions**, and analytic and synthetic **judgments**. The necessary/contingent distinction is drawn in terms comparable to current **possible worlds** approaches, and Kant claims that this distinction yields the same division of propositions as the *a priori*/empirical distinction (with only necessary propositions being knowable *a priori*). The **analytic/synthetic distinction** is drawn in terms of **concept** inclusion. A judgment is analytic only if its predicate is included in the subject concept and synthetic if the predicate is not included in the subject. Concept *A* is said to be included in concept *B* if *A* can be logically derived from *B*. Kant argues that some synthetic judgments can be known *a priori* (e.g., 5 + 7 = 12, a straight line is the shortest distance between two points, each event has a cause). The primary task undertaken in this work is to determine how such synthetic *a priori* knowledge is possible.

Kant argues that knowledge results from a combination of **intuitions** and concepts. Concepts, which are manipulated by our mental faculty of understanding, represent objects in virtue of shared features. Intuitions, which are the province of our mental faculty of sensing, directly represent single objects or states of affairs. Both are required for knowledge; Kant puts it this way: "Thoughts without content are empty, intuitions without concepts are blind" (*Critique of Pure Reason* A51/B75). Reference and the propositional structure of knowledge require the involvement of both intuition and concepts.

Kant's approach to the issue of *a priori* knowledge is so innovative that he calls it his "**Copernican revolution**." Copernicus sought to explain the movement of stars and planets in terms of the motion of the earthbound observer rather than in terms of the motions of the heavenly bodies. Similarly, instead of focusing on the nature of the synthetic *a priori* judgments, Kant examines the nature of the conscious mind of the knower. All spatial and temporal features of objects are said to be features of **appearances** in the mind and not of the objects as they are in themselves. This emphasis on appearances is the key to his **transcendental idealism**. We form judgments about concepts on the basis of pure intuition, a sort of mental visualization. Knowable objects are shaped by this faculty of intuition, and this allows us to have synthetic *a priori* knowledge of them. Some concepts are themselves *a priori* rather than abstracted from experience. Kant calls these the categories; they include the concepts of substance, cause, and temporal relations of events. *See also* CONSCIOUSNESS; CONTINGENCY; NECESSITY; SKEPTICISM; TRANSCENDENTAL ARGUMENTS.

KEYNES, JOHN MAYNARD (1883–1946). English economist whose theories greatly influenced how economics is applied to government policy. His *A Treatise on Probability* (1921) breaks with the subjectivist tradition and treats probabilities as objective statements of evidential value. He also argues that some **probability** claims are incommensurable. *See also* BAYESIANISM.

KIERKEGAARD, SØREN AABYE (1813–1855). Danish writer and Christian existentialist, sometimes regarded as the father of existentialism. Christianity, he says, is accepted not on the basis of **arguments** or **evidence** but in a "**leap of faith**." This failure of **rationality** results from the paradoxical nature of the divine incarnation. Kierkegaard also criticizes **G. W. F. Hegel**'s absolute **idealism**. Kierkegaard says our finiteness and human limitations prevent us from grasping a complete and final system of reality. The response to **skepticism** should be a will to believe, not an exercise of reason. *See also* CREDULITY; FAITH; RELIGIOUS KNOWLEDGE; VOLUNTARISM.

KK THESIS. The thesis that if one knows that p, then one also knows that one knows that p. This thesis takes its name from the way in which this is symbolized in **epistemic logic**: $Kap \rightarrow KaKap$, where "K" represents knowing, "a" the knower, and "p" the known **proposition**. The KK thesis was first stated explicitly by **Jaakko Hintikka** in his *Knowledge and Belief* (1962). Defenders of the KK thesis claim that if one knows that p, one ought to be able to give an account of that **knowledge** and defend it against **skeptics**. Thus, one would establish that one knows that one knows that p. Critics argue that this sets the standards for knowledge too high, for there are many cases (e.g., of children) who are plausibly said to have knowledge but who cannot explain or defend it. In addition, the KK thesis seems to lead to an infinite regress of knowledge claims (as each iteration of its application yields a new knowledge claim to which it is then applied), and this is psychologically implausible. *See also* EPISTEMIC LEVELS; EXTERNALISM/INTERNALISM; PROBLEM OF THE CRITERION.

KNOWER PARADOX. A self-referential **paradox** presented most clearly by Kaplan and Montague (1960). It begins with sentence (S): The negation of this sentence is known to be true. If we suppose that (S) is true, then its negation must also be true. If the negation of (S) is true, then we can deduce that (S) must be false. Thus, assuming the **truth** of (S) results in a contradiction; this is thus an **indirect proof** for the conclusion that (S) is false. By providing this compelling **argument** for the negation of (S), we have fulfilled the conditions for (S) being true. Thus, we have shown that (S) is both true and false.

A number of solutions have been proposed to this paradox, but none stands out as definitive. **Saul Kripke** helped develop one of the more promising approaches, known as the truth value gap, which says that (S) is neither true nor false because it does not express a **proposition**. Critics respond that the knower paradox can be restated using a sentence that clearly does express a proposition.

KNOWLEDGE. A wide-ranging and disputed **concept**, traditionally descriptive of a situation in which a subject holds a true **belief** strongly supported by **evidence** or **experience**, perhaps involving **certainty**. Knowledge differs from **epistemic justification** in that it is a more positive claim of epistemic success and is not regarded as admitting of degree. It is widely held that one may be justified to a greater or lesser extent in holding a belief, but either one knows something or one does not. A justified belief may be false, but one could not *know* that which is false.

Knowledge is often divided into **propositional knowledge, procedural knowledge, knowledge by description**, and **knowledge by acquaintance**. It can also be divided into *a priori* **knowledge** and *a posteriori* knowledge. Propositional knowledge is knowledge *that* some proposition is true; this form of knowledge has been the focus of much attention among analytic philosophers. It is with regard to propositional knowledge that most of the debate about *a priori* (nonempirical, not based on experience) knowledge and *a posteriori* (empirical, based on experience) knowledge has taken place. Procedural knowledge is knowledge of *how* to do something. Knowledge by acquaintance, sometimes known as nonpropositional knowledge, results from the knower's encounter with and experience of something and cannot be reduced to propositional knowledge. *See also* CAUSAL THEORIES OF KNOWLEDGE AND JUSTIFICATION; COHERENTISM; EPISTEMOLOGY; FOUNDATIONALISM; GETTIER CASES; KK THESIS; RELIABILISM; SKEPTICISM.

KNOWLEDGE BY ACQUAINTANCE. **Knowledge** of things (as distinct from knowing *about* things) by direct awareness of them; this is rooted in **sense perception**. In order for this knowledge to be about things (and not merely about **sensations**), it involves some form of reference or **intentionality**, often claimed to be unmediated by our **concepts**. Because no representations or other stages are involved, **William James**, **Bertrand Russell**, and others argued that knowledge by acquaintance is epistemically more fundamental and more secure than **propositional knowledge** or **knowledge by description**. The alleged nonpropositional character of what is known by acquaintance raises questions about whether it can be communicated to others. *See* *also* DIRECT REALISM; EMPIRICISM; FOUNDATIONALISM; GIVEN, THE.

KNOWLEDGE BY DESCRIPTION. According to **Bertrand Russell**, **knowledge** of things that is mediated by our mental representations of them. Knowledge by description is typically contrasted with **knowledge by acquaintance** and is said to be less epistemically fundamental or secure. It is typically thought to be a form of **propositional knowledge**.

KNOWLEDGE *DE DICTO*. Propositional knowledge or **knowledge** of **facts**. Unlike **knowledge *de re***, which is knowledge of a particular object, knowledge *de dicto* does not attribute particular properties or relations to a specified object. *See also* KNOWLEDGE *DE SE*; PROPOSITION; PROPOSITIONAL ATTITUDE.

KNOWLEDGE *DE RE*. Knowledge of things themselves; knowledge that a specified object has a particular property or stands in a particular relationship with other things. This is contrasted with **knowledge *de dicto***, which is knowledge of propositions. *See also* KNOWLEDGE *DE SE*.

KNOWLEDGE *DE SE*. Knowledge of oneself. This is not equivalent to **knowledge *de re*** about oneself. To qualify as knowledge *de se*, one must recognize this in a self-attributive manner; it is knowledge that *I* am (or have) some specified property. *See also* KNOWLEDGE *DE DICTO*.

KOTARBIŃSKI, TADEUSZ (1886–1981). Polish philosopher and cofounder (with **Jan Łukasiewicz** and Stanislaw Leśniewski [1886–1939]) of the Warsaw Center of Logical Research. He argued, notably in his *Elements of Theory of Knowledge, Formal Logic, and Scientific Methodology* (1929), that the only genuine philosophical method is the **logic** and **analysis** used in the empirical **science**s, geometry, and so on.

KRIPKE, SAUL (1940–). American philosopher, educated at Harvard University, and professor at Princeton University. His work has been very influential, particularly in modal **logic**, philosophy of language, and the interpretation of **Ludwig Wittgenstein**. In his *Naming and Necessity* (1980), he argues that some necessary **truths** are known *a posteriori*, for example, that Cicero is Tully, and other cases in which one learns through **experience** that two or more terms refer to the same thing. His *Wittgenstein on Rules and Private Language* (1982) addresses Wittgenstein's response to **skepticism**, although critics argue that Kripke's discussion has little to do with Wittgenstein. *See also A PRIORI/A POSTERIORI* KNOWLEDGE; PRIVATE LANGUAGE ARGUMENT.

KUHN, THOMAS SAMUEL (1922–1996). American philosopher and scientist; he studied physics at Harvard University and then taught at Harvard, the University of California at Berkeley, Princeton University, and the Massachusetts Institute of Technology. His *The Structure of Scientific Revolutions* (1962) shed important new light on the nature of change in **science** and introduced the **concepts** of scientific revolutions and paradigm shifts. He also contributed to the understanding of the **incommensurability** of scientific theories. *See also* FEYERABEND, PAUL.

– L –

LAKATOS, IMRE (1922–1974). Hungarian-born mathematician whose flight from Nazi and then Soviet invasions eventually led him to England; he taught at the London School of Economics. His *Proofs and Refutations* (1963) explores the role of **counterexamples** or refutations in both mathematics and **science**. Drawing on the work of **Karl Popper** and **Thomas Kuhn**, he argues that science should be understood in terms of research programs rather than theories and proposes criteria for progress and degeneration of research programs. *See also* FEYERABEND, PAUL; MATHEMATICAL KNOWLEDGE; SCIENTIFIC METHOD; THEORY.

LAPLACE, PIERRE SIMON DE (1749–1827). French astronomer and mathematician, noted for his contributions to the **theory** of **probability**. Laplace argued that the world is deterministic (i.e., the past and the laws of nature jointly dictate a unique future—one in which probabilities have no place), but we must often deal in probabilities because of our limited **knowledge** of it. His *Théorie analytique des probabilités* (*Analytic Theory of Probability*, 1812) includes the principle of indifference, which states that all possible states or outcomes are equally probable. *See also* BAYESIANISM.

LAW OF NATURE. *See* NATURAL LAW.

LAWS, SCIENTIFIC. *See* NATURAL SCIENCE.

LEAP OF FAITH. In the work of **Søren Kierkegaard**, the deliberate and essentially irrational choice of Christianity despite the absence of conclusive **evidence** for its **truth** or for **God**'s existence. One's commitment to **faith** should be maintained despite one's intellectual awareness of the **logical** and evidential problems facing one's position. *See also* CREDULITY; RELIGIOUS KNOWLEDGE; VOLUNTARISM.

LEHRER, KEITH (1936–). American philosopher, emeritus at the University of Arizona. He was elected as a member of the American Academy of Arts and Sciences in 2005. Lehrer's contributions in epistemology are many and wide ranging and include work on the **problem of the criterion** (in response to the **Gettier problems**), responses to **skepticism**, the philosophy of **Thomas Reid**, and various issues in **metaepistemology**. His recent work develops and defends **coherentism**. Notable works include *Knowledge* (1974), *Thomas Reid* (1989), and *Self-Trust: A Study of Reason, Knowledge and Autonomy* (1997).

LEIBNIZ, GOTTFRIED WILHELM (1646–1716). A German rationalist philosopher; he was born in Leipzig and worked much of his life in Hanover. Leibniz claimed that although all true **propositions** are conceptually true (i.e., the predicate **concept** is contained within the subject concept), not all are **necessarily** true. The concepts in a necessarily true proposition can be shown to be identical using a finite number of **logical** steps. The logical **analysis** of **contingently** true propositions requires infinitely many steps and converges on the identity only of the component concepts. Only necessary **truths** can be known *a priori*. Our **knowledge** of contingent truths is rooted in perceptual **experience**. Despite this apparently empiricist stance, he argued that minds cannot exist without thought and that the empiricists' *tabula rasa* is impossible. People have **innate ideas** of existence, possibility, and identity.

The mind or soul is a monad: an unextended, simple substance that does not causally interact with other monads. Each substance reflects the entire world but from its own point of view. Thus, because ideas cannot enter minds from the outside, there is a sense in which every idea is innate. Although minds always have perceptions, they are not always aware of them. Moreover, minds have innate concepts (e.g., those of **causation** and substance), and these make possible our knowledge that a proposition is necessarily true. Much of his epistemology can be found in his *Monadologie* (*Monadology*, 1714) and *Nouveaux essais* (*New Essays*, 1704); the latter is an examination of **John Locke**'s *Essay Concerning Human Understanding. See also A PRIORI/A POSTERIORI* KNOWLEDGE; EMPIRICISM; PRINCIPLE OF SUFFICIENT REASON; RATIONALISM.

LEWIS, CLARENCE IRVING (1883–1964). An American empiricist philosopher who graduated from Harvard University and spent much of his life teaching there. He developed a version of **foundationalism** according to which we can be certain about our current sensory **experiences** but not about any claims regarding the **external world**. He argues that **certainty** about our current experiences is required if our **beliefs** about the external world are to be true (or even probably true), but this seems to rely on faulty reasoning about the nature of probabilities and **evidence**.

Lewis also defended a form of **phenomenalism**: He held that all empirical judgments can be reduced to large sets of conditional **judgments** about which **perceptions** would follow, given specified combinations of perceptions and volitions. He argues that these conditionals can be tested and conclusively confirmed, thus confirming our beliefs about the external world. *See also* CONDITIONAL PROOF; CONFIRMATION; EMPIRICISM; GIVEN, THE.

LIGHT OF REASON. *See* NATURAL LIGHT.

LINEAR JUSTIFICATION. The **epistemic justification** provided for a particular **belief** in the form of one or more other beliefs, **experiences**, or mental processes. This understanding of justification, which is characteristic of **foundationalism**, regards it as being transmitted from one belief (or experience and so on) to another by means of inductive or deductive relationships. This is often confronted with the **regress argument**: One's belief that P is supported by one's belief that Q, which is supported in turn by one's belief that R and so on. How can one rule out the possibility that none of these beliefs is true (or well justified)? *See also* COHERENTISM; HOLISM.

LOCKE, JOHN (1632–1704). English philosopher, brought up in a Puritan family and educated at Oxford University. His principal work on **epistemology** is *An Essay Concerning Human Understanding* (1690) in which he argues against **innate ideas** and sets out his empiricist system. This system employs the analogy of the mind beginning as a blank page or tablet, a ***tabula rasa***, that acquires **ideas** only through **experience**. **Knowledge** results from the operation of our faculty of reason on these ideas. Reason's role is to arrive at the agreements or disagreements of ideas; this is accomplished by intuitively perceiving these relationships or by arriving at them using other ideas in a deductive process. (Locke rejected the Scholastic claim that specific forms of syllogistic reasoning are required for scientific knowledge.) Knowledge consists in the recognition of these relationships; without this we have only **belief** or **opinion**. Although knowledge is generally *accompanied* by belief, the two are not identical. Knowledge is the direct perception of the agreement of ideas, whereas belief is taking a **proposition** to be true. We are obligated to regulate our minds so as to maximize true beliefs that are of practical value and minimize false beliefs. The strength with which one holds a belief should be guided by the weight of the evidence supporting it.

The study of objects in the external world does not result in these relationships (e.g., we are unable to deduce a relationship between a substance's being gold and its being yellow), so in this area we have only belief and not knowledge. If we knew the real essences of substances, we would be able to grasp these relationships, and scientific knowledge could be worked out without further observation. The study of the properties of objects will never be a true *science* because we are unable to have knowledge of these matters. By contrast, the study of arithmetic or geometry does yield knowledge because we are able to grasp the essences of the entities involved. Locke deviates from this high standard he has set for knowledge when he insists that we can have "sensitive knowledge" that the **external world** exists, even though this does not involve grasping relations among ideas.

Religion and ethics are also areas in which reasoning can yield knowledge. We can know the real essences of ethical ideas and so grasp the **necessary** connections among these ideas; this process yields ethical rules and principles. Locke claims that ethical principles express the will of **God** and that our natural faculties enable us to arrive at knowledge of God's existence and nature. The conclusions we reach in this manner correspond to that which is revealed by God by means of **revelation**. *See also* BAYESIANISM; EMPIRICISM; INFERENCE TO THE BEST EXPLANATION; MATHEMATICAL KNOWLEDGE; REPRESENTATIVE REALISM.

LOGIC. The systematic investigation of reasoning. Logic studies the structures of **propositions** and **arguments** and makes assessments of **consistency**, validity, and soundness. When a **belief** is defended by appealing to other beliefs or **evidence**, logic identifies the principles connecting the evidence with the belief supported by it. Logic is generally held to be separate from the examination of the **psychological** processes involved in forming and defending beliefs; the rules of logic are not the laws of thought. *See also A PRIORI/A POSTERIORI* KNOWLEDGE; BELIEF-FORMING PROCESS; RATIONALITY.

LOGIC OF DISCOVERY. A **logic** or method of discovery is a systematic procedure for gaining new **knowledge** about a particular subject, usually in mathematics or **science**. This logic, which could be either deductive or inductive, would both reveal new **truths** and provide **evidence** or **epistemic justification** for the investigator. **Francis Bacon**, **René Descartes**, Isaac Newton, and others proposed various logics of discovery, but these have generally been supplanted by the **hypothetico-deductive method**, which places the epistemic emphasis on the testing of claims rather than on the means by which they are formulated or discovered. *See also* ABDUCTION; SCIENTIFIC METHOD; TESTABILITY.

LOGICAL CONSTRUCTION. An object constructed of simpler constituents by means of a logical process. If all sentences apparently referring to objects of type *A* can be paraphrased without any change in meaning so that they refer only to objects of type *B*, then objects of type *A* may be said to be logical constructions out of objects of type *B*. **Bertrand Russell** used this technique in his **theory** of descriptions to reduce his ontological commitments and resolve philosophical issues. For instance, he argued that material, extramental objects are nothing but logical constructs whose constituents are **sense data**. He believed that this allowed him to avoid the challenge of **skepticism** regarding the **external world**. *See also* CARNAP, RUDOLF.

LOGICAL EMPIRICISM. *See* LOGICAL POSITIVISM.

LOGICAL POSITIVISM. A philosophical school of thought (also called logical empiricism) that began in Vienna in the 1920s, was influential in the English-speaking world until the 1960s, but now is largely discredited. It was heavily influenced by British **empiricism** and claimed that only **science** can generate genuine **knowledge**; any issues that cannot be stated and addressed in scientific terms are cognitively meaningless. The logical positivists regard a sentence as cognitively meaningful only if it is **analytic**, or if **experiences** (actual or possible) can verify or falsify it. This claim that the meaning of a statement is its method of verification is known as the **verification theory** of meaning, and it is used to reject as meaningless sentences about ethics, esthetics, religion, metaphysics, and other matters. All normative statements are unverifiable and thus meaningless, and all meaningful statements are factual and value free.

The **epistemology** of logical positivism is **foundationalism**; all justified **beliefs** are justified either by their own nature (these are **basic beliefs**, sometimes referred to as **protocol statements**) or by their relationships with basic beliefs. The central goal of logical positivism is to clarify the nature and structure of human knowledge, particularly in the sciences. This is accompanied by a commitment to reductionism, according to which ontological commitments would be minimized by describing some types of entities as **logical constructions** of other types of entities. *See also* CARNAP, RUDOLF; REDUCTION SENTENCE; VIENNA CIRCLE; VERIFICATIONISM.

LOGICISM. The thesis that mathematics is, at least to a significant degree, a part of **logic**. Expressibility logicism states that mathematical statements are (or are reducible to) logical statements. It claims that the fundamental **concepts** of mathematics are also those of logic and that the **proof** procedures in mathematics and logic are structurally identical. Derivational logicism states that the axioms and theorems of mathematics can be derived from the principles of logic. Different versions of logicism arise from disagreements about what should count as logic or as a derivation from pure logic. Notable logicists include **Gottlob Frege**, **Bertrand Russell**, and **Rudolf Carnap**. *See also* MATHEMATICAL KNOWLEDGE.

LOTTERY PARADOX. A **paradox**, formulated by Henry Kyburg (1928–), intended to show that common assumptions about **epistemic justification** or **rational acceptance** result in a rational person justifiably believing clearly contradictory **propositions**. To generate this paradox, begin by considering a large, one-winner lottery. You justifiably believe that there will be exactly one winner; call this proposition "W." Furthermore, because of the large number of lottery tickets involved, you are justified in believing of each ticket that it will not be the winner. Thus, you believe that ticket 1 is not the winner, that ticket 2 is not the winner, that ticket 3 is not the winner, and so forth for all the tickets in the lottery. If you are justified in believing each of these propositions about individual tickets, then you should also be justified in believing their conjunction (a proposition we will call "T"). T is equivalent to the proposition that no ticket will win, but one is also justified in believing that one of those tickets *will* win. Thus, one is justified in believing the conjunction T and W, which is clearly contradictory.

This conclusion is undesirable and has led epistemologists to question the assumptions that lead to it. One of these assumptions, called the deductive **closure principle** for justification, is that one is justified in believing the deductive consequences of what one justifiably believes. Kyburg recommends that we reject this assumption, although Mark Kaplan has argued that without this assumption we would be unable to recognize the force of *reductio ad absurdum* **arguments**. A second assumption is that one is never justified in believing a set of propositions that are clearly logically inconsistent. A third assumption at work here is that one is justified in accepting a proposition as true if the **probability** of its **truth** is great but not **certain**. The second and third assumptions have been questioned by some, but there is widespread reluctance to abandon them. *See also* BAYESIANISM; CLOSURE PRINCIPLE.

ŁUKASIEWICZ, JAN (1878–1956). A Polish philosopher and logician, he was the most notable member of the Warsaw School. He developed many-valued **logics**, invented bracket-free Polish notation, formulated a superior interpretation of Stoic logic, and developed a unified account of **Aristotle**'s assertoric and **modal logics**. He used a third truth value, *possible*, to defuse philosophical problems about future contingencies, free will, and universal determinism.

LYCAN, WILLIAM G. (1945–). American philosopher who was educated at the University of Chicago and teaches at the University of North Carolina, Chapel Hill. *Knowing Who* (1986), written with Steven Boër, examines how we know who someone is. Lycan's *Judgment and Justification* (1993) examines the nature of **beliefs** and links this to work in the cognitive sciences. **Epistemic justification** is explained in terms of natural selection. *See also* NATURALIZED EPISTEMOLOGY.

– M –

MACH, ERNST (1838–1916). An Austrian physicist and philosopher of **science**. In 1867 he became chair of the physics department at Prague and in 1895 returned to Vienna (where he had been a student) to teach philosophy. He significantly influenced the **Vienna Circle** and was one of the founders of **logical positivism**.

Mach's *The Science of Mechanics* (1883) argues that mechanics is based on **sensations** and that the **external world** can be understood as a **logical construction** of sensations. Mechanics, like other areas of **science**, is inductive and descriptive. Scientific **theories** may appear to provide **explanations**, but this is misleading. A theory only aids in predicting **observations**, and the entities that theories postulate should not be regarded as having independent existence. *See also* ABSTRACT ENTITY; INDUCTION; THEORETICAL ENTITY.

MAIMON, SALOMON (1753–1800). German Jewish philosopher, born in Lithuania. He was a friend of **Moses Mendelssohn** and a critic of **Immanuel Kant**. He argues that Kant's philosophy is inadequate as a response to **skepticism**. He also rejects the claim that the "thing-in-itself" is a genuine object underlying phenomena and argues against Kant's distinction between sensibility and understanding.

MALCOLM, NORMAN (1911–1990). An American philosopher, he was a biographer and interpreter of **Ludwig Wittgenstein**. He taught at Cornell University and was later associated with King's College, London. He wrote articles and books on various epistemic topics, including criticisms of **G. E. Moore**'s alleged **proof** of the existence of (and our **knowledge** about) the **external world**. He also wrote about Wittgenstein's **private language argument** and influenced the latter's *On Certainty* (1969).

MALEBRANCHE, NICOLAS (1638–1715). French philosopher and theologian. In his *De la recherche de la vérité* (*The Search after Truth*, 1674) he agrees with **René Descartes** that **ideas** are central to **sense perception** and understanding but argues that the ideas perceived by humans are actually in the mind of **God**. Ideas exist independently of finite, human minds and are what make it possible for us to grasp necessary **truths**. *See also* RATIONALISM.

MANIFEST IMAGE. *See* HOLISM; SELLARS, WILFRID; WEB OF BELIEF.

MANNHEIM, KARL (1893–1947). Hungarian-born German social theorist. He introduced and established the study of **sociology of knowledge**, a new branch of study that investigates the social *causes* of **beliefs** as distinct from the reasons people have for holding those beliefs.

He argued that there can be no objective **knowledge** of society. *See also* BELIEF-FORMING PROCESS; OBJECTIVE/SUBJECTIVE; REASONS FOR BELIEF.

MANSEL, HENRY LONGUEVILLE (1820–1871). British philosopher and clergyman; professor at Oxford University and dean of St. Paul's Cathedral in London, England. Strongly influenced by **Immanuel Kant**, he argues that **logic** is the study of the laws of thought (*Prolegomena Logica*, 1851), that the true nature of things is unknowable (*Metaphysics*, 1860), and that the human mind is incapable of understanding **God**, so **rationality** is incapable of properly criticizing religious doctrine (*The Limits of Religious Thought*, 1858). *See also* FAITH; PSYCHOLOGY; RELIGIOUS KNOWLEDGE.

MANY PROPERTIES PROBLEM. *See* ADVERBIAL THEORY OF PERCEPTION.

MARITAIN, JACQUES (1882–1973). French philosopher and neo-Thomist. He developed an account of **knowledge** that unifies the **empirical sciences** with metaphysics, theology, and **mysticism** (*Distinguish to Unite, or The Degrees of Knowledge*, 1932).

MARXISM. Based on the work of Karl Marx (1818–1883), a German economic theorist, philosopher, and revolutionary, Marxist **theory** rejects many of the practices and **presuppositions** of mainstream **epistemology**. Marx's own epistemic views are found chiefly in his *Economic and Philosophical Manuscripts of 1844*, "Theses on Feuerbach" (1845), and *German Ideology* (1845–1846, coauthored with Friederich Engels).

Marx claims that each individual is situated in a historical setting that molds both self-understanding and the understanding of one's world. One interacts with one's society and environment, and understanding this interaction is central to epistemology. The **external world** is material and exists independently of us; we know of it through **sense perception**. There is disagreement among Marxists about whether we are directly aware of objects themselves or aware of the external world only by means of representations or **sensations** it causes in the observer's mind. These **observations** are the basis for one's **knowledge** of objective **truth**. Theories based on these observations can be only partly or relatively true; as history progresses, theories will become more completely true. Some Marxists take a different approach, arguing that the world is transformed and created by "human sensuous activity, practice." Thus, both humans and their world are constituted by human social activity. This approach rejects the traditional epistemic assumption that there can be a neutral, privileged standpoint from which the epistemologist can assess **beliefs**. *See also* CONTEXTUALISM; DIRECT REALISM; EPISTEMIC RELATIVISM; HISTORICISM; OBJECTIVE/SUBJECTIVE; REPRESENTATIVE REALISM; SOCIOLOGY OF KNOWLEDGE.

MATHEMATICAL INDUCTION. A method of definition and **proof** used to define a collection of objects and to establish the characteristics of members of that set. For example, mathematical induction can be used to define the set of natural numbers, N, by means of a basic clause ("0 is in N") and an inductive clause ("For any x in N, the successor of x is also in N"). To show that all members of an inductively defined set have a particular property, the method is to show that the members specified by the basic clause have that property and that this property is preserved in the inductive process. Although mathematical induction provides important **evidence** for the conclusions it generates, it may not be capable of generating **knowledge**. *See also* INDUCTION; MATHEMATICAL KNOWLEDGE.

MATHEMATICAL INTUITIONISM. A twentieth-century school of thought founded by **L. E. J. Brouwer** that interprets mathematics in the light of **Immanuel Kant**'s metaphysics. Classical **logic**, particularly the principles of excluded middle (every **proposition** is either true or false) and noncontradiction (no proposition is both true and false), is rejected as a tool for mathematical reasoning. Mathematics is regarded as a languageless activity of the mind, rooted in the **intuition** of time. The fundamental mathematical act is mentally distinguishing between two events in one's flow of **consciousness**, and from this basis it is claimed that all mathematical objects can be constructed. Some of these mathematical objects may not have determinate properties—a suggestion rejected by classical mathematics. *See also* MATHEMATICAL KNOWLEDGE.

MATHEMATICAL KNOWLEDGE. Knowledge of mathematics is essential for scientific knowledge and is one of the few areas in which very high levels of **certainty** are possible. Several conflicting accounts have been offered of how mathematical knowledge is possible.

Immanuel Kant argues that mathematical knowledge arises from **perceptions** of time and space and that this knowledge is essential for any **empirical** knowledge. The world in itself is unknowable, however, and mathematical knowledge is rooted in the structure of **experience** and the mind. This Kantian approach spawned intuitionism and formalism, both views that the subject matter of mathematics is ultimately **mathematical intuition**.

Logicist interpretations of mathematics claim that it is a branch of **logic** and thus that its **truths** are **analytic**. Difficulties have arisen, however, in attempts to reduce mathematics to analytic statements of logic.

John Stuart Mill takes an empiricist approach to mathematical knowledge, arguing that it is a branch of physics (rather than of logic) and that our **evidence** for the truth of mathematical statements lies in the widespread **confirmation** they receive in experience.

Mathematical realists suggest that numbers, pure sets, or other entities have mind-independent (albeit nonphysical) existence and that knowledge of them is gained by means of a noncausal, quasi-perceptual awareness. **Kurt Gödel**, for example, claims that "mathematical intuition" provides one with knowledge of some mathematical truths. In this way, one could know a mathematical truth independently of any **proof** procedure. Other mathematical realists argue that ordinary **sense perception** can provide one with knowledge of mathematical truths, perhaps by observing structures or patterns in the natural world.

Pragmatism begins with the **observation** that mathematics is essential for the physical sciences and concludes that because of this we are warranted in accepting its claims as true. **W. V. O. Quine** takes a similar approach, stating that mathematical theories are **justified** by their success in predicting observations. Quine, however, adds to this an **ontological commitment** to mathematical objects.

Conventionalism states that the axioms and theorems of mathematics are true by convention. According to this view, genuine mathematical knowledge is impossible; we can know only about our arbitrarily selected practices. **Ludwig Wittgenstein** is often regarded as a conventionalist, although his view also includes a role for the observation of empirical regularities that are then "hardened" into rules. *See also A PRIORI/A POSTERIORI* KNOWLEDGE; ABSTRACT ENTITY; ANALYTICITY; EPISTEMIC WARRANT; MATHEMATICAL INTUITIONISM.

McCOSH, JAMES (1811–1894). Scottish philosopher and clergyman; he served as a professor at Queen's College, Belfast, and later as president of the College of New Jersey (which is now Princeton University). His *Intuitions of the Mind* (1860) defines **intuitions** as rules that the mind follows in forming **beliefs** on the basis of **observations** of external objects. He argues that we have immediate **knowledge** both of our own minds and of external objects. *See also* BELIEF-FORMING PROCESS; EXTERNAL WORLD; IMMEDIACY.

MEAD, GEORGE HERBERT (1863–1931). American philosopher, educated at Harvard University, who taught at the University of Michigan and the University of Chicago. He was an important member of the American **pragmatism** school, along with **William James**, **John Dewey**, and **Charles Peirce**. He is noted for his work on human communication, the formation of the "self" in child development, and his contributions to the sociology of symbolic interactions.

MEASUREMENT. Measurements play an important role in information and **evidence**, but complex issues underlie our practices. How should a scale or system of representation be chosen? Once it has been selected, how is it applied to or used to represent the phenomena being measured? Absolute measurement involves using numbers to represent, for example, the number of members in a set. Ratio measurement, by contrast, represents the measured phenomenon on an interval; the measurement of temperature is an instance of this. Ordinal measurement, as exemplified by Moh's hardness scale, employs an arbitrary ordering of labels or categories.

Measurement often involves the use of laboratory instruments, and this raises further questions about the **theory ladenness** of **observations**. Furthermore, measurements often involve margins of **error**, thus limiting their effectiveness in testing **predictions** or assessing **theories**. *See also* TESTABILITY.

MECHANISTIC EXPLANATION. A form of **explanation** rooted in the mechanics of masses in motion, avoiding any reference to final causes, vital forces, or other nonnatural factors. Although this form of explanation is widely used in the physical **sciences**, it faces difficulties in explaining **consciousness** and **intentional** behavior. *See also* CAUSATION.

MEMORY. The capacity to retain or recall past **experience** or previously acquired information. **Aristotle, David Hume, Bertrand Russell**, and others claim that memory consists in the retention and recall of mental images. Adherents of this view disagree with regard to what it is about an image that establishes its "pastness," its being about the past rather than being simply a current mental image. Critics point out that memory need not involve images at all.

There is disagreement about memory's role in providing **evidence** for **beliefs** or as a basis for **knowledge**. These issues are dealt with in particular **theories** of knowledge and **epistemic justification** and are not unique to the issue of memory. Memory plays a significant role in assessing new information: We are more likely to accept a **proposition** as true if it is **consistent** with (and stands in **explanatory** relations with) the information and experiences we remember. Thus, memory can be a source of evidence. Skeptics challenge this, however, pointing out that our memories may be inaccurate. As **Bertrand Russell** observed (*An Outline of Philosophy*, 1921), it could be that the entire world, complete with historical records, fossils, memories, and overdue library books, sprang into existence only five minutes ago. Therefore, memory does not seem to be adequate as a basis for knowledge. *See also* IMAGINATION; SKEPTICISM; TRUTH.

MENDELSSOHN, MOSES (1729–1786). German Jewish philosopher and Talmudic scholar; sometimes called "the Jewish Socrates." He argues that the immortality of the soul and the existence of **God** can be proven (*Phaedo, or on the Immortality of the Soul*, 1767; *Morning Hours, or Lectures on the Existence of God*, 1785). **Immanuel Kant** criticizes Mendelssohn's arguments in his *Critique of*

Pure Reason (1781/1787). He also argues that Judaism consists not in a set of **beliefs** for which **evidence** must be provided but in a set of practices. *See also* PROOF; RELIGIOUS KNOWLEDGE.

MENTALISM. Any **theory** that posits the existence of mental states or processes (regardless of whether these are physical or immaterial). Mentalistic theories thus posit the existence of **beliefs**, desires, **memories**, emotions, and so forth. Nonmentalistic theories, such as behaviorism, avoid such references and talk only of brain states, behavior, and other nonmental states or processes. *See also* BEHAVIORISM, ANALYTIC; BEHAVIORISM, METHODOLOGICAL; ELIMINATIVE MATERIALISM; FOLK PSYCHOLOGY; NATURALIZED EPISTEMOLOGY; PSYCHOLOGY.

MERCIER, DÉSIRÉ-JOSEPH (1851–1926). Belgian Catholic philosopher and neo-Thomist, founder of the Institut Supérieur de Philosophie at Louvain (1889), which was devoted to the study of **Thomas Aquinas**. In his *Critériologie générale ou Théorie générale de la certitude* (1906), Mercier argues against **skepticism** by describing the motives and rules that govern **judgment** and claiming that judgment establishes **truth** by abstract apprehension; this employs a distinct cognitive faculty of the soul. *See also* BELIEF-FORMING PROCESS.

MERLEAU-PONTY, MAURICE (1908–1961). French philosopher, chair of the Child Psychology Department at the Sorbonne and later professor of philosophy at the Collège de France. Influenced by the **phenomenology** of **Edmund Husserl** and the existentialism of **Martin Heidegger**, Merleau-Ponty developed a philosophy of the lived body or the body subject and stressed the **ambiguity** of **truth**. His *Phénoménologie de la Perception* (*Phenomenology of Perception*, 1945) argues that all higher cognitive functioning is rooted in **perception**, the subject's prereflective bodily existence. He rejects the traditional philosophical accounts of perception, particularly intellectualism and **empiricism**, claiming that they fail to deal adequately with the phenomenal nature of perception. The lived body is not an object in the world about which we learn; instead, it is the subjective point of view from which all **knowledge** is derived. His subsequent writings defend his position against criticisms that it amounts to an unacceptable reductionism. He criticizes the subject/object dichotomy characteristic of traditional philosophy and introduces a notion of "the flesh" as a means of reconceptualizing Being and intersubjectivity.

Merleau-Ponty understands perception as a skill one develops, not as a mechanism for forming particular beliefs. Perception, action, and bodily movement are all united in discovering the features of objects and the environment. Our awareness of others is more fundamental than, and forms a basis for, our awareness of ourselves.

Merleau-Ponty rejects mind–body dualism and the traditional **epistemological** concern with responding to **skepticism**, claiming that the latter project involves an unacceptable expectation regarding **certainty** and **objectivity**. It also, he argues, requires an untenable separation between perception and the world. Thus, he says, "we must not, therefore, wonder whether we really perceive a world, we must instead say: the world is what we perceive" (*Phenomenology of Perception*). *See also* ACT/OBJECT ANALYSIS; BELIEF-FORMING PROCESS; CONSCIOUSNESS; EXPERIENCE; EXTERNAL WORLD; OBJECTIVE/SUBJECTIVE; PERCEPTUAL KNOWLEDGE.

MERSENNE, MARIN (1588–1648). French priest, noted for his correspondence with Galileo, **René Descartes**, **Thomas Hobbes**, and others. He collected the objections and responses that were published with Descartes's *Meditations on First Philosophy* (1641). He argues that a limited form of **skepticism** is a valuable basis for scientific investigation and that we cannot know the true essences of things. He supported the use of **mechanistic explanation** and mathematical models in **science**. *See also* SCIENTIFIC METHOD.

METAEPISTEMOLOGY. A branch of metaphilosophy, the study of the nature of **epistemology**, the **objectivity** or relativity of epistemic claims, and the conditions in which those claims are meaningful, warranted, or true. It also examines the methods employed in epistemology and their relationship to those used in other areas of study. *See also* EPISTEMIC RELATIVISM; EPISTEMIC WARRANT; TRUTH.

METHOD OF DOUBT. *See* DESCARTES, RENÉ.

METHODISM. *See* PROBLEM OF THE CRITERION.

MIDDLE KNOWLEDGE. *See* MOLINA, LUIS DE.

MILL, JOHN STUART (1806–1873). British philosopher, economist, and social theorist. He defends a **naturalized epistemology** according to which all **evidence** for our **beliefs** about the world must originate in **experience**. In his *System of Logic* (1843), Mill distinguishes between "real" and "verbal" **propositions**, a distinction that parallels that between analytic and synthetic propositions. Verbal propositions, which Mill says have no real content, do *not* include the truths of mathematics or **logic**. Mill uses his **analysis** of language to show that real knowledge is provided by statements of logic or mathematics, making them "real" propositions.

Because these propositions are real, Mill claims the evidence supporting them must originate in experience; ultimately, this evidence is rooted in **enumerative induction**. Although these **inferences** are **fallible** and cannot eliminate all **doubt**, they can nonetheless generate **knowledge**; Mill's position is thus an early form of fallibilism. The principle "Enumerative induction is **reliable**" is said to be neither verbal nor real; Mill simply says that people generally accept and use it. He holds that we are **immediately** aware only of the contents of our own **consciousness** and that these contents are the fundamental subjects of our inferences. Physical objects, then, can be known only as well-established "Possibilities of **Sensation**." *See also* ANALYTICITY; INDUCTION, PROBLEM OF; MATHEMATICAL KNOWLEDGE.

MĪMĀMSĀ. An orthodox school of thought within Hinduism; also known as Pūrva Mīmāmsā. It regards **sense perception**, **inference**, and **testimony** as **reliable** sources of **knowledge**. Knowledge can also arise from explanatory postulations. *See also* INDIAN EPISTEMOLOGY; INFERENCE TO THE BEST EXPLANATION.

MODAL KNOWLEDGE. *See* CONTINGENCY; NECESSITY; POSSIBLE WORLDS.

MODAL LOGIC. *See* CONTINGENCY; LOGIC; NECESSITY; POSSIBLE WORLDS.

MOLINA, LUIS DE (1535–1600). Spanish Jesuit theologian and philosopher. In his *Concordia liberi arbitrii cum gratiae donis* (*Free Will and Grace*, 1588), he argued that free will is compatible with **divine foreknowledge** of a free agent's actions. This is his doctrine of "middle **knowledge**," so called because it lies between **God**'s knowledge of what has existed, exists, and will exist and God's knowledge of what has not existed, does not exist, and will not exist. That is, God's middle knowledge is of **contingent** future events, based on divine knowledge of our **dispositions**—how we would behave in any specified set of circumstances. This allows God to arrange the circumstances that will bring about a particular action without actually predetermining that action.

MOLYNEUX QUESTION. Also called Molyneux's problem, it was posed by William Molyneux (1656–1698) in a letter to **John Locke**. It begins by having us consider a person, blind from birth, who has learned to distinguish cubes from spheres by means of touch. Suppose that this person is now able to see, and a cube and a sphere are placed in front of him. Would this person be able to tell—without touching either object—which is the cube and which the sphere? Locke included this question in his *Essay Concerning Human Understanding* (1694, bk. 2, chap. 9, sec. 8) and agrees with Molyneux that this person would *not* be able to make this distinction. Locke argues that one must learn through **experience** how to associate a particular visual appearance with a particular tactile **sensation**, and our formerly blind person has not yet had a chance to do this. At issue here are whether the sensations generated by different sense modalities resemble one another and whether we have any innate ability to determine shapes visually.

A similar question was posed by Denis Diderot (*Lettre sur les aveugles*, 1749), who asked whether a person blind from birth would, on receiving sight as an adult, be able to recognize different two-dimensional figures (e.g., a circle and a square) on the basis of prior tactile experiences. This version of the problem eliminates the issue of depth cues available from vision. The issue is whether primary quality **concepts** are linked to a particular sense modality or with combinations of these modalities. *See also* INNATE IDEA; PRIMARY AND SECONDARY QUALITIES; SENSE PERCEPTION.

MONTAIGNE, MICHEL DE (1533–1592). French essayist and philosopher; born near Bordeaux and later mayor of that city. Influenced by **Sextus Empiricus** and **Cicero**, Montaigne developed and defends a tolerant **skepticism** on many issues. He argues that we are unable to establish appropriate criteria for **knowledge**, that our ethical views are unsupported by objective **evidence**, and that religious **beliefs** should be held on **faith** rather than on the basis of inadequate evidence. **Science** does not provide convincing evidence for its conclusions; scientists of the past are rejected by those of today, and those of today will be rejected tomorrow. He argues that one should accept traditional beliefs and follow customs not because we have good evidence for their **truth** but because we have no adequate reason for changing them. This should be accompanied by tolerance of others' views and practices. Montaigne's views, a form of **Pyrrhonian skepticism**, influenced **Francis Bacon**, **René Descartes**, **Blaise Pascal**, and others. *See also* OBJECTIVE/SUBJECTIVE; PROBLEM OF THE CRITERION; REASONS FOR BELIEF; RELIGIOUS KNOWLEDGE.

MOORE, GEORGE EDWARD (G. E.) (1873–1958). British philosopher, educated at Cambridge University and later a professor at that institution. He was also the editor of the journal *Mind*. He argues against **skepticism** and defends a form of **commonsensism**. In *Some Main Problems of Philosophy* (1953), he argues that we are more **certain** that the conclusions of skeptical **arguments** are false than we are that their premises are true; thus, we are warranted in rejecting skepticism. Indeed, the very fact that those premises lead to skepticism undermines our reasons for accepting them.

Moore also argues that skeptics cannot present arguments in support of their position without risking self-contradiction: One who presents an argument asserts **knowledge** of the premises and their **implications**, but the skeptics claim that we do not have such knowledge. The skeptic can avoid this problem by presenting the premises as ones to which the nonskeptic is committed, so that the nonskeptic ought also to accept skepticism.

Moore famously "proved" the existence of an **external world** by claiming that it would be unreasonable to question whether his two hands were there in front of him (*Philosophical Papers*, 1959). It is not clear whether this is intended to establish merely the existence of the external world or its existence as well as our knowledge of its existence. Either way, it hardly seems to **defeat** the skeptic. Moore claims, however, that one can know that *p* without being able to prove that skeptical arguments against one's knowledge of *p* are unsound.

In giving an account of how we know about the external world, Moore usually endorses **representative realism**, although he sometimes supports **direct realism** or **phenomenalism**. His accounts of **sense perception** include discussions of how **sense data** are related to physical objects. He also discusses the distinction between **knowledge by acquaintance** and **propositional knowledge**. *See also* DEFEASIBILITY; EPISTEMIC WARRANT; MOORE'S PARADOX; PROOF; REASONS FOR BELIEF.

MOORE'S PARADOX. G. E. Moore presented a set of apparently paradoxical sentences, such as "Socrates was a philosopher, but it is not the case that I believe that Socrates was a philosopher" or "Socrates was a philosopher, but I believe that Socrates was not a philosopher." The first section of each sentence implies that the speaker believes what is asserted, but the second section either denies that the speaker believes this or presents a contradictory **belief**. Moore regarded these sentences as illustrating the difference between an assertion and an **implication**. The first section of each sentence implies that the speaker believes what is said, but the second half asserts the speaker's beliefs (or lack of belief). Some regard these sentences as being unassertable because they violate the principles governing speech acts or as being logically **consistent** but impossible to believe. *See also* GRAMMAR; PARADOX; PARADOX OF THE KNOWER; PRINCIPLE OF CHARITY.

MORAL EPISTEMOLOGY. The study, drawing on both **epistemology** and ethics, of the epistemic status of moral principles and **judgments**. It seeks to determine what **evidence** supports our moral views and whether any of our moral **beliefs** qualify as **knowledge**. This involves related issues, such as whether normative claims are either true or false.

Noncognitive **theories** of ethics hold that moral judgments are neither true nor false because there are no moral properties or **facts** to which these judgments might correspond. Thus, this view implies that moral knowledge and **justified** belief are impossible. Most moral theories, however, claim that moral judgments are either true or false; it is here that moral epistemology is generally applied.

A particularist approach to moral epistemology takes our judgments about particular cases or our awareness of particular moral facts to be epistemically fundamental. From this basis we can then generalize to formulate moral rules, principles, and theories. A generalist approach to moral epistemology takes our grasp of moral rules or principles to be epistemically fundamental. We then apply these general **truths** to particular cases to arrive at moral judgments. **Immanuel Kant** takes a generalist approach, claiming that moral laws are universalizable principles of action (*Groundwork of the Metaphysics of Morals*, 1785). The evidence for moral laws, then, lies in the fact that negating them results in a logical contradiction. Henry Sidgwick (1838–1900) and others argue that a faculty of moral **intuition** allows us to grasp fundamental moral principles (*The Methods of Ethics*, 1874), although critics claim that appeals to intuition are nothing more than an admission that one is unable to provide any compelling evidence in support of one's position.

W. D. Ross (1877–1971) is a particularist, holding that one recognizes in particular cases that a certain factor of the situation is morally significant; one then uses a process of intuitive induction to reach the conclusion that this factor will be morally significant in any situation in which it appears (*The Right and the Good*, 1930). Ross, however, admits that we can never know what ought to be done in particular cases; we may know which factors are morally relevant but not how to balance out their conflicts to arrive at our "final duty" in that situation. **C. D. Broad** and others take a different particularist approach, arguing that **sense perception** provides evidence of the rightness or wrongness of actions ("Some Reflections on Moral-Sense Theories in Ethics," in *Broad's Critical Essays in Moral Philosophy*, ed. D. Cheney, 1971). Observers (of the proper sort) respond to actions in ways that are analogous to responding to ordinary observable properties of objects or situations. Once again, this moral **perception** would yield evidence regarding particular cases, and this provides the basis for moral generalizations.

John Rawls (1921–2002) proposes a **coherentist** approach to moral epistemology according to which we seek rational equilibrium. This is a middle-ground position between the particularists and the rationalists, balancing both our confident judgments about particular cases and our confidently held moral rules and principles. This stance resembles epistemic forms of coherentism.

MOSER, PAUL K. (1957–). American philosopher who was trained at Vanderbilt University (Nashville, Tenn.); professor at Loyola University (Chicago, Ill.). His work in **epistemology** includes examinations of **objectivity**, the nature of **evidence**, the *a priori/a posteriori* distinction, and **religious knowledge**. His notable works include *Empirical Justification* (1985), *Knowledge and Evidence* (1989), and *Philosophy after Objectivity* (1993).

MYSTICISM. The view that **knowledge** can be gained by means of mystical **experience**, which is independent of and inaccessible to **sense perception** or **rationality**. Although it is typically associated with religion, mysticism may take theistic or nontheistic forms. Mystical experiences may reveal that the distinction between the subject and the world (or perhaps between the subject and **God**) are illusory. The content of these experiences is sometimes claimed to be ineffable. *See also* CERTAINTY; CREDULITY; FAITH; RELIGIOUS KNOWLEDGE.

MYTH OF THE GIVEN. *See* FOUNDATIONALISM; GIVEN, THE; SELLARS, WILFRID.

– N –

NĀGĀRJUNA (second century A.D.). Indian Mahayana **Buddhist** philosopher and founder of the Mādhyamika school of thought. His *Mūlanadhya-makārikā Prajñā* (*The Fundamental Verses on the Middle Way*) and *Sūnyātasaptati* (*The Septuagint on Emptiness*) distinguish between two **truths**. Conditional truth is the everyday truth of ordinary **experience**, but final truth has to do with the existence of an ineffable ultimate **reality**. Enlightenment requires shifting one's attention from the former to the latter. *See also* INDIAN EPISTEMOLOGY.

NAGEL, ERNEST (1901–1985). Czech-born philosopher, educated at Columbia University, New York, who taught at that institution for four decades. His work focuses on the philosophy of **science**, dealing particularly with **probability** and the nature of scientific **explanation**. Nagel argues that **concepts** of probability, reduction, and explanation are properly applied only to scientific **theories** and not to the phenomena themselves (*Principles of the Theory of Probability*, 1939). *See also* COVERING LAW MODEL OF EXPLANATION; SCIENTIFIC METHOD.

NAIVE REALISM. *See* DIRECT REALISM.

NATURAL LAW. Also called "law of nature," it is an **objective** norm or standard, often thought to have been established by **God**. The Stoics believed that such laws are evident in the structure of the cosmos, a view later incorporated by **Thomas Aquinas** and others into Christian legal, moral, and political theories. Natural laws, they claim, can be discovered by means of reason alone, without need for **revelation**. **John Locke** asserts that revelation and reasoning would lead to the same conclusions about such laws. In current legal theory, the natural law approach holds that there are objective legal standards to which all human lawmaking must be held.

NATURAL LIGHT. Also called the "light of reason," this phrase reflects the claim that some foundational intellectual **intuitions** can be known with **certainty**. Rooted in the work of **Plato**, **St. Augustine**, and **René Descartes**, the natural light is often said to be of divine origin, with **God** acting as the guarantor of the **truth** of **beliefs** formed with its aid. *See also* CLEAR AND DISTINCT IDEA; REVELATION.

NATURAL SCIENCE. The scientific investigation of the natural world incorporates physics, chemistry, biology, geology, and astronomy. It is of epistemic importance because these endeavors provide an unusually broad, **coherent**, systematic, and **reliable** body of **belief**. The epistemic assessment of natural **science** sheds light on the nature of **knowledge**, **evidence**, and **epistemic justification**.

Although science relies on perceptual **observations**, it is widely held that the uncertainty inherent in **sense perception** does not prevent beliefs about science from qualifying as knowledge. **Sense-data** theories attempt to provide **certainty** for our observations, but efforts to bridge the gap between sense data and an **external world** of material objects have not been successful. Natural science proceeds on the assumption that although sense perception is not **infallible**, its **errors** and inadequacies can be identified and compensated for. Thus, science incorporates a **fallibilist** account of knowledge.

Natural science generates generalizations by means of **enumerative induction**, and these face **David Hume**'s questions regarding the **problem of induction**. Science uses past observations as a basis for claims about future and unobserved events. Hume points out that this requires the unwarranted assumption that nature is uniform; thus, our generalizations and **predictions** are unjustified. This problem also arises when science formulates laws that are said to apply to all relevant cases (including future and unobserved cases).

The **hypothetico-deductive method** has been widely endorsed as an account of how scientific laws are formulated and confirmed. Observation leads one to formulate a **hypothesis**, and this hypothesis (in conjunction with a statement of the initial conditions) generates a **testable** prediction. If that prediction is true, then the hypothesis is said to receive some degree of **confirmation** as a result. If the prediction is false (and one is confident that the statement of initial conditions is true), then the hypothesis is rejected as false. **Karl Popper** claims that testing predictions can allow us only to reject false hypotheses and cannot provide those hypotheses evidence of their **truth**. **Probability theory** is now often used in exploring how observations provide evidence for or against hypotheses.

The sciences often posit the existence of unobserved entities or events, and this raises important epistemic questions. **Logical positivism** claims that statements about these theoretical entities cannot be observationally tested and thus are meaningless. **Rudolf Carnap** and others argue that although statements about theoretical entities are meaningful within a scientific **theory**, this does not settle the "external" question of whether those entities exist. A strong case has been made in support of the existence of theoretical entities by examining Avogadro's number and Jean Perrin's account of Brownian movement. By observing the movements of visible particles in water, Perrin concluded that these movements resulted from collisions with smaller, unobservable particles. He was then able to calculate the approximate value of Avogadro's number (the number of molecules in a mole of a substance, approximately 6.02×10^{23}). Other observations in other settings also form the basis for calculations of this number, and these results are very close to one another. If the unobservable particles posited in these cases did not really exist, the similitude of these calculations would be exceedingly difficult to explain. *See also* ABSTRACT ENTITY; BAYESIANISM; EMPIRICISM; EPISTEMIC WARRANT; INDUCTION, PROBLEM OF; KUHN, THOMAS; QUINE, W. V. O.; UNIFORMITY OF NATURE.

NATURALIZED EPISTEMOLOGY. An approach to **epistemology** that regards human **beliefs** as a natural phenomenon and employs the **sciences** in addressing epistemological questions. The phrase "naturalized epistemology" was introduced by **W. V. O. Quine** in his "Epistemology Naturalized" (in *Ontological Relativity and Other Essays*, 1969), where he argues that epistemology ought to be entirely replaced by empirical **psychology**. This approach contrasts strongly with the traditional approach found in **René Descartes's** *Meditations on First Philosophy* (1641). According to that view, a proper account of **epistemic justification** and **knowledge** must be developed *before* we can investigate the world and thus arrive at knowledge, and that **logic** could enable one to find a firm **foundation** for belief in immediate **experience**. Quine rejects the **implication** that epistemology is prior to science and claims instead that epistemology is the study of how human beings interact with their environment and that this is part of the empirical sciences. The normativity in epistemology is preserved only in the technology or "engineering" of predicting **observations**; apart from this, epistemology would become descriptive. **Causal theories of knowledge and justification** carry out at least part of this naturalizing project by submitting the processes of belief formation and maintenance to empirical examination.

In addressing **skepticism**, the traditional epistemic approach prohibits making use of scientific resources; doing so would require the illicit assumption that science can provide knowledge and epistemic justification—precisely the claims the skeptics deny. Quine, however, argues that skeptical questions arise only within the practice of science and that it is perfectly appropriate to appeal to science in addressing these questions. Thus, naturalized epistemology has little difficulty in dealing with the challenge of skepticism, although critics argue that it has avoided the skeptical issue rather than resolved it.

Naturalized epistemology would include a scientific examination of how **scientific methodology** has been developed and employed; in this way, these methodologies could be improved. It could also include the examination of communities of knowers, studying the social practices and influences that shape beliefs. *See also* BELIEF-FORMING PROCESS; EMPIRICISM; FIRST PHILOSOPHY; RATIONALISM; SOCIOLOGY OF KNOWLEDGE.

NECESSITY. A necessary **truth** is one that must be true, one whose negation could not possibly be true. A **contingent** truth is one that is not necessary, one whose negation could possibly be true. Necessity and contingency are modal properties often expressed in terms of **possible worlds**: A necessary truth is one that is true in all possible worlds (and whose negation is true in no possible world), and a contingent truth is one that is true in the actual world but false in at least one possible world. Necessary truths are generally held to include truths of **logic**, mathematics, and geometry. Every **proposition**, whether true or false, has that truth value either necessarily or contingently; this is known as the proposition's modal status.

Gottfried Leibniz defines a necessary truth as one whose negation is contradictory and claims that all necessary truths are either identity statements or reducible to them. The truth of identity statements is **self-evident**, so, according to Leibniz, all necessary truths *can* be known *a priori* (although we do not *in fact* know all necessary truths). Later critics have argued, however, that not all necessary truths are reducible to identity statements and have sought other accounts of how we can know them. **A. J. Ayer**, for example, claimed that only analytic statements are necessarily true, and this **analyticity** is rooted in our commitments to use words in certain ways. This linguistic approach to analyticity has been widely criticized, and **W. V. O. Quine** has argued that the analytic/synthetic distinction cannot be salvaged.

Necessity and contingency can also be predicated of objects and their properties; this applies these modal properties *de re* (to objects) rather than *de dicto* (to statements or propositions). An object has a property necessarily if there is no possible world in which that object exists lacking that property. Similarly, an object has a property contingently if the object has that property in the actual world but lacks it in at least one possible world. A necessary property of an object is sometimes described as an essential property; such properties are sometimes described as being part of the object's essence. *See also A PRIORI/A POSTERIORI* KNOWLEDGE; TRUTHS OF REASON/ TRUTHS OF FACT.

NEO-KANTIANISM. A school of thought in German philosophy, beginning in the 1860s and lasting into the 1930s, that developed and reinterpreted **Immanuel Kant**'s **epistemology** and metaphysics. Neo-Kantianism was motivated particularly by criticisms of Kant's **theories** by Hegelian **idealism** and materialism. The Marburg School of neo-Kantianism, founded by Hermann Cohen (1842–1918), emphasized the *a priori* nature of **science**, ethics, and aesthetics. The Southwest German School, founded by Wilhelm Windelband (1848–1915), emphasized the critical examination of norms and values. *See also A PRIORI/A POSTERIORI* KNOWLEDGE; HEGEL, G. W. F.

NEO-PLATONISM. The reformulation of **Plato**'s **theories** by Plotinus (A.D. 205–270), Porphyry (233–ca. 305), Syrianus (d. ca. 437), Proclus (412–485), and others. This school of thought lasted at least until Justinian's closing of the Platonic School in Athens (A.D. 529), with remnants and influences lasting much longer, particularly in Arabic and Latin medieval philosophy. **Epistemologically**, the neo-Platonists were concerned more with theoretical than with **empirical knowledge**. Empirically, one comes to know that an object has a particular property by mentally comparing what one sees (described as an abstracted sensible form) with an innate standard or ideal (cf. Plato's Form). **Error** arises when one's grasp of this standard is obscured. Theoretical knowledge is developed by clarifying one's grasp of the innate standards or ideals. This process leads eventually to direct participation in Intellect, the **ideas** in which are identical with **truth** itself. *See also* INNATE IDEA.

NEURATH, OTTO (1882–1945). Austrian philosopher; a member of the **Vienna Circle** and a leading figure in **logical positivism**. He made great contributions to sociology and the understanding of **scientific method**. He rejects the **foundationalist** approach to **epistemology** typified by **René Descartes** in favor of an epistemological **coherentism**. Instead of trying to ground **knowledge** in the **certainty** of **experience**, he begins with the existence of an **external world** of physical objects and argues that **observations** of these objects could be intersubjectively confirmed. He is noted for his comparison of the scientific enterprise with a boat being rebuilt while at sea. There is no "dry dock" of absolute, unquestionable **truth** in which **science** can be given its foundation. Instead, the project of science must make improvements and adjustments as it goes along. This is accompanied by Neurath's **coherence theory of truth**. *See also* QUINE, W. V. O; SCIENTIFIC METHOD.

NEW REALISM. *See* PERRY, RALPH BARTON.

NEWCOMB'S PARADOX. Also known as Newcomb's problem, it is a situation in which two plausible and widely accepted principles of **rational** decision making conflict. This problem was first formulated in about 1960 by physicist William Newcomb and **analyzed** by Robert Nozick in his "Newcomb's Problem and Two Principles of Choice" (1969). One of the principles involved is the principle of *maximizing expected utility*, which states that one should make the choice that yields the best outcome. The other principle is the principle of *dominance*. This states that if the results or outcomes of the options are **causally** independent of those options and if there is an option that is better than the others in each state, then that is the option one should choose.

Newcomb describes a situation in which you are presented with two boxes; you may take only the first box or take both of them. The first box contains either $1,000,000 or nothing, and the second contains $1,000. The content of the first box is decided by someone who is very good at **predicting** your behavior. If he predicts that you will take only the first box, he will put $1,000,000 into it. If he predicts that you will take both boxes, he will leave the first box empty.

The expected utility of an option is calculated by multiplying the value or utility of the outcome by the **probability** of obtaining that result. Because the person predicting your behavior is quite **reliable**, the probability of getting $1,000,000 if you take only the first box is high, but the probability of getting $1,001,000 if you take both boxes is low. Therefore, the principle of maximizing expected utility indicates that you should take only the first box. The principle of dominance, however, indicates that you should take both boxes. The reason for this is that your choice does not causally influence the content of the first box, and choosing both boxes results in $1,000 plus the contents of the first box (whatever that turns out to be). *See also* BAYESIANISM; CAUSATION; DECISION THEORY.

NEWMAN, JOHN HENRY (1801–1890). English theologian and philosopher. He was a member of the Anglican Oxford Movement while a fellow at Oriel College, Oxford, but converted to Roman Catholicism in 1845 and became a cardinal in 1879. His *Grammar of Assent* (1870) distinguishes between formal reasoning and the natural activity of the mind in identifying **truths** about concrete or historical matters. One may, with education and **experience**, develop an **illative sense**, a cognitive ability to be certain of the truth of a **judgment** even though the objective **evidence** shows that it is only probably true. *See also* CERTAINTY; HISTORICAL KNOWLEDGE; OBJECTIVE/SUBJECTIVE; PROBABILITY.

NIETZSCHE, FRIEDRICH (1844–1900). German philosopher and cultural critic. He argues that humans cannot have **knowledge** because "we simply lack any organ for knowledge, for 'truth'" (*Die fröliche Wissenschaft* [*The Gay Science*], 1887). We cannot have knowledge of **facts** because "facts are precisely what there is not, only interpretations" (*Der Wille zur Macht* [*The Will to Power*], 1906). There is no privileged perspective that is uniquely correct; instead, we each function within a perspective from which we cannot escape and which may well be false; there can be no knowledge that transcends these perspectives. Nietzsche also denies that **beliefs** can be regarded as true when they prove to be useful; this is also something about which we may be mistaken. What we think of as useful "is ultimately also a mere belief, something imaginary and perhaps precisely that most calamitous stupidity of which we shall perish some day" (*The Gay Science*). The scientific perspective may be suitable for the purposes it serves, but this perspective is not objectively superior to the others. Thus, scientific **theories** can be regarded as true only in relation to the structure of **science**. *See also* CONTINENTAL EPISTEMOLOGY; REALISM/ANTIREALISM; TRUTH.

NIHIL EST IN INTELLECTU QUOD NON PRIUS FUERIT IN SENSU. Latin: "Nothing is first in the understanding that had not previously been in the senses." This statement is fundamental to **empiricism**. There are two common interpretations of this claim. The weaker (endorsed by **John Locke**) states that any **concept** in the mind must have been gained by means of **experience**; no concepts are *a priori*. The stronger (endorsed by **John Stuart Mill**) states that all **propositional knowledge** is derived from sense experience. *See also A PRIORI/A POSTERIORI* KNOWLEDGE; INNATE IDEA.

NOETIC. From the Greek *noētikos*, "perceiving," that which relates to apprehension by the intellect, particularly the cognitive grasp of non-sensuous content. **Plato** claimed that we have noetic apprehension of the **Forms**. *See also A PRIORI/A POSTERIORI* KNOWLEDGE; NATURAL LIGHT; PERCEPTION.

NOUMENAL/PHENOMENAL. These adjectives are used to distinguish between things as they are in themselves (noumenal) and things as they appear to an observer (phenomenal). This distinction plays an important role in the **epistemology** of **Immanuel Kant**, who argues that the noumenal world exists but is unknowable. Even such features of the world as space, time, and **causation** are phenomenal, he claims, and are part of the structure imposed on **experience** by the mind. Although traditional interpretations of Kant have envisioned the noumenal and phenomenal worlds as separate, more recent interpretations present a one-world or double-aspect view. According to this, there is only one world of objects, and these may be understood or discussed either noumenally or phenomenally. *See also* APPEARANCE/REALITY; EXTERNAL WORLD; HUSSERL, EDMUND; OBJECTIVE/SUBJECTIVE; PHENOMENOLOGY.

NYĀYA. A school of Hindu thought in Indian philosophy, originating in Gotama's *Nyāyasûtras* (ca. A.D. 150) and commentaries on them by Vatsyāyana (fourth century A.D.). Major figures in this school include Uddyotakara (sixth century A.D.), Vacaspati (ninth century A.D.), Udayana (eleventh century A.D.), and Gangeśa (fourteenth century A.D.). Its central concerns include understanding the nature of thought or cognition, providing an account of true cognition, and analyzing the structure of propositional cognitions. It also includes **theories** of **inference** and **perception**. *See also* INDIAN EPISTEMOLOGY; *PRĀMĀṆYA*; PROPOSITIONAL ATTITUDES.

– O –

OBJECTIVE/SUBJECTIVE. The distinction between objective and subjective is that between impartiality and bias, or between that which is independent of the mind and that which is mind dependent. When applied to standards for **epistemic justification**, externalist **theories** (e.g., most formulations of **reliabilism**) employ objective standards such as reliability or **truth** conduciveness. Internalist theories generally employ subjective standards (e.g., is the subject *aware* of the **evidence**—a question that can be answered only from the subject's point of view). *See also* EXTERNALISM/INTERNALISM; NOUMENAL/PHENOMENAL; OBJECTIVITY.

OBJECTIVITY. In an ontological sense, objectivity refers to something's mind-independent existence. This is contrasted with the subjective, mind-dependent existence of **sensations** and secondary qualities. In an **epistemological** sense, objectivity refers to **beliefs** or mental processes that are not influenced by one's own goals or attitudes. An objective belief may be understood as one that corresponds to an ontologically objective feature of the world or as one based on **evidence** whose support for that belief would be acknowledged by any reasonable person. It is sometimes claimed that only objective beliefs can qualify as **knowledge**. Objective beliefs or statements have also been said to be those that do not reflect or incorporate any particular point of view. *See also* NOUMENAL/PHENOMENAL; OBJECTIVE/SUBJECTIVE.

OBSERVATION. Observation is central to **science** as a source of information about the **external world**, but it raises important **epistemological** questions. Observations provide **evidence** for **hypotheses** or **theories**, but, as **David Hume** points out, neither is deducible from observations. In addition, observations are used to test theories, but the observations themselves seem to make various theoretical **presuppositions**. This is particularly true when observations involve mechanisms such as X-ray machines, radio telescopes, or particle detectors. The use of such mechanisms requires a conceptual framework about what is being observed and how various entities interact with one another (and with observers). As the history of **science** illustrates, the **theory-laden** nature of observation does not prevent it from providing evidence for the falsehood of scientific theories. *See also* EPISTEMIC CIRCULARITY; EXPERIENCE; SCIENTIFIC METHOD; SENSE PERCEPTION.

OCKHAM, WILLIAM OF (1285–1347). English Scholastic philosopher educated at Oxford University. Ockham (also spelled "Occam") reinterpreted the work of **Aristotle**, simplifying the latter's accounts of the soul, cognitive **psychology**, and **perception**. Ockham agrees with Aristotle that, in the right conditions, our sensory systems are free of **errors**; therefore, he argues that we can have **knowledge** of the **external world** and of our own mental states. His **theory** includes an account of **intuitive** (as opposed to abstract) cognitions, which produce clearly true **judgments** about their objects. Our knowledge is **certain** in the sense that one has no **doubt** of its **truth**; this is not taken as implying that there is no possibility of error. Risk of error does not lead Ockham into **skepticism**, however; he takes **Duns Scotus** to have adequately refuted the **arguments** of the Academic skeptics. Ockham is also noted for his principle of ontological parsimony, "Ockham's razor." Also found in **Aristotle**, this principle states that entities should not be multiplied beyond **necessity**. Oddly, Ockham does not seem to have asserted this principle explicitly.

OMNISCIENT OBSERVER. *See* IDEAL OBSERVER.

ONTOLOGICAL COMMITMENT. A **theory** is ontologically committed to the existence of an object (or type of object) if its existence is required in order for the theory to be true. **W. V. O. Quine** claims that the ontological commitments of a theory can be determined by expressing the theory in terms of first-order **logic** and then examining the values of the variables. Any object (or type of object) among these values must exist in order for the statements that employ that variable to be true. If two or more different ontologies would fulfill a theory, then the theory is committed to the existence only of those objects (or types of objects) common to all those ontologies. Critics argue that Quine's approach is complicated by disagreements about quantification, the nature of kinds, **intentionality**, and other matters. *See also* ABSTRACT ENTITY.

OPEN TEXTURE. Introduced by Friedrich Waismann (1896–1959) in his "Verifiability" (1945), this means the ineliminable **vagueness** of all **empirical** terms. There is vagueness about when the term applies, and our attempts to clarify its application may not address all future questions of its application. In addition, when there are two or more criteria for the application of a term, they may yield different results; the consequence is vagueness about the proper application of the term. Waismann concludes from this that it is impossible conclusively to verify experiential statements and that statements about physical objects cannot be adequately translated into **phenomenal** terms. *See also* PROBLEM OF THE CRITERION; VERIFICATIONISM.

OPERATIONALISM. The attempt in philosophy of **science** to interpret all scientific **concepts** in terms of experimental procedures and **observations**. This was later incorporated into **logical positivism**'s requirement that theoretical terms be defined by means of observation conditions. These attempts are complicated by the **fact** that different **measurement** or detection procedures can be used for the same concept. It is widely held that observational consequences cannot exhaustively convey the content of scientific concepts and that more than one **theory** or set of concepts could account for a particular set of procedures and observations. *See also* REDUCTION SENTENCE; VERIFICATIONISM.

ORDINARY LANGUAGE PHILOSOPHY. A philosophical movement that flourished among English-speaking philosophers from the

1940s until the 1960s, according to which the content of **concepts** (including those of **truth** and **knowledge**) is determined by linguistic practice. Notable figures in this movement include **G. E. Moore**, **Ludwig Wittgenstein**, **Gilbert Ryle**, and **John Austin**. According to this approach, an account of a concept is tested by comparing it with how the relevant terms are actually used in ordinary language. Many philosophical puzzles are said to arise from misunderstanding the nature or use of language; ordinary language philosophers set out to identify and eliminate them. *See also* GRAMMAR.

ORTEGA y GASSET, JOSÉ (1883–1955). Spanish philosopher, professor of metaphysics at the University of Madrid from 1910 until 1936. His wide-ranging interests included the view that something is real for me only insofar as it is a part of my life (which includes myself, my **experiences**, and my circumstances). The self is not sharply separate from its surroundings and circumstances; these are woven together to form one's reality. Each self has a unique perspective, and **truth** can be assessed only from some individual perspective. No perspective is privileged above the others. *See also* OBJECTIVE/SUBJECTIVE; PERCEPTION; PERCEPTUAL RELATIVITY.

OTHER MINDS, PROBLEM OF. There are two versions of this problem. The first addresses whether we have sufficient **evidence** to ground our **belief** that other people are conscious and have minds. The second is about the meaning of mental terms and addresses whether our attribution of mental states to others can be meaningful.

Each of us is aware of (at least some of) his or her own mental states, but we have no direct **access** to the mental states of others. Our evidence that others have minds comes from an **argument from analogy**: Other people resemble me in many anatomical ways and exhibit similar types of behavior, particularly in responding to their surroundings. My behavior is linked to my mental states, so the behavior of others is probably linked to mental states as well. The problem is that this feels uncomfortably like a hasty **generalization** from a single case, and the possibility that there are no other minds cannot be dismissed. **Logical positivism** and **psychological** behaviorism seek to avoid this problem by arguing that mental states are nothing more than one's actual and **dispositional** behavior.

The second version of the problem begins with the assumption that **mentalistic** terms such as "pain," "fear," and so forth get their meaning from their connection with our own **experiences**. The problem arises because this irreducibly first-person account of the meaning of mentalistic terms does not seem to allow for mental attributions to others. **John Stuart Mill** argues that one's conscious states are the root of the meaning of the mental attributions we make to them (*An Examination of Sir William Hamilton's Philosophy*, 1865). However, **Ludwig Wittgenstein** points out that the conscious states that give meaning to mentalistic terms in one's own case are not available when those terms are applied to others (*Philosophical Investigations*, 1953). Wittgenstein's **argument** against the possibility of a private language challenges the assumption that mentalistic terms can be defined in terms of one's own experience (because this does not allow for the possibility of one's being mistaken about the proper application of those terms). *See also* BEHAVIORISM, ANALYTIC; BEHAVIORISM, METHODOLOGICAL; CONSCIOUSNESS; GRAMMAR; INDUCTION, PROBLEM OF; INTROSPECTION; PRIVATE LANGUAGE ARGUMENT; SELF-KNOWLEDGE.

OVERRIDER. A **defeater** of which one is aware; a **fact** or piece of **evidence** that has been added to my stock of **information** and that, as a result, defeats or overrides my **epistemic justification** for a **belief**. *See also* DEFEASIBILITY; GETTIER CASES; *PRIMA FACIE* REASONS.

– P –

PARACONSISTENCY. The property of a system of **logic** that not all statements can be derived from a contradiction. Relevance logic, for example, is able to isolate contradictions to prevent them from entailing all other statements. Paraconsistent logics allow one to work within an inconsistent **theory** and still place limits on which statements are implied. *See also* CONSISTENCY; IMPLICATION.

PARADIGM. As this term is used by **Thomas Kuhn** (*The Structure of Scientific Revolutions*, 1962), it is a theoretical framework comprising scientific **beliefs** and practices, ontological claims, and other background assumptions. This framework allows scientific theories to be developed, tested, and revised. Kuhn argues that scientific change does not occur in a smooth, gradual manner but involves revolutions in which one paradigm is replaced by another. This paradigm shift brings with it a fundamental change in scientific vocabularies, concepts, and practices. *See also* PRESUPPOSITION; SCIENCE; SCIENTIFIC METHOD; TESTABILITY.

PARADIGM CASE ARGUMENT. A type of **argument**, often presented as a response to some form of **skepticism**, intended to demonstrate that entities of a certain type exist or have a particular property. Paradigm case arguments typically use common sense or ordinary language to establish a paradigmatic or exemplary case showing the existence or properties in question. Such an argument might be used to defend the claim that some actions are free, that some material objects exist, or that some **beliefs** qualify as **knowledge**. *See also* COMMONSENSISM; KUHN, THOMAS; ORDINARY LANGUAGE PHILOSOPHY.

PARADOX. An apparently sound **argument** whose conclusion is contradictory or in some other way unacceptable. In some cases, a paradox may involve only a single statement. For example, "This sentence is false" is true only if it is false and false only if it is true. Paradoxes are often used to expose flaws in commonly accepted premises or forms of argument. *See also* ANTINOMY; HEMPEL, KARL; KNOWER PARADOX; LOTTERY PARADOX; MOORE'S PARADOX; NEWCOMB'S PARADOX; PARADOX OF ANALYSIS; PREFACE PARADOX; UNEXPECTED EXAMINATION PARADOX.

PARADOX OF ANALYSIS. A **paradox** about how an **analysis** of a term or **concept** can be informative for someone who is already able to use the term (or apply the concept) correctly. If the analysis expresses the same meaning or content as the term being analyzed, then the result should be trivially true and not informative. However, it seems clear that an analysis *can* be informative. That is, an analysis of the concept of being an *a* may state, "An *a* is a *b*." This analysis will be true provided *a* and *b* have the same meaning or content. But if they have the same meaning, then the analysis is **equivalent** to "An *a* is an *a*," and this is not informative.

One response to this paradox is to distinguish between *tacit* and *explicit* **knowledge**: One may have tacit knowledge of the content of the term being analyzed, but the analysis makes this explicit; thus, the analysis can still be informative for someone who is already able to use the term correctly. Another response distinguishes between the term or concept being analyzed and the ways in which that concept is expressed linguistically. According to this view, the value of the analysis lies in the **fact** that it reveals previously unrecognized facts about the meanings and usage of expressions; less well understood expressions are connected with better understood expressions. *See also A PRIORI/A POSTERIORI* KNOWLEDGE; GRAMMAR.

PARADOX OF THE KNOWER. *See* KNOWER PARADOX.

PARADOX OF THE RAVENS. *See* CONFIRMATION; HEMPEL, KARL.

PARALLEL DISTRIBUTED PROCESSING. *See* CONNECTIONISM; NATURALIZED EPISTEMOLOGY; PSYCHOLOGY.

PARAPSYCHOLOGY. The study of psychological capacities and events that are not accounted for (and are generally not recognized) by the established study of **psychology**. The aspects of parapsychology that are of particular epistemic interest are the study of extrasensory perception (ESP) and of the survival of mental functioning after death. Parapsychologists claim that their work challenges current psychological **theories** as well as our understanding of minds and **causation**. Precognition, for example, is said to be the **knowledge** of an event before it happens, with the apparent causation running backward in time.

Experimental data in this field have often been challenged, and there has been great difficulty in establishing reliable, repeatable demonstrations that parapsychological phenomena exist. Apart from this, there is the question of whether such phenomena (assuming they exist) could be a source of genuine knowledge or **justified true be-**

lief. For instance, a subject whose performance on an "identify the card someone else is looking at" test is well above chance would not be plausibly described as *knowing* the correct answer. In fact, the subject's responses may not even reflect actual **beliefs**. If parapsychological phenomena produce beliefs without causal connections to the events or states they are about, then most theories of **evidence** would conclude that these beliefs are unjustified. **Reliabilism** would say that these beliefs are justified (and perhaps qualify as knowledge) provided the process by which they are formed is sufficiently reliable. Reliabilists, however, generally expect these to be *causal* processes, an assumption challenged by some parapsychologists. *See also* BELIEF-FORMING PROCESS; CREDULITY; INTUITION.

PARTIAL BELIEF. A term used to describe degrees of **belief**. The degree to which one believes that *p* ought to correspond to the strength of one's **evidence** that *p*. **Frank Ramsey** argues that **probability** calculus should serve as the **logic** of partial belief. *See also* BAYESIANISM; BELIEF-FORMING PROCESS; EPISTEMIC JUSTIFICATION; JTB THEORY OF KNOWLEDGE; TRUTH.

PARTICULARISM. *See* PROBLEM OF THE CRITERION.

PASCAL, BLAISE (1623–1662). French philosopher, mathematician, scientist, and writer. His *Pensées* (unfinished and fragmentary, published posthumously in 1670) explore **skepticism** regarding Christianity and argue that although **certainty** about religious **beliefs** is not within our reach, we can still have **knowledge** of **God**'s existence. This knowledge cannot be fully **justified** rationally and rests partly on the explanatory power of religious doctrines and on **pragmatic** considerations. The latter are summed up in Pascal's wager, which uses his work on **probability** and **decision theory** to show that when faced with uncertainty about the truth of Christianity's claims, it is rational to "wager" that these claims are true. Having made this wager, Pascal says one should then seek "inspiration," a religious **experience** that is the primary basis of **religious knowledge**. *See also* RATIONALITY.

PEIRCE, CHARLES SANDERS (1839–1914). American philosopher, logician, and founder of **pragmatism**. He received a degree in chemistry from Harvard University in 1863 and spent three decades working for the U.S. Coast and Geodetic Survey. During this time he also worked on issues in **logic** and philosophy. In **epistemology**, Peirce rejects **René Descartes**'s method of **doubt** and insistence that the proper grounding for **knowledge** is to be found in an *individual's* mental states and processes. Instead, Peirce argues that the pursuit of knowledge involves an entire community of inquirers and that the process should begin with those things we are incapable of doubting. A **belief** is understood as "that which a man is prepared to act upon," and although each of these initial beliefs may be mistaken, the fact that they jointly form an interrelated **web of belief** provides them with **epistemic justification**. Furthermore, Peirce claims that **sense perception** is **theory laden** and thus not an **objective** source of data. His position is thus a form of **fallibilism** akin to **coherentism**.

His paper "Pragmatism" (1905) presents and defends his principle of pragmatism: The meaning of an "intellectual conception" is a set of "practical consequences" or **conditional propositions** describing the **observations** that would follow from various actions or experimental conditions.

Beginning with the assumption that there is a mind-independent world of physical objects, Peirce argues that employing the **scientific method** will result in our eventual agreement about what that world is like. This scientific method employs **abduction**, **deduction**, and **induction**. Abduction, which Peirce regards as the **logic of discovery**, is a system for determining which **hypotheses** are worth exploring and developing. It involves tentatively accepting and testing a hypothesis that, if true, would make the phenomena in question intelligible. Induction, another crucial component of the **hypothetico-deductive method**, may be unreliable in particular instances, but when it is used over a long period by an entire community of inquirers, **errors** that result from its use will be identified; it has a self-correcting nature.

Peirce regards logic as part of a broader theory of signs, also called semiotic(s); he made large contributions in this area. He describes the sign relation as a triad of the sign itself, the object the sign stands for, and an interpretant that determines how the sign represents its object. The interpretant is itself a sign with its own interpretant and object.

The resulting regress terminates in an "ultimate logical interpretant" that is "a change of habit of conduct."

Peirce's position on **truth** is that it is "stable opinion" that need never be changed because of new inquiries or **observations**. **Reality** is independent of our opinions, but the scientific process will eventually lead to truth. *See also* ACT/OBJECT ANALYSIS; BELIEF-FORMING PROCESS; COLLECTIVE BELIEF; CONTEXTUAL-ISM; DEWEY, JOHN; INDUBITABILITY; JAMES, WILLIAM; SCIENCE; SOCIOLOGY OF KNOWLEDGE.

PERCEPTION. *See* SENSE PERCEPTION.

PERCEPTUAL KNOWLEDGE. Knowledge acquired by means of **sense perception**; a large portion of our knowledge falls into this category. Most theorists have adopted an **act/object analysis** of **perception**, assuming that each instance of perception involves both a perceiving subject and an object being perceived. Perception involves a collection of sensory surfaces (e.g., retina, tongue, fingertips) that respond to various properties of the object being perceived, conveying information about that object to the perceiver.

It is helpful to distinguish between perceiving an object and perceiving *that* it has certain properties. Seeing an object, for instance, differs from seeing the object *as* being a member of a particular class or seeing *that* it has a particular feature. Seeing *as* and seeing *that* generate **propositional knowledge** and depend on the perceiver's having relevant background **beliefs**. (Internalist theories of knowledge generally require that these background beliefs meet the criteria for knowledge if the beliefs that arise from perception are to be knowledge. Externalist theories are much less likely to include this requirement.)

Perception thus requires a background of propositional knowledge in order to generate (and provide **evidence** for) propositional knowledge. If **direct realism** is true and we are directly aware (in at least some cases) of the **external world**, then some propositional knowledge is generated by perception without the need for background beliefs. One would be able to determine the colors, shapes, smells, and so forth of objects; this information could then be used in conjunction with background beliefs to identify objects as having properties that cannot be **immediately** perceived. If **representative realism** is true and we are directly aware only of our own current mental contents, then all propositional content about the external world is inferred from one's examination of **sense data** or other mental contents. On this view, our perception of the external world is always indirect and **theory laden**. **Skepticism** about our perceptual beliefs is typically rooted in the many ways in which background beliefs might be false or sensory systems might yield misleading information. *See also* EXTERNALISM/INTERNALISM; FALLIBILITY; NATURALIZED EPISTEMOLOGY.

PERCEPTUAL RELATIVITY. The variation of some perceived qualities of an object from one observer to another or from one time to another for a single observer. For example, the room may feel cold to Bob but warm to Jane, or the orange juice may taste sweet to Bob but bitter to Jane. This variation typically involves secondary qualities such as taste, smell, and sound. **John Locke** and others argue that in such cases perceptual relativity results from variation in the sensory systems of the observers (*Essay Concerning Human Understanding*, 1690); thus, it need not imply that any observer is in **error**. This view is typical of **representative realism**. **George Berkeley**, however, argues that all qualities of objects can vary from observer to observer, even the so-called primary qualities such as size and shape; this discussion of perceptual relativity is one part of his **argument** against the primary/secondary quality distinction and in support of his **idealism**. *See also* PRIMARY AND SECONDARY QUALITIES.

PERRY, RALPH BARTON (1876–1957). American philosopher; he taught at Harvard University from 1902 until 1946. He received a Pulitzer Prize in 1936 for his *The Thought and Character of William James*. He argues against **dualism** and **idealism** and defends a form of **direct realism** called "New Realism." He claims that observers have unmediated **access** to the **external world**; other views, he said, lead to **skepticism**. Perry and E. B. Holt developed the **"specific response" theory** of **belief** and **perception**; these are construed in terms of the subject's behavior and bodily adjustments. *See also* BE-

HAVIORISM, ANALYTIC; BEHAVIORISM, METHODOLOGI-
CAL; REALISM/ANTIREALISM; SENSE PERCEPTION.

PERSONAL IDENTITY. The philosophical issue of personal identity
has focused on the criteria for the survival of a particular individual
through time. This involves understanding the type of entity a person
is. This has an important epistemic aspect: **John Locke** and others argue that one's **memory** of one's past plays a key role (along with
other **psychological** factors) in determining whether a person at a
later time is the same individual as a person at some earlier time. Because of the physical and psychological changes people undergo over
time, diachronic personal identity has posed a persistent challenge for
epistemology and metaphysics. *See also* PROBLEM OF THE CRI-
TERION.

PERSPECTIVISM. *See* TEICHMÜLLER, GUSTAV.

PHANTASIA. Greek term meaning "appearance" or "imagination."
This term is used to refer both to the state of having something appear to one to be the case and to the **psychological** capacity for being in this state. "*Phantasia*" is not limited to images; it can apply to
anything that one takes to be the case. It has also been described as
our capacity to understand claims about geometry by forming mental
images. *Phantasia* includes the possibility that such an appearance or
attitude might be mistaken. **Plato** describes *phantasia* as a combination of **sensation** and **belief**, and **Aristotle** claims that it is the faculty
that makes **truth** and falsehood possible. The Stoics regard it as the
most fundamental type of mental state; other mental states are explained in terms of it. *See also* APPEARANCE/REALITY; ILLU-
SION; IMAGINATION.

PHENOMENAL PROPERTY. *See* QUALIA.

PHENOMENAL WORLD. *See* KANT, IMMANUEL; NOUMENAL/
PHENOMENAL.

PHENOMENALISM. The view that any **proposition** about the existence of physical objects is **equivalent** to a collection of propositions

about the **sensations** that individual subjects would **experience** in specified circumstances (where those circumstances are also expressed in terms of the sensations of those individuals). The **truth** of these **conditional propositions** about sensations is independent of our minds, so phenomenalism is able to retain something of the mind independence of physical objects. Although phenomenalism is compatible with many different views of sensations, it is commonly associated with **sense-data** theories. Phenomenalism is defended by **John Stuart Mill** (*The Examination of Sir William Hamilton's Philosophy*, 1865) and gained popularity with the rise of **logical positivism**.

Phenomenalism is often associated with epistemic **foundationalism** and **empiricism**. If one begins with the assumption that the only **contingently** true propositions of whose truth one can be **certain** are those about the contents of one's own mind and that **beliefs** about the **external world** must be inferred from or based on this **knowledge** of one's own experiences, then phenomenalism provides a straightforward connection between the two. Without such a connection, one faces the skeptical conclusion, defended by **David Hume** (*A Treatise of Human Nature*, 1739–1740), that our mental states provide no **evidence** for our beliefs about the external world.

Roderick Chisholm argues that the conditional propositions generated by phenomenalism are not equivalent to propositions about physical objects ("The Problem of Empiricism," 1948). For any set of conditional propositions presented by phenomenalists, Chisholm describes how to generate a hypothetical situation in which those propositions are true but in which the corresponding proposition about physical objects is false. What sensations one would experience depends, he claims, on the physical circumstances. Phenomenalists respond that this problem can be avoided by adding an "in normal or standard conditions" clause to each conditional proposition about sensations. However, it is difficult to see how this could be done successfully without at some point making reference to physical objects. *See also* DIRECT REALISM; FIRTH, RODERICK; LEWIS, CLARENCE IRVING; LOGICAL CONSTRUCTION.

PHENOMENOLOGICAL REDUCTION. *See* HUSSERL, EDMUND.

PHENOMENOLOGY. A diverse philosophical movement, originated by **Edmund Husserl** and others, that gives a central place to the nature and structure of lived **experience**, as it is prior to philosophical theorizing and reflection. This direct examination of experience deliberately sets aside any questions about **psychology** or causal **explanation**. The individual's subjective experience is taken as the starting point for an investigation into the "meaning and Being" of beings. An important aspect of phenomenology is its claim that all conscious states have **intentionality**; they are directed toward those things that **consciousness** is of or about. Some phenomenologists (e.g., **Martin Heidegger** and **Maurice Merleau-Ponty**) rejected this **act/object analysis** of consciousness and developed an account of the "natural conception of the world."

Because phenomenology examines the subject's lived experience in the world and not merely the contents of the mind, it includes how subjects act in their world. The intentionality of consciousness links it with one's actions in the world. One **implication** of this is that **procedural knowledge** is more fundamental than **propositional knowledge**; knowing *how* lays the foundation for knowing *that*. *See also* CONTINENTAL EPISTEMOLOGY; EPOCHÉ; EXTERNAL WORLD; OBJECTIVE/SUBJECTIVE; SENSATION.

PHILOSOPHICAL KNOWLEDGE. Knowledge of philosophical issues or produced by philosophical methods. There are grounds for **skepticism** regarding this type of knowledge. Unlike **science** or mathematics, philosophy does not have any universally accepted methodology or an established body of accepted **truths**. As a result, philosophers often disagree about who won a philosophical dispute or whether a particular **argument** provides strong **evidence** for its conclusion. Some of the conclusions drawn by philosophers are highly counterintuitive (e.g., arguments for skepticism), and this adds to the **doubt** about whether there is much philosophical knowledge.

Defenders of philosophical knowledge point out that it has (in at least some cases) secure, *a priori* foundations and employs rigorous standards for its arguments. **René Descartes** and others have attempted to put philosophy on the same firm **epistemological** footing as mathematics or the sciences by emphasizing the importance of the **certainty** of one's premises and the **deductive** nature of one's arguments. This approach, which is commonly associated with **foundationalist theories** of knowledge, has not been widely adopted in practice and greatly restricts the theorizing of its adherents. *See also A PRIORI/A POSTERIORI* KNOWLEDGE.

PI. Chinese term meaning "shelter" or "cover." Hsün Tzu uses this as a metaphor for anything that prevents the mind from functioning properly. When the mind is in the state of *pi*, one is unable to reason, remember, judge, or perform other cognitive processes properly. One must avoid *pi* in order to acquire **knowledge**.

PIAGET, JEAN (1896–1980). Swiss psychologist and epistemologist, noted for his **theory** of cognitive development. His position is a form of **genetic epistemology**; he argues that an account of **knowledge** could and should be developed by examining how our behavioral interactions with the **external world** become more complex as we develop cognitively. Children at different developmental stages understand themselves and their world in radically different ways. This study of children served as a basis for his theorizing about the epistemic processes of other organisms. Rather than adopting traditional **rationalism** or **empiricism**, Piaget argues that knowledge arises from complex interactions between organisms (including humans) and their environment. His works include *Biology and Knowledge* (1967), *Genetic Epistemology* (1970), and *Psychology and Epistemology* (1970). *See also* GENETIC EPISTEMOLOGY; NATURALIZED EPISTEMOLOGY; PSYCHOLOGY.

PIEN. Chinese Mohist term meaning "disputing conflicting claims." It involves making **judgments** about what fits with the **facts**, distinguishing between different types of mental states, and identifies the proper objects of each sensory system. *Pien* is particularly involved in justifying ethical judgments.

PLANTINGA, ALVIN (1932–). American philosopher who was educated at Yale University; he has taught at Calvin College (Grand Rapids, Mich.) and the University of Notre Dame (Notre Dame, Ind.). In **epistemology**, he is noted for his defense of the existence of **God** and of the **rationality** of **belief** in God. His *God and Other*

Minds (1967; rev. ed., 1990) examines the **problem of other minds** and concludes that the same **justification** underlies both our belief that there are other minds and that God exists. His *Warrant: The Current Debate* (1993) and *Warrant and Proper Function* (1993) examine **epistemic warrant** and defend belief in God. *See also* RELIGIOUS KNOWLEDGE.

PLATO (ca. 429–347 B.C.). Greek philosopher; a student of **Socrates**, and founder of the Academy (in Athens). He notes that *elenchus* (the process of rational examination or refutation) is capable of building a case against most of our beliefs and makes it difficult to establish that a **belief** qualifies as **knowledge**. In *Theaetetus* 200–210, Plato famously considers whether knowledge might consist in having a belief that one can defend by offering reasons. He regards this proposal as a failure, but it later became influential as the **JTB theory of knowledge**.

Plato argues that we have knowledge only of the **Forms** (*eide*), nonphysical objects that we do not sense in the ordinary ways but with which we were familiar in our preexistence. Thus, this knowledge arises from a direct acquaintance with or intellectual grasp of its object. At a number of points, Plato argues that we are unable to have genuine knowledge about the **external world**, or knowledge that is based on **sense perception**. *See also* A *PRIORI/APOSTERIORI* KNOWLEDGE; ANAMNESIS; REASONS FOR BELIEF.

POINCARÉ, JULES HENRI (1854–1912). French mathematician and philosopher of **science**. Initially trained as a mining engineer, he completed a doctoral degree in mathematics (1879) and taught at the University of Paris (beginning in 1881). His influential work in the philosophy of science includes his proposal that making choices among competing sets of scientific axioms is merely a matter of choice and convention. Axioms, he said, should be understood as definitions, and no particular set of them can be regarded as uniquely correct. Similar conventions and choices must be made at various levels of science, so science cannot be said to reveal the true underlying nature of the world. Instead, it is a system for exploring the relationships among sets of **experiences**, enabling us to make **predictions** and offer **explanations**. *See also* CONVENTIONALISM.

POLLOCK, JOHN L. (1940–). American philosopher; professor at the University of Arizona (Tucson, Arizona). In addition to directing the OSCAR project, an attempt to formulate a **theory** of **rationality** and create an artificial rational agent, Pollock has made a number of contributions to **epistemology**. Much of his recent work in this area involves attempts to formalize or naturalize **beliefs**, their relationship with **sensory perception**, **induction**, and the processes of belief revision. Notable works include his *Knowledge and Justification* (1974), *Language and Thought* (1982), and *Nomic Probability and the Foundations of Induction* (1990).

POPPER, KARL RAIMUND (1902–1994). Austrian-born philosopher who lived and worked in England, noted for his contributions to philosophy of **science** and political philosophy. He rejected **logical positivism**'s verifiability criterion of cognitive significance and studied the nature of the **scientific method**. In his *The Logic of Scientific Discovery* (1959; originally *Logik der Forschung*, 1934) he takes science as the leading **example** of the growth of **knowledge** and examines the pitfalls of drawing **inferences** from **experience**. Even ordinary **observational** statements, such as "There are chairs in this room," are **theory laden** and include terms (e.g., "room") that imply the law-like behavior of objects. Our experience is unable to establish the **truth** of these **implications**, so experience is inadequate to verify that there are chairs in this room.

Accepting Humean **skepticism** about **beliefs** based on **induction**, Popper attempts to devise an **epistemology** that avoids its use. Although experience is capable of disproving a **theory**, it cannot establish that a theory is true (although it can provide a theory with "corroboration"). Science grows by generating and testing (i.e., attempting to falsify) a sequence of **hypotheses** and theories (*Conjectures and Refutations*, 1963). One should avoid **dogmatism** and bear in mind that the currently accepted theories may turn out to be false. *See also* FALSIFIABILITY; INDUCTION, PROBLEM OF; PROBLEM OF THE CRITERION; TESTABILITY; VERIFICATIONISM.

PORT-ROYAL LOGIC. Written by **Antoine Arnauld** and Pierre Nicole (possibly with the assistance of **Blaise Pascal**) and originally titled

La logique, ou L'art de penser, it is a treatise on **logic**, language, and pedagogical method. The first edition appeared in 1662, and six editions had been published by 1685. The book takes its name from the convent at Port-Royal-des-Champs (the home of French Jansenism), with which the authors were associated. Logic is presented as "the art of directing reason" so that one may develop **knowledge** and discern **truth** from **error**. The book examines the mind's four fundamental operations: conceiving, judging, reasoning, and ordering.

POSIT. *See* INDUCTION, PROBLEM OF; REICHENBACH, HANS.

POSITIVISM. *See* LOGICAL POSITIVISM.

POSSIBLE WORLDS. Alternative ways in which things might have been (including the actual world), a framework for understanding **necessity**, **contingency**, and possibility. Possible worlds are sometimes understood to be maximally **consistent** sets of **propositions** or perhaps as actual, physical entities (David Lewis, *On the Plurality of Worlds*, 1986). According to the possible worlds semantics for modal **logic**, a **proposition** is true if it is included in the actual world, contingently true or false if it is included in some possible worlds but not others, necessarily true if it is included in all possible worlds, and necessarily false if it is not included in any possible world.

POSTMODERNISM. A diverse, multidisciplinary movement opposed to **foundationalism**, realism, essentialism, and other aspects of modern philosophy. Philosophers within this movement include **Friedrich Nietzsche** (1844–1900), **Martin Heidegger** (1889–1976), **Michel Foucault** (1926–1984), **Jacques Derrida** (1930–2004), and Ferdinand de Saussure (1857–1913). In the area of **epistemology**, postmodernism rejects the possibility of an objective or transcendent standpoint for **observation** or **knowledge**. The rejection of realism includes denying that knowledge consists in the accurate representation of reality and denying that **truth** consists in correspondence with reality. All our **beliefs** and attitudes are shaped by the subject's gender, historical context, and socioeconomic situation. The task of epistemology, then, becomes that of the **sociology of knowledge**. *See also* CONTEXTUALISM; CONTINENTAL EPISTEMOLOGY;

DEATH OF EPISTEMOLOGY; DECONSTRUCTION; HISTORICISM; REALISM/ANTIREALISM; REPRESENTATIVE REALISM.

PRAGMATISM. A diverse philosophical school of thought, based largely in America, founded by **Charles Peirce** and **William James**; it also includes **John Dewey**. Its central tenet, the pragmatic maxim, states that the meaning of a **concept** is rooted in **experience** (the ongoing interaction of an organism with its environment) and the practical results of applying that concept. The **Cartesian** strategy of overcoming **skepticism** by establishing a foundation of **certainty** for **knowledge** is rejected by pragmatism. In its place, it proposes a **fallibilist** account of knowledge that is linked with actions and **observations**. By this standard, most philosophical discussion of metaphysical ontology is meaningless, and the pragmatists say that only scientific metaphysics can be salvaged. The methods and **observations** of **science** are emphasized, and the only genuine questions are those that can (at least in principle) be settled by scientific investigation.

Belief is understood as a **disposition** to behave in certain ways in certain sorts of situations; **doubt** is similarly behavioral. Inquiry is motivated by the desire to eliminate doubt, and science is particularly well suited to this task of "fixing belief." Our knowledge is guided by our goals and interests and is valuable because of the role it plays in organizing experience. Science progresses by means of **abduction** (proposing suitable **hypotheses** for testing), **deduction** (for arriving at **testable** consequences of hypotheses), and **induction** as a method for testing those consequences. The knowledge that results from this process is not **infallible**. Although it is not immune from the feigned doubt of the traditional Cartesian approach, it will be free from genuine doubt. Science, if carried out long enough and carefully enough, will eventually result in a stable body of belief that qualifies as true. James argues that a true belief is one that "works" and is verifiable; he says this is not adequately captured by the common claim that **truth** consists in correspondence with **reality**. Some pragmatists, such as Dewey, prefer to replace our talk of truth with talk of **warranted assertability**.

The influences of pragmatism have been widespread and have left their mark on the work of **W. V. O. Quine** (e.g., his rejection of the analytic/synthetic distinction) and **Richard Rorty**. *See also* ANALYTICITY; BEHAVIORISM, ANALYTIC; BEHAVIORISM, METHODOLOGICAL; CONTEXTUALISM; EMPIRICISM; EVOLUTIONARY EPISTEMOLOGY; HYPOTHETICODEDUCTIVE METHOD; NATURALIZED EPISTEMOLOGY; VERIFICATIONISM.

PRAMĀ. A Sanskrit word meaning "**knowledge**"; a central concept in **Indian epistemology**.

PRĀMĀṆYA. A Sanskrit word meaning "**truth**." Some theorists define this in terms of epistemic **concepts**, explaining that each cognition is true in itself and that falsehood consists in the failure to distinguish between distinct cognitions. Others claim that a thought or cognition is true provided it has not been shown to be false. This allows for the demonstration of falsehood but not of truth. The *Nyāya* **theory** of *prāmāṇya* resembles the **correspondence theory of truth** in that the attribution of a property to an object, for instance, is true only if that object has that property. *See also* INDIAN EPISTEMOLOGY.

PRATYAKṢA. A Sanskrit word meaning "**sense perception**;" an important **concept** in **Indian epistemology**. *Pratyakṣa* is the mental state or event that is caused by the functioning of the sensory systems when they are in contact with the objects of perception. There is disagreement among the various Indian schools of thought about whether these mental states have a linguistic structure, with the Grammarians saying that they do; the **Buddhists** that these are ineffable, nonlinguistic states; and the *Nyāya* that an initial nonlinguistic state is quickly replaced by a linguistically structured perceptual **judgment**. *See also* INDIAN EPISTEMOLOGY.

PREANALYTIC BELIEFS AND JUDGMENTS. *See* PRETHEORETIC BELIEFS AND JUDGMENTS.

PREDICTION. *See* NATURAL SCIENCE.

PREFACE PARADOX. First presented by D. C. Makinson ("The Paradox of the Preface," 1965), this **paradox** challenges our usual standards regarding rational **belief** and believing contradictions. It begins by considering an author who presents a collection of rationally held beliefs, $b_1, b_2, b_3, \ldots, b_n$. The author reasonably recognizes the possibility that mistakes have been made and so prefaces these assertions with the claim that there is at least one false claim in the collection; this can be stated thus: $\sim(b_1 \; \& \; b_2 \; \& \; b_3 \; \& \; \ldots \; \& \; b_n)$. The author thus seems committed to believing a contradiction: $(b_1 \; \& \; b_2 \; \& \; b_3 \; \& \; \ldots \; \& \; b_n) \; \& \; \sim(b_1 \; \& \; b_2 \; \& \; b_3 \; \& \; \ldots \; \& \; b_n)$. It seems that one cannot reasonably believe something that is clearly contradictory, yet the author reasonably believes each component of this complex belief. It is noteworthy that this paradox can be crafted using many different sorts of **evidence** to support the component beliefs; in this way, it differs from the **lottery paradox** (which relies on statistical evidence).

We ordinarily expect that any belief that is clearly deducible from a rationally held belief is also rationally held. However, all **propositions** can be deduced from a contradiction, but not all propositions can be rationally believed. We must either reject the claim that one can rationally believe a contradiction or radically alter the role deductive **logic** plays in generating beliefs and providing **evidence**. Earl Conee, for example, argues that some deductive consequences of our rationally held beliefs are not rationally acceptable ("Evident, but Rationally Unacceptable," 1987). It is difficult, however, to establish a principled boundary between the deductive consequences of our beliefs that can be held rationally and those that cannot. *See also* BELIEF-FORMING PROCESS; DEDUCTION; PARACONSISTENCY; RATIONAL ACCEPTANCE; RATIONALITY.

PRESENCE. *See* IMMEDIACY.

PRESOCRATIC EPISTEMOLOGY. Among the early Greek philosophers (e.g., Xenophanes of Colophon, Herodotus, Heraclitus of Ephesus, Pythagoras of Samos) who were not influenced by **Socrates**, **knowledge** is often equated with first-person acquaintance with **facts** or states of affairs; one could be said to know only what one had personally seen. This implies **skepticism** regarding our knowledge of universal principles and other matters beyond our **experience**. Although one may have opinions on these matters, they do not qualify as genuine understanding. Some pre-Socratics (e.g., Parmenides) note the limitations and inadequacies of **sense perception** and argue that only **necessary truths** are knowable.

PRESUPPOSITION. Either a relationship among **propositions** or what one takes to be understood or accepted when one makes a statement.

As a relationship among propositions, *p* presupposes *q* if *q* is entailed both by *p* and by *not-p*. Thus, *q* is presupposed by *p* if *q* is a condition that must be met for *p* to be either true *or* false. This position is presented by **P. F. Strawson** in his criticism of **Bertrand Russell's theory** of descriptions. Strawson argues that "The present King of France is bald" presupposes "There is a present King of France." He disagrees with Russell's claim that the latter statement is entailed by the former; instead, Strawson claims that presupposition is similar to but distinct from entailment. Therefore, although Russell claims that "The present King of France is bald" is false, Strawson claims that it is neither true nor false.

In its second sense, a presupposition is distinct from one's utterances or assertions and reflects what one expects one's audience already to believe or accept. Presuppositions are, in this sense, **beliefs** that one takes for granted. *See also* CONVERSATIONAL IMPLICATURE; IMPLICATION.

PRETHEORETIC BELIEFS AND JUDGMENTS. A pretheoretical **judgment** or **belief** is one that is independent of **theory** or not rooted in explicit theorizing. Such **propositions** are plausible for "commonsense" reasons independent of one's acceptance of a theory. It is widely held that pretheoretical judgments play an important role in testing theories: A theory ought to account for the relevant pretheoretical judgments and ought not to conflict with them. Many philosophers also accept that in some cases our attempts to achieve **reflective equilibrium** will lead us to reject or **override** some of our pretheoretic judgments. *See also* COMMONSENSISM; INTUITION; ORDINARY LANGUAGE PHILOSOPHY.

PRICHARD, HAROLD ARTHUR (1871–1947). English philosopher and Oxford professor; founder of the Oxford school of ethical **intuitionism**. His *Knowledge and Perception* (1950) presents a form of

direct realism and claims that our **experience** of particular cases provides the foundation for our **knowledge** of universals and **necessary truths**. He also extends his account of **perception** to account for our **moral knowledge** of our obligations in particular situations ("Does Moral Philosophy Rest on a Mistake?" 1912).

***PRIMA FACIE* REASONS.** From the Latin phrase meaning (roughly) "at first sight," a *prima facie* reason is one that initially seems to constitute significant **evidence** but that may be undermined by the results of further examination. *See also* DEFEATER; OVERRIDER.

PRIMARY AND SECONDARY QUALITIES. A distinction among the qualities of an object or the object's capacity to produce effects or **sensations** in observers. Philosophers have not always used these terms in the same way, and individual philosophers (e.g., **John Locke**) are sometimes inconsistent in how they draw this distinction. Typically, primary qualities include an object's size, shape, state of motion or rest, number, and microphysical structure. Secondary qualities are usually said to include the object's color, smell, taste, and sound. Some also include wet/dry, warm/cold, heavy/light, rough/smooth, and hard/soft as secondary qualities, although these are closely linked to microphysical structure (a primary quality). Secondary qualities depend on both the object's primary qualities and the observer's sensory systems. Locke notes that primary qualities can each be observed with two or more sense modalities (e.g., touch and vision), while secondary qualities can be observed with only one. He also suggests that our **ideas** of primary qualities resemble those features of the object itself, while our ideas of secondary qualities do not; **George Berkeley** rejects this, arguing that ideas can resemble other ideas but not external, material objects.

From an epistemic standpoint, some philosophers (e.g., **René Descartes**) hold that primary qualities are those that the object "really" has and that secondary qualities are those we mistakenly attribute to the object. This view has its roots in ancient Greece, as it was held by Democritus and others. **Perceptual relativity** (the variation of some perceived qualities from one observer to another) is widely held to occur only with secondary qualities (although Berkeley rejects this claim as well). The general stability of an agreement regarding primary qualities has been taken by some to indicate that primary qualities are really "out there" in the object, while secondary qualities are only in the mind. *See also* APPEARANCE/REALITY; MOLYNEUX'S QUESTION; OBJECTIVE/SUBJECTIVE; SENSE PERCEPTION.

PRINCIPLE OF CHARITY. Proposed by **Donald Davidson** ("Radical Interpretation" in his *Inquiries into Truth and Interpretation*, 1984), a principle used in translating or determining the meaning of statements. It states that one should assume that most of the statements made by speakers of a language are true, particularly those statements ascribing physical properties to objects. Critics charge that this principle has the effect of assuming that most forms of **skepticism** are false.

PRINCIPLE OF CLOSURE. *See* DEDUCTIVE CLOSURE PRINCIPLE.

PRINCIPLE OF CREDULITY. Formulated by **Thomas Reid** (*An Inquiry into the Human Mind*, 1846), it states that people are generally inclined to believe what they are told by others. This principle is said to be "original" in the sense that this **disposition** is natural rather than learned. This, along with his principle of veracity (which states that people are disposed to speak truthfully), is of great practical value and enables other forms of learning.

Richard Swinburne (*The Existence of God*, 1979) also presents a principle of **credulity** according to which our perceptual **beliefs** are likely to be true and can rationally be accepted (although this may be overridden by contrary **evidence**). He then uses this principle to argue that our religious **experiences** are **reliable** and provide good evidence for **God**'s existence. *See also* COMMONSENSISM; CREDULITY; OVERRIDER; PERCEPTION; RATIONAL ACCEPTANCE; RELIGIOUS KNOWLEDGE; TESTIMONY.

PRINCIPLE OF INDIFFERENCE. A rule for assigning **probabilities** to events. It states that when the **evidence** or reasons that one event will occur are of equal strength as the evidence that another event will occur, these events should be assigned equal probability. *See also* APORIA; BAYESIANISM.

PRINCIPLE OF INDUCTION. *See* INDUCTION, PRINCIPLE OF.

PRINCIPLE OF SUFFICIENT REASON. Formulated by **Gottfried Leibniz**, it states that there must be a sufficient reason for every choice and for any state of affairs (and thus for the **truth** of any **proposition**). In his *An Essay on Free Will* (1983), Peter van Inwagen argues that one can identify a **contingently** true proposition for which the principle of sufficient reason is unable to account. *See also* CONTINGENCY; REASONS FOR BELIEF.

PRINCIPLE OF VERACITY. *See* PRINCIPLE OF CREDULITY.

PRINCIPLE OF VERIFIABILITY. The claim that a sentence is meaningful only if some **experience** or experimental situation could verify it. Typically associated with **logical positivism**, this principle is used as a basis for dismissing metaphysics, theology, ethics, and other matters as "pseudo-problems." *See also* VERIFICATIONISM.

PRIVACY OF MENTAL STATES. It is commonly held that only *I* can directly **experience** my own mental states; any access that others have to them is indirect, typically mediated by my behavior. In this sense, mental states are private. This raises **skeptical** challenges regarding the existence of mental states in others. *See also* GIVEN, THE; INTROSPECTION; OTHER MINDS, PROBLEM OF; PRIVATE LANGUAGE ARGUMENT; PRIVILEGED ACCESS.

PRIVATE LANGUAGE ARGUMENT. An **argument** intended to show the impossibility of a language having only one speaker. Presented by **Ludwig Wittgenstein** (*Philosophical Investigations*, 1953; especially §§243–315), this argument can be formulated in a variety of ways. A common formulation begins by considering someone who assigns signs to **sensations** or mental states. The **privacy of these mental states** makes ordinary and ostensive definitions impossible. Wittgenstein argues that this attempt at language building is doomed to fail because standards cannot be formulated for the proper application of those signs. Without such standards, a language cannot exist. This runs contrary to the long-held view that all languages involve, at bottom, an individual's association of words with mental states. *See also* INTROSPECTION; OTHER MINDS, PROBLEM OF; PRIVACY OF MENTAL STATES.

PRIVILEGED ACCESS. One's first-person, unmediated awareness of one's own mental states and **experiences**. Because of this access, many regard **beliefs** about one's own mental states as self-justifying, **infallible**, **incorrigible**, or **indubitable**. **René Descartes** and other **foundationalists** employed this privileged access in establishing a foundation for other **knowledge**. *See also* BASIC BELIEF; CERTAINTY; GIVEN, THE; IMMEDIACY; INTROSPECTION; PRIVACY OF MENTAL STATES; SELF-EVIDENCE.

PROBABILITY. A numerical value (typically a proportion or ratio) used to measure relative frequency, the likelihood of an event or state of affairs, degree of **belief**, or the strength of **evidence**.

As a measure of degree of belief, probability is closely linked to the strength of one's evidence. **Frank Ramsey** ("Truth and Probability" in his *The Foundations of Mathematics and Other Essays*, 1926) and others argue that the calculus of probability should be used as a **logic** for **partial belief**. This is also a central feature of **Bayesianism**.

As a measure of relative frequency, probability is determined by the proportion of cases in which a specified event or state of affairs arises in an infinite sequence of fair samples or trials. Thus, if I flip a coin ten times and it comes up "heads" seven times, the relative frequency or probability of its coming up "heads" may still be 50 percent (or 0.5). The brief actual sequence of coin tosses may not be a good indicator of the event's true probability. In a closely related matter, probability can be used as a measure of chance. Here it is determined by the tendency or propensity of an event's occurring or a state of affairs obtaining (or of its occurring randomly or of its occurring on the next sample or trial). The focus here may be on a particular case or sample, not on an infinite sequence of them.

A subjective interpretation of probability uses probability to measure one's partial belief and is commonly measured by (and even defined in terms of) one's betting behavior. The more one is willing to bet on the **truth** of a **proposition**, the greater subjective probability it has for one and the greater the strength of one's belief that this proposition is true. A rational person will hold partial beliefs in such a way that it is impossible to make a **Dutch book** against him or her. *See also* INDUCTION; OBJECTIVE/SUBJECTIVE.

PROBLEM OF INDUCTION. *See* INDUCTION, PROBLEM OF.

PROBLEM OF OTHER MINDS. *See* OTHER MINDS, PROBLEM OF.

PROBLEM OF THE CRITERION. The difficulty of determining both the criteria of **knowledge** and the extent of our knowledge. In order to determine whether someone knows that *p*, we need to know the criteria of knowledge. However, in order to determine the criteria of knowledge, we must already be able to identify clear instances of knowledge. The **JTB theory of knowledge** was commonly regarded as at least a close approximation of the criteria of knowledge until the **Gettier cases** disproved it and focused more attention on the problem of the criterion.

Some attempts to resolve this problem begin with cases that we confidently regard as knowledge; these were labeled by **Roderick Chisholm** as particularism. Attempts to resolve it that begin with criteria we confidently accept for knowledge he labels as methodism (*Theory of Knowledge*, 2nd ed., 1977). **David Hume** is a methodist; he is more confident about the criteria of knowledge than of its extent. **Thomas Reid** and **G. E. Moore** are particularists; they are confident that many of our common beliefs qualify as knowledge and use this as a basis for formulating the criteria of knowledge. Chisholm's **critical cognitivism** is a form of particularism: He identifies clear cases of knowledge and **justified true belief** (without using any criteria) and then evaluates proposed criteria by seeing how well they fit with these particular instances. Methodists charge that this approach makes the unfounded assumption that **skepticism** is false. *See also* COMMONSENSISM; REFLECTIVE EQUILIBRIUM; SEXTUS EMPIRICUS.

PROBLEM OF THE SPECKLED HEN. *See* SPECKLED HEN PROBLEM.

PROCEDURAL KNOWLEDGE. Knowing *how*; one's confident ability to accomplish a task. The distinction between this and **propositional knowledge** was first drawn by **Gilbert Ryle**, who argues that both forms are best understood in terms of the subject's behavioral **dispositions**. Procedural knowledge has received surprisingly little attention from most epistemologists, although it has a central place in **phenomenology**. *See also* BEHAVIORISM, ANALYTIC; BEHAVIORISM, METHODOLOGICAL.

PROJECTIBILITY. A predicate is projectible if **observations** of it in some cases provide **evidence** about it in unobserved cases (when used in **ampliative inferences**, such as inductive or hypothetical reasoning). The **grue paradox**, presented by **Nelson Goodman**, illustrates this. Observing that all the emeralds we have encountered are green provides evidence that unobserved ones are also green. But that the observed emeralds are also grue (the property of being either observed before a particular time t and found to be green or not examined prior to t and being blue) does not provide evidence that unobserved emeralds are grue. "Green" is projectible, but "grue" is not. There is no general agreement about what makes a predicate projectible. *See also* INDUCTION, PROBLEM OF.

PROOF. A set of **evidence** and reasoning demonstrating, without the possibility of **error**, that a particular **proposition** or **theory** is true. In mathematics, proofs are used to demonstrate that a particular theorem is **necessarily** true. The apparent impossibility of providing proofs in support of most of our ordinary **beliefs** has greatly fueled **skepticism**. *See also* DEDUCTION; LOGIC; PROOF THEORY.

PROOF BY RECURSION. *See* MATHEMATICAL INDUCTION.

PROOF THEORY. A branch of mathematical **logic** developed by **David Hilbert** that he uses to formalize important areas of mathematics and prove their **consistency**. This involves showing that contradictory formulae cannot be derived within a strict formalization of logic and mathematics. *See also* MATHEMATICAL KNOWLEDGE.

PROPOSITION. An **abstract entity** that expresses the meaning of a declarative sentence and is often said to be the bearer of **truth** values. Propositions have **logical** and semantic structure; they can be conditional, disjunctive, universal, existential, and so forth. Propositions are the objects of our **propositional attitudes**; for example, my **belief** that cats are mammals is my attitude that the proposition expressed by the sentence "Cats are mammals" is true. Problems regarding meaning, reference, indexicals and so forth are generally problems about propositions as well. *See also* CONDITIONAL PROPOSITION; GRAMMAR.

PROPOSITIONAL ATTITUDE. Any of various **psychological** states whose content includes a **proposition** and an attitude regarding that proposition's **truth**, falsehood, likelihood, or desirability. Propositional attitudes include **beliefs**, **doubts**, hopes, fears, and others. A belief is the propositional attitude of accepting a proposition as true and as such is subject to epistemic evaluation. **Paul Churchland** and other critics argue that our common views about propositional attitudes are incompatible with the neurosciences. *See also* CONNECTIONISM; ELIMINATIVE MATERIALISM; EPISTEMIC JUSTIFICATION; FOLK PSYCHOLOGY; PSYCHOLOGY; RATIONAL ACCEPTANCE.

PROPOSITIONAL KNOWLEDGE. The type of knowing that is the central focus of most work in **epistemology**: knowing that a **proposition** is true. This is also called knowing *that* (commonly represented as "*S* knows that *p*," where "*S*" represents a subject and "*p*" a proposition). Propositional knowledge has traditionally been thought to require that the proposition be true, that the subject believe that *p*, and that the subject's **belief** be adequately justified. This approach, known as the **JTB theory of knowledge**, has been seriously challenged by Edmund Gettier's **counterexamples** and by continuing disagreements regarding the nature of **epistemic justification**. *See also* CERTAINTY; EXTERNALISM/INTERNALISM; GETTIER CASES; KNOWLEDGE *DE DICTO*.

PROPRIOCEPTION. A mode of **sensory perception** that provides **information** about the relative position of body parts and bodily movement.

PROTOCOL SENTENCES. This term was introduced by **Rudolf Carnap** (*The Unity of Science*, 1932) and refers to those sentences that record an observer's **experiences** without any use of **induction** or reliance on **presuppositions**. **Foundationalist theories** of knowledge and **epistemic justification** regard protocol sentences as **basic beliefs** and thus non**inferentially** justified. *See also* EMPIRICISM; LOGICAL POSITIVISM.

PSYCHOLOGISM. The view that a specified philosophical problem or area of research can be reduced to psychological phenomena. Although influential in the latter part of the nineteenth century, it has been criticized by **Edmund Husserl**, **Gottlob Frege**, **Ludwig Wittgenstein**, and others. **W. V. O. Quine** famously argues that **epistemology** can be reduced to or replaced by **psychology** ("Epistemology Naturalized" in his *Ontological Relativity and Other Essays*, 1969). *See also* NATURALIZED EPISTEMOLOGY.

PSYCHOLOGY. The study of human thought and behavior, thought by some to be relevant to **epistemology**. Although some epistemologists regard their discipline as purely *a priori*, others (such as **David Hume** and **Immanuel Kant**) appeal to **empirical** psychology in developing or defending their epistemic **theories**.

    Reliabilism and other **causal theories of knowledge** draw on psychological descriptions of our cognitive processes to develop their theories. Epistemologists commonly make claims about psychology (e.g., about whether all of one's mental states are available to **introspection**, whether introspection is **infallible**, or how we go about drawing **inferences**) in presenting their theories, and empirical investigation by psychologists is valuable in supporting or refuting those claims. **W. V. O. Quine** argues that psychology should replace epistemology ("Epistemology Naturalized" in his *Ontological Relativity and Other Essays*, 1969), and **Paul Churchland** contends that neuropsychology will eventually provide a system of **concepts** to replace the **folk psychological** ones (such as the concepts of **belief** and desire) currently employed in epistemology. Epistemology also influences psychology; for example, there is an ongoing debate among psychologists, hermeneuticians, and others about the appropriate evidential standards that should be employed in developing and evaluating psychological theories. *See also A PRIORI/APOSTERIORI* KNOWLEDGE; BELIEF-FORMING PROCESS; ELIMINATIVE MATERIALISM; EVIDENCE; FREUD, SIGMUND; HERMENEUTICS; NATURALIZED EPISTEMOLOGY.

PUTNAM, HILARY (1926–). American philosopher, trained at the University of California at Los Angeles (working with **Hans Reichenbach**), and professor at Harvard University. He has made a variety of important contributions to **epistemology**, among them his critique of **verificationism** and his claim that **truth** is best understood as idealized **warranted assertability** (*Meaning and the Moral Sciences*, 1978; *Reason, Truth and History*, 1981). This makes truth an epistemic **concept**.

Putnam uses his causal **theory** of reference to refute those forms of **skepticism** that dismiss all our usual **evidence** about the world by saying that it could all be misleading. Putnam argues that if one were a **brain in a vat** (with all one's **experiences** generated by a computer, resulting in one's having false **beliefs**), one's beliefs would refer to the computer and its actions, not to the **external world**. Thus, if such a brain were to believe that it is a brain in a vat, that would be false; it would refer only to the computer's actions, not to the state of affairs (in the external world) of its being in a vat. And if "I am a brain in a vat" is always false, the skeptic who asserts that it may be true must be mistaken. *See also* TRANSCENDENTAL ARGUMENTS.

PYRRHO OF ELIS (ca. 365–ca. 270 B.C.). Greek philosopher whose attack on **knowledge** was widely influential. His work is known chiefly through the writings of his student Timon of Philius. Pyrrho argues that knowledge is impossible because our senses are unreliable and because the world itself lacks determinate qualities. For any **argument** supporting a particular conclusion, Pyrrho holds that an equally compelling argument can be produced for the opposite conclusion. Thus, the reasonable response is to suspend **judgment**.

Rather than producing anxiety, Pyrrho shows that this could lead to tranquility (a view that influenced the Stoics). *See also* APORIA; RELIABILITY; SENSE PERCEPTION; SEXTUS EMPIRICUS; SKEPTICISM.

PYRRHONIAN SKEPTICISM. *See* PYRRHO OF ELIS; SKEPTICISM.

– Q –

QUALIA. (Singular: quale). The qualitative features or phenomenal qualities of mental states or events; qualia determine what it is like to **experience** that state or event. *See also* GIVEN, THE; INTROSPECTION; OBJECTIVE/SUBJECTIVE; SENSATION; SENSE PERCEPTION.

QUINE, WILLARD VAN ORMAN (W. V. O.) (1908–2000). American philosopher and professor at Harvard University. His work has been very influential in many areas of philosophy, including **epistemology**. In "Two Dogmas of Empiricism" (in his *From a Logical Point of View*, 1953), Quine attacks the **analytic/synthetic distinction** and the claim that all meaningful statements can be reduced to statements about **experience**. This leads him to redescribe the relationships among **beliefs**. Instead of regarding analytically true beliefs as immune to revision regardless of any experiences one might have, Quine claims that no belief has a claim to this special status. Instead, any belief may be maintained in the face of experience, provided we are willing to make appropriate (and sometimes drastic) changes elsewhere in the system of beliefs. Therefore, experience is incapable of proving that any particular belief is false. We tend to respond to new and surprising **observations** in such a way that our system of beliefs is altered as little as possible; this leads to the mistaken **impression** that some of our beliefs are vulnerable to change while others are not.

Quine visited the **Vienna Circle** in the 1930s, and this contact with **empiricism** and **logical positivism** proved to be a persistent influence (although he clearly rejects many of their central tenets). One important point of agreement Quine has with these schools of thought is that epistemology is a part of the broader enterprise of **science**. In "Naturalized Epistemology" (in his *Ontological Relativity and Other Essays*, 1969), he argues that epistemology is the study of how the stimulation of one's sensory surfaces leads to the production and evaluation of **theories**. This is a psychological issue; thus, epistemology should be replaced by **psychology** and thus take its place within **natural science**. The traditional search for **Cartesian certainty** is rejected, and epistemology is described as an undertaking that arises (and makes sense) only within the context of science. There is no need to try to refute radical **skepticism**; the only legitimate challenges to a theory are those that are based on scientific reasons. *See also* COHERENTISM; CREDULITY; EMPIRICISM; HOLISM; INDETERMINACY OF TRANSLATION; NATURALIZED EPISTEMOLOGY; PSYCHOLOGISM; WEB OF BELIEF.

– R –

RAMSEY, FRANK PLUMPTON (1903–1930). British philosopher and mathematician; he also made notable contributions to economics. In **epistemology**, he developed a quantitative account of how decisions are made in circumstances of uncertainty and explores the role in this of the strength of one's **beliefs** and desires. His view also supports the **reliabilist** position that a **justified true belief** is one that is true and formed in a **truth**-conducive manner. Beliefs are understood in terms of the influence they have on our behavior. *See also* BAYESIANISM; BELIEF-FORMING PROCESS; RELIABILISM.

RATIONAL ACCEPTANCE. The degree to which one is rationally warranted in believing a particular **proposition** given the **evidence** available. Some regard the degree of rational acceptance to be **equivalent** to the degree of **epistemic justification**. *See also* BAYESIANISM; EPISTEMIC WARRANT; LOTTERY PARADOX; PARTIAL BELIEF.

RATIONALISM. A diverse philosophical school of thought according to which reason is the most important (or perhaps the only) means of acquiring **knowledge**; it is opposed to **empiricism**. Rationalists disagree about the nature of reason and the role of **experience** in **epistemology**. They often regard mathematics as the **paradigm** of knowledge, and some argue that all knowledge arises from a small set of **truths** known by means of reason, along with the principles of **deduction**. (Rationalists typically reject **fallibilism**.) The philosophers most commonly regarded as rationalists are **René Descartes**, **Baruch Spinoza**, and **Gottfried Leibniz**. Rationalism is sometimes described as the view that there is at least one synthetic **proposition** that can be known *a priori*. *See also A PRIORI/A POSTERIORI* KNOWLEDGE; ANALYTICITY.

RATIONALITY. Behavior and **beliefs** (and perhaps desires) are said to be rational when they are guided by proper reasoning. The standards of logical reasoning are not altogether clear, however. It seems clear that an adequate account of rationality will need to go well beyond the principles of **deduction**, including, for instance, **probabilistic** guidelines for **ampliative inferences** and rules of **conversational implicature**. Some argue that rationality includes the nature and activities of a faculty of rational **intuition**.

David Hume, Karl Popper, and others argue that rationality does not extend beyond deductive **logic** (along with some strict forms of mathematical and semantic reasoning) and thus that rationality can provide only a relatively narrow body of **knowledge**.

RATIONALIZATION. A pseudo-**explanation** of a person's **belief** or behavior that purports to **justify** it or present it as innocuous. In addition, according to **Donald Davidson**, rationalization is a genuine explanation of a person's behavior by adducing desires and reasons, presenting it as rational from that person's standpoint. *See also* OBJECTIVE/SUBJECTIVE.

RAVEN PARADOX. *See* CONFIRMATION; HEMPEL, CARL.

REALISM/ANTIREALISM. Realism is the view that which (types of) entities exist and what they are like is independent of our minds and **observations**. Antirealism denies this. One might be a realist about one set of entities or properties (e.g., physics or history) while being antirealist about another (e.g., aesthetics or ethics). The traditional distinction—now increasingly challenged—has it that realists determine a sentence's (or **proposition**'s) **truth** by reference to mind-independent reality and that antirealists determine truth in epistemic terms, referring to assertability conditions or the convergence of research programs.

Hilary Putnam ("Two Philosophical Perspectives" in his *Reason, Truth and History*, 1981) argues that no sense can be made of the question of whether the entities posited by a particular theoretical framework really exist apart from that framework. He proposes that we replace this incoherent sense of realism with "internal realism" according to which entities are real from the standpoint of a particular theoretical framework if that **theory** is committed to the existence of such entities. Although Putnam calls this a form of realism, most would classify it as a form of antirealism because it makes existence dependent on theories or standpoints.

Michael Dummett ("Realism" in his *Truth and Other Enigmas*, 1978) has proposed that realists are those who link a sentence's meaning with its truth conditions and that antirealists are those who link meaning with assertability conditions. This puts the realism/antirealism distinction into semantic rather than ontological or epistemological terms. *See also* APPEARANCE/REALITY; IDEALISM; SCIENTIFIC REALISM/ANTIREALISM; THEORETICAL ENTITY.

REALITY. *See* APPEARANCE/REALITY.

REASONS FOR BELIEF. There are three ways of understanding reasons for **belief**. First, these may be the **cause** or basis of one's belief (to which one may or may not have **introspective** access). **Reliabilism** examines this cause to determine the belief's epistemic status. Second, a reason for belief may be a body of **evidence** in one's possession that implies and supports the belief. To possess a reason in this sense requires grasping the evidential relation it has with the belief in question. Third, a reason for belief may be the defense or **explanation** one offers when that belief is questioned. The reasons one presents may not match up with the actual causes of that belief, and one's reasons may not provide any significant evidence for the belief being defended. *See also* EXTERNALISM/INTERNALISM; IMPLICATION.

REDUCTION SENTENCE. The process of reduction allows one to replace a sentence with a reduction sentence that has the same meaning but makes reference to different (types of) entities. For example, some have argued that all statements about the **external world** can be replaced with reduction sentences about **sense data**. Others argue that all mathematical statements can be replaced with reduction sentences about **logic**. *See also* CARNAP, RUDOLF; PHENOMENALISM.

REFLECTIVE EQUILIBRIUM. First introduced by **Nelson Goodman** (*Fact, Fiction and Forecast*, 1955), it is a procedure for finding a carefully reasoned balance between confidently held assessments of particular cases (e.g., assessments of the epistemic status of individual **beliefs**) and appealing general principles (e.g., standards of **knowledge** or **epistemic justification**). It is a system of mutual adjustment in which no principle or **judgment** is epistemically immune from revision. John Rawls (*A Theory of Justice*, 1971) develops this further and applies it to ethics and political philosophy. *See also* COHERENTISM; CONFIDENCE.

REGRESS ARGUMENT. *See* EPISTEMIC REGRESS ARGUMENT.

REICHENBACH, HANS (1891–1953). German philosopher of **science** and a major figure in a movement known as logical **empiricism**. He received his doctoral degree in philosophy from Erlangen (1915) but left Germany in 1933 and eventually joined the faculty of the University of California at Los Angeles. Reichenbach rejects **Immanuel Kant**'s claims regarding the *a priori* nature of time, space, and **causation**, arguing that they are inconsistent with Albert Einstein's relativistic physics (*Relativitätstheorie und Erkenntnis Apriori*, 1920; translated as *The Theory of Relativity and A Priori Knowledge*, 1965). He also argues against **phenomenalism** and **logical positivism** (*Experience and Prediction*, 1938).

He made important contributions to the understanding of **probability** and **induction** (*Wahrscheinlichkeitslehre*, 1935; translated as

The Theory of Probability, 2nd ed., 1949). His defense of induction against **David Hume**'s skeptical criticisms stresses a **pragmatic** approach to the problem; Reichenbach argues that it is reasonable to employ induction even though we cannot be assured that nature is uniform. *See also A PRIORI/A POSTERIORI* KNOWLEDGE; CARNAP, RUDOLF; INDUCTION, PROBLEM OF; UNIFORMITY OF NATURE; VIENNA CIRCLE.

REID, THOMAS (1710–1796). Scottish philosopher; he was a regent and lecturer at King's College (Aberdeen) before succeeding Adam Smith as the chair of moral philosophy in the Old College at Glasgow. He is notable as a defender of common sense and critic of the **skepticism** of his contemporary **David Hume**. In his *Inquiry into the Human Mind on the Principles of Common Sense* (1764), Reid argues that Hume's **theory** of **ideas** fails to explain how an observer can have ideas of an object's qualities, and he replaces Hume's conjecture with his own theory of the innate powers or faculties of the human mind. These faculties account for our ability to conceive of qualities, nonexistent objects, past objects we have not **experienced**, and so forth. Although these conceptions arise as the result of sensory stimulation, they are not reducible to **sensations** or **impressions**.

These innate faculties of the mind generate **beliefs** and do so in accordance with "first principles" of the mind. These first principles account for the very early development of such beliefs in children, the universality of such beliefs in the human population, and our inability to resist or seriously **doubt** these beliefs. Such beliefs are **immediately** justified and form the foundation or source for the **justification** of our **inferential beliefs**; thus, Reid's **epistemology** incorporates important elements of **foundationalism**. Reid's conclusion is that we are justified in regarding our mental faculties (including our faculty for making moral judgments) as **reliable**, although our senses are fallible and this justification may be **overridden** in particular cases. Reid criticizes Hume for his willingness to trust one of our mental faculties (reason) but not the others. Reid argues that our faculties should be treated equally; Hume should either stop trusting reason or trust his other faculties as well. *See also* COMMONSENSISM; FALLIBILISM; INNATE IDEA; SENSE PERCEPTION; THEORETICAL ENTITY.

RELATIVISM. *See* EPISTEMIC RELATIVISM.

RELEVANT ALTERNATIVES. A **skeptical alternative** (i.e., a situation **consistent** with one's **evidence** but in which the **belief** being evaluated is false) that is relevant to the belief or **knowledge** claim being assessed. Some propose that a belief qualifies as knowledge if the evidence supporting it suffices to rule out all relevant alternatives, even though there are other skeptical alternatives that it cannot rule out (**Fred Dretske**, "Epistemic Operators," 1970, and "The Pragmatic Dimension of Knowledge," 1981; Stewart Cohen, "How to Be a Fallibilist," 1988). This is used as an **argument** against some forms of **skepticism**, claiming that knowledge does not require that one's evidence rule out all skeptical alternatives; instead, only relevant alternatives must be eliminated by the available evidence. Critics of this relevant-alternatives approach point out that no clear account of relevance has yet been provided and that it violates the **closure principle** (because one could know that *p* without knowing that a skeptical alternative is false, even though the negation of that skeptical alternative is trivially entailed by *p*). *See also* FALLIBILISM; PRAGMATISM; PROBLEM OF THE CRITERION.

RELIABILISM. The view that a **belief**'s epistemic status is determined (in large part, at least) by the reliability of the means by which it was formed or maintained. There are reliabilist accounts of both **knowledge** and **epistemic justification**. This emphasis on **causation** can be traced to **Frank Ramsey**'s "Knowledge" (in his *The Foundations of Mathematics and Other Essays*, 1931), where he defends the claim that a belief qualifies as knowledge if it is true, **certain**, and formed by a reliable process. Other early causal accounts were formulated by Peter Unger ("An Analysis of Factual Knowledge," 1968) and **David Armstrong** (*Belief, Truth and Knowledge*, 1973). Reliabilist **theories** are typically externalist in that a belief's status depends on something external to the subject's viewpoint.

Reliabilist theories of epistemic justification may focus on the **evidence** on which the belief is based or on the process of belief formation and maintenance. The former are called reliable indicator theories, which say that a belief is justified to the degree that the evidence or indicator central to its formation is reliable. This is often put **counterfactually**: If the belief had been false, this indicator would not have been present (or would not have caused the belief). Formulations of the latter type are called reliable process theories and say that a belief is justified to the degree that the **psychological** process by which it is formed (or maintained) is reliable. Either sort of theory has the consequence that one might know that *p* without knowing that one knows that *p* (because one is unaware of the reliability of the indicator or psychological process involved).

Critics have presented various problems for reliabilism. Some attack the externalist nature of the theory, while others find technical challenges. The technical problems include identifying and describing belief-forming (and belief-maintaining) processes and determining how reliability is to be measured. *See also* BELIEF-FORMING PROCESS; CAUSAL THEORIES OF KNOWLEDGE AND JUSTIFICATION; EXTERNALISM/INTERNALISM; KK THESIS; NATURALIZED EPISTEMOLOGY.

RELIGIOUS KNOWLEDGE. The study of **beliefs** about **God**'s existence, nature, or commands has long been an important **epistemological** issue. In the Western philosophical tradition, this discussion has focused almost exclusively on the Judeo-Christian conception of God. Those who believe that we do have **knowledge** (or justified beliefs) of these matters have traditionally relied on **arguments** for God's existence or **revelation**. Those who are **skeptical** of these claims have traditionally relied on the **argument from evil** (for the conclusion that God does not exist) or on alternative **explanations** of the persistent reports of religious **experience** and belief. Some theists seek to avoid the usual epistemological standards by claiming that religious belief is based on **faith**, not **evidence**. *See also* CREDULITY; EPIPHANY; LEAP OF FAITH; MYSTICISM.

REPRESENTATIVE REALISM. The view that there is a mind-independent **external world** and that we perceive this world indirectly by means of mental representations. Contrary to **direct realism**, representative realism states that we are directly aware only of our own mental states. One learns about external objects by drawing **inferences** from the examination of their mental representations. **John Locke**, whose presentation of representative realism has been very influential (*Essay Concerning Human Understanding*, 1690), holds that not all the properties that appear in our mental representations of objects actually resemble those objects. He accounts for this by distinguishing between **primary and secondary qualities**. Other representative realists, noting the differences between **appearance and reality**, have suggested that in **perception** one is directly aware of **sense data**, mental objects that actually possess the properties (e.g., being bent, being red) that external objects appear to have.

Critics have challenged the **act/object analysis** of perception that is implicit in representative realism and the claim that we are only indirectly aware of the external world. Representative realists, it is argued, are unable to avoid **skepticism**. *See also* BERKELEY, GEORGE; EXPERIENCE; PERCEPTUAL KNOWLEDGE; SENSE PERCEPTION.

RESCHER, NICHOLAS (1928–). German-born American philosopher, educated at Princeton University, and professor at the University of Pittsburgh. He is an extraordinarily prolific writer and has made important contributions in **epistemology**, ethics, metaphysics, and other areas. He adopts a **pragmatist**'s stance, emphasizing **scientific method** as the standard for acquiring empirical **knowledge**. None of our **beliefs** are immune from revision as scientific investigation continues. Beliefs begin as working **hypotheses** and qualify as **knowledge** only when they have stood the test of long **experience**; even these beliefs, however, may one day be rejected in favor of a promising new hypothesis. *See also* FALLIBILISM.

REVELATION. A source of **religious knowledge** whereby **God** reveals **truths** to humans. **Beliefs** formed in this manner are held by some to be **certain** and immune from rational revision. Skeptics offer alternative **explanations** of alleged revelations that theists have difficulty ruling out. *See also* CREDULITY; GIVEN, THE; SKEPTICAL ALTERNATIVES.

RORTY, RICHARD (1931–). American philosopher, educated at the University of Chicago and Yale University. He has taught at Yale, Wellesley College, Princeton, and the University of Virginia. His early work was largely on the philosophy of mind, and he defended

eliminative materialism. His *Philosophy and the Mirror of Nature* (1979) began a very different, critical trend in his thought. He now argues that **epistemology** is an artificial and misleading enterprise founded on false assumptions about the nature of mind and the role of language. Once we abandon the conception of mind as representing and interpreting **reality**, he says we will find that the epistemological enterprise has evaporated. *See also* DEATH OF EPISTEMOLOGY; POSTMODERNISM; REPRESENTATIVE REALISM.

RUSSELL, BERTRAND (1872–1970). British philosopher and logician; a founder of analytic philosophy. His understanding of **epistemology** links it closely with virtually all other areas of philosophy, particularly with the philosophical study of mind, language, metaphysics, **science**, and **truth**. His early work takes a broadly **Cartesian, foundationalist** approach to understanding **knowledge**; he begins with the content of **experience** and considers how it could provide a foundation for **beliefs** about the **external world**. He explores different positions at different times, including a version of **phenomenalism** that regards material objects as **logical constructs** of **sense data** (*Our Knowledge of the External World*, 1914), arguing that we have *a priori* **knowledge** of scientific principles (*Human Knowledge: Its Scope and Limits*, 1948), and a form of **representative realism** (*Problems of Philosophy*, 1912). His mature work, reflected in *Human Knowledge*, incorporates elements of both **coherentism** and a weak formulation of foundationalism. In addition, he regards moral **judgments** as subjective expressions of desire and thus not as candidates for knowledge. In *Human Knowledge*, Russell cedes some territory to **skepticism** in acknowledging the limits on the degree to which our beliefs are **justified**; **certainty** is beyond our reach. He concludes that "all human knowledge is uncertain, inexact, and partial." *See also* ANALYTICITY.

RYLE, GILBERT (1900–1976). British philosopher, professor at Oxford University. He sees the role of philosophy as analyzing and organizing **concepts** and categories, and he employs this in his famous rejection of the **Cartesian** dualist understanding of mind (*The Concept of Mind*, 1949). The phrase "the mind," he argues, is misleading in that it does not refer to a particular type of entity. This is an **example** of how grammatical and logical structures can diverge and lead to confusion. In **epistemology**, Ryle argues that the traditional focus on **propositional knowledge** ("knowing that") has detracted epistemologists from the equally important issue of **procedural knowledge** ("knowing how"). *See also* ANALYSIS; GRAMMAR; LOGICAL CONSTRUCTION.

– S –

SANCHES, FRANCISCO (ca. 1551–1623). Portuguese-born philosopher and physician, trained at the University of Montpellier (France), where he was later professor of philosophy and then of medicine. His *Quod nihil scitur* (*That Nothing Is Known*, 1581) is a skeptical critique of the **epistemologies** of **Aristotle** and **Plato**. Scientific investigation cannot produce **certainty**, for our faculties are unreliable and the **truth** of the premises used in alleged demonstrations cannot be ascertained. *See also* SCIENTIFIC METHOD; SKEPTICISM.

SANTAYANA, GEORGE (1863–1952). Spanish-born philosopher and writer, educated at Harvard University and later professor there. His *Scepticism and Animal Faith* (1923) employs **René Descartes**'s methodological **doubt** to show that anything can be doubted (apart from our unhelpful **consciousness** of universals). Santayana rejects this **skepticism** as dishonest and impractical, insisting that no philosophical position should be adopted that cannot be acted on in practice. He proposes instead that we begin with what he calls "animal **faith**," the commitment to the **external world** that humans and other animals reveal in their behavior. (This emphasis on action seems to reveal the influence of **William James** and **John Dewey**.) **Knowledge** is true **belief** presented in mental symbols. The objects of consciousness that arise from our senses are used as symbols of material objects in our environment and enable us to grasp and contemplate pure **Forms** or essences. This platonic view of universals is tied to an irreducibly organic account of our sensory systems. *See also* ACT/OBJECT ANALYSIS; SENSE PERCEPTION.

SARTRE, JEAN-PAUL (1905–1980). French philosopher and writer, a leading figure in existentialism. *L'être et le Néant* (*Being and Nothingness*, 1943), his major philosophical work, rejects the notion of the self as merely self-consciousness. Sartre draws on **G. W. F. Hegel**'s terminology to contrast **consciousness** (*pour soi*, "being-for-itself") with the existence of objects (*en soi*, "being-in-itself"). Consciousness is not a substance, contrary to **René Descartes**'s assertion, but is instead an activity, "a wind blowing from nowhere toward the world." In this way, Sartre rejects both the **rationalist** and the **empiricist** traditions; the mind does not contain **ideas** or representations of the **external world**.

Consciousness can never examine itself the way it does other objects; thus, consciousness is not a thing, a point Sartre expresses by saying that it is nothingness. Consciousness is also free from the constraints of **causality** and is completely self-determining; this is the essence of human freedom. This freedom results in one experiencing objects in terms of their "potentialities-for-me," the ways in which one may use them; this is expressed in terms of the "nothingnesses" of objects. *See also* CONTINENTAL EPISTEMOLOGY.

SCHMITT, FREDERICK F. (1951–). American philosopher, trained at the University of Michigan (Ann Arbor, Michigan); he has taught at the University of Illinois at Urbana–Champaign and Indiana University (Bloomington, Indiana). His work in **epistemology** includes examinations of the **externalism/internalism** debate, **reliabilist** theories of **epistemic justification**, **naturalized epistemology**, **social epistemology**, the nature of **truth**, and the **problem of the criterion**. He has also written about the work of **René Descartes**, **David Hume**, and **C. S. Peirce**. His notable works include *Knowledge and Belief* (1992) and the edited collection *Socializing Epistemology: The Social Dimensions of Knowledge* (1994).

SCIENCE. An outgrowth of philosophy, science is the careful and organized study of the natural world. It is also a major epistemic success story: Science has generated a systematic and carefully examined body of **evidence**, **inferences**, and **theories**. The nature of scientific **knowledge** has long been a central concern of **epistemology**.

Science relies on **observation**, and this raises epistemological questions. If observation sentences are taken to be about the **external world**, then it is difficult to see how they could be theory neutral, and they also **presuppose** the falsehood of many **skeptical alternatives**. This casts considerable **doubt** on the security of science's epistemic foundations. In response, some philosophers have argued that observation sentences are only about the observer's **experiences**; this is sometimes accompanied by the claim that material objects are **logical constructions** of such experiences. This conflicts, however, with the **scientific realism** endorsed by many scientists.

Another epistemological question in science addresses the **credibility** of scientific **hypotheses**. **Inductivism** is the view that hypotheses gain credibility from their success in predicting **observations**. The **hypothetico-deductive method** sees hypotheses as the products of the scientist's **imagination** that are then subjected to empirical testing. In either case, an **inference to the best explanation** is used to draw the conclusion that the hypothesis's predictive success indicates its **truth**. *See also* EXPLANATION; KUHN, THOMAS; OBJECTIVITY; POPPER, KARL; PREDICTION; QUINE, W. V. O.; SCIENTIFIC METHOD; TESTABILITY; THEORY LADEN.

SCIENTIFIC METHOD. The set of strategies and procedures employed in acquiring scientific **knowledge** or **evidence**; these involve formulating **theories** or models and testing them by means of **observation** or **experiment**. In the physical **sciences**, theory testing has focused on identifying and testing **predictions**. This approach differs from those used in other areas of investigation—chiefly in the use of mathematics in formulating theories, the use of quantitative data, and the use of experimental situations.

The use of experiments in testing theories or hypotheses developed most clearly during the scientific revolution of the seventeenth century. **Thomas Kuhn** points out that the observations made in experimental situations and elsewhere are **theory laden**, and thus experimental observations are unable to function as **objective** tests. More recent theorists argue that experimental activity can be understood as independent of fundamental scientific theories. The sociology of science, the nature of scientific and educational institutions, and the influence of religion and politics all have an impact on the methods and results of science. *See also* ABDUCTION; CRUCIAL EXPERIMENT; MEASUREMENT; OBJECTIVITY; TESTABILITY; THEORY.

SCIENTIFIC REALISM/ANTIREALISM. Scientific realism is the view that the objects of scientific **knowledge** are mind-independent entities in the **external world**. Scientific antirealism takes a variety of forms (including constructivism, **instrumentalism**, and **phenomenalism**), all of which share the view that the objects of scientific knowledge are *not* mind independent. For instance, realists hold that **theoretical entities** (e.g., electrons) are really constituents of the external world, while antirealists argue that they have no existence apart from the **theories** that posit them. Realists ask whether a scientific theory is true, but antirealists may ask only whether it is **reliable** or empirically adequate. *See also* ABSTRACT ENTITY; KUHN, THOMAS; PUTNAM, HILARY; REALISM/ANTIREALISM; SCIENCE; TRUTH.

SELF-CONSCIOUSNESS. *See* CONSCIOUSNESS; INTROSPECTION; OBJECTIVE/SUBJECTIVE.

SELF-EVIDENCE. A self-evident **proposition** is one that requires no other support or **evidence** for its **truth** to be apparent. When one grasps the content of such a proposition, one automatically knows it or is **justified** in believing it. Such **knowledge** is sometimes said to be based on **intuition**. Self-evident propositions include simple truths of **logic** or **arithmetic** and perhaps propositions about one's current sensory states. *See also* A PRIORI/A POSTERIORI KNOWLEDGE; ANALYTICITY; BASIC BELIEF; EPISTEMIC JUSTIFICATION; GIVEN, THE; SENSE PERCEPTION.

SELF-PRESENTING. A property said to be possessed by at least some mental states such that they are **immediately** present to one's **consciousness**. One who is in a self-presenting mental state knows that he or she is in that state; self-presentingness is a source of **certainty**. *See also* EXPERIENCE; GIVEN, THE; INTROSPECTION.

SELLARS, WILFRID (1912–1989). American philosopher, son of Roy Wood Sellars; professor at the University of Pittsburgh. Particularly noteworthy is his critique of what he called the "Myth of the Given" ("Empiricism and the Philosophy of Mind" in his *Science, Perception and Reality*, 1963). This **argument** also attacks **sense data** and even the claim that **empirical knowledge** has any clear foundation. **Foundationalist** formulations of **empiricism** claim that our **beliefs** about the **external world** are **justified** because they are supported by our **perceptions**, and perception does not involve cognition or the application of **concepts**. **Sense experience** is thus taken to be a form of **knowledge** that can provide a basis for other inferential knowledge. Sellars challenges this approach, arguing that sensory **experience** involves cognition and the application of **concepts** and that such experiences do not qualify as basic knowledge. Instead, the nature of one's sensory experience and the **context** in which it takes place jointly provide one with **evidence** that it is veridical. Sellars's account of knowledge and **epistemic justification** is **holistic**: Beliefs and patterns of **inference** are warranted by their role within a systematic epistemic structure. He describes the dynamics of **rational acceptance** and change within such systems and explains how the commonsense network of beliefs (which he calls the "manifest image") contains tensions and **errors** that are eventually eliminated by **science** (resulting in what he calls the "scientific image"). *See also* BASIC BELIEF; COHERENTISM; EPISTEMIC WARRANT; GIVEN, THE; INFERENTIAL BELIEF; SENSE PERCEPTION; WEB OF BELIEF.

SENSATION. A type of mental state, typically thought to be non-propositional, in which **qualia** are presented to **consciousness**; it is a mental state with a felt or phenomenal quality. Some theorists claim that sensation is the awareness of **sense data**, but critics argue that these entities are metaphysically puzzling and unnecessary. There is ongoing debate about the role of cognition in sensation and about sensation's role as an epistemic foundation for **empirical** beliefs. *See also* ACT/OBJECT ANALYSIS; BASIC BELIEF; EXPERIENCE; FOUNDATIONALISM; GIVEN, THE; INTROSPECTION; QUALIA.

SENSATIONALISM. The view that **sensation** is the source of all content in other mental states. It is often linked with forms of **foundationalism** that regard sensations as **basic beliefs** that provide the **evidential** support for all other **beliefs**. **Thomas Hobbes**, for instance, claims that there is nothing in the mind that is not first in the senses. *See also* ACT/OBJECT ANALYSIS; CONSCIOUSNESS; EMPIRICISM; EXPERIENCE; GIVEN, THE; QUALIA.

SENSE DATA. The objects of **immediate** perceptual awareness; mental entities of whose qualities one can be **certain**. Sense data were first discussed by **Bertrand Russell** (*Our Knowledge of the External World*, 1914) and **G. E. Moore** ("Sense Data" in his *Some Main Problems of Philosophy*, 1953). When one observes a partly submerged stick, for instance, the stick appears to bend at the water line, but we recognize that the stick itself is not bent. If one perceives something bent but the object in the **external world** is not bent, then the bent object of one's awareness must be in the mind. This, it is proposed, is the sense datum.

Sense data are sometimes employed in **foundationalist theories** of **knowledge**: One can be certain that sense data are as they appear, and **beliefs** about sense data are **basic beliefs** from which beliefs about external objects derive their **epistemic justification**. The connection between these two sets of beliefs has, however, been difficult to establish.

Critics have raised challenges about how sense data are to be individuated, how long they last, what properties they have, what their metaphysical status is, and their relationships with external objects. *See also* ACT/OBJECT ANALYSIS; APPEARANCE/REALITY; FOUNDATIONALISM; GIVEN, THE; REPRESENTATIVE REALISM; SENSE PERCEPTION.

SENSE PERCEPTION. Gathering information about oneself and one's environment by means of one's sensory systems. The external senses (vision, touch, smell, taste, and hearing) have been the subject of most philosophical investigations, with vision receiving the lion's share of the attention, but the internal senses (**proprioception**) are also significant. **Perception** acquaints one with both objects (e.g., the table) and **facts** (e.g., that the table is near the door). **Direct realism** is the view that objects are perceived directly, and **representative realism** is the view that objects are perceived indirectly via mental representations. A distinction is drawn between perceiving an object (sometimes referred to as nonepistemic perception) and perceiving *that* it has a particular quality or falls under a particular **concept** (epistemic perception).

Most **theories** of sense perception are **causal**: In order for one to perceive an object, it must cause (directly or indirectly) some change in one's sensory surfaces. If true, then one cannot perceive future states of affairs or causally inert entities (such as pure sets). **Kurt Gödel** and others report perceiving numbers and other entities thought to be abstract, and this may be taken as **evidence** against the causal theories of perception.

The **act/object analysis** of perception separates the act of perceiving and the object being perceived. This raises several epistemic questions: If one is directly aware of an external material object, how can we account for perceptual **error**? If one is directly aware of **impressions** or **sense data**, how are we to explain what these objects are and the role they play in perceiving the **external world**? Although the act/object approach is widespread, it is challenged by the **adverbial theory of perception**, which examines the different ways in which one can perceive and **analyze** these in terms of adverbs. Instead of saying that Jill perceives a red circle, the adverbial theory would say that Jill perceives red-circlely. This avoids awkward questions about the nature of the objects of perception but has difficulty analyzing perceptions involving many properties.

The veridicality of sense perception has been the subject of much consideration by epistemologists; how can we bridge the gap between **appearance** and **reality**? Ongoing **empirical** research reveals that "top-down" factors (e.g., **beliefs** and expectations) can significantly influence the phenomenal character of at least some of one's sensory **experiences**. In many circumstances, this top-down influence helps to speed processing and deal with perceptual **ambiguity**. It can also, however, be a source of error. **Illusions** and hallucinations teach us that our sensory systems sometimes err, and skeptics have exploited this to raise the worry that sense perception might be often or always in error. The difficulty of ruling out such **skeptical alternatives** has led some (e.g., **George Berkeley**) to explore **idealism**, **phenomenalism**, and other positions that reduce the possibilities for perceptual error. *See also* CONSCIOUSNESS; EXPERIENCE; GIVEN, THE; PERCEPTUAL RELATIVITY; THEORY OF APPEARING.

SENSIBILIA. (Singular: Sensible.) As used by **Bertrand Russell** (*Our Knowledge of the External World*, 1914), a sensible is an entity of the sort a perceiver can be aware of but that is not (at the moment) being perceived by anyone. Russell argues that in **sense perception** one is directly aware of **sense data**, so sensibilia would be unsensed sense data. This is problematic: Sense-data theorists generally claim that sense data exist only when they are being perceived. (As **George Berkeley** puts it, their *esse est percipii*.) For **direct realism**, sensibilia would simply be external objects that are not presently being observed.

SENSORIUM. In the psychological **theories** of the seventeenth and eighteenth centuries, that faculty of the mind that enables one to have **perceptions**. Some theorists also credited this faculty with the capacity (when excited) to cause muscular contractions and activity. *See also* SENSE PERCEPTION.

SENSUS COMMUNIS. In **Aristotle**'s *On the Soul* (II.1–2), this is described as the cognitive faculty to which the various sensory systems report. This faculty is said to account for common sensibles, qualities that can be sensed by means of two or more sense modalities (e.g., size). The *sensus communis* is also said to monitor the senses to determine whether they are functioning properly and to make one aware that one is alive (*De anima* II, 13.370). The action of this faculty prepares **experience** for the action of the mind's cognitive faculties.

SEXTUS EMPIRICUS (ca. A.D. 200). Greek philosopher and physician, a skeptic of the Pyrrhonist school. His *Outlines of Pyrrhonism* (in three books) and *Against the Mathematicians* (in eleven books) present his **Pyrrhonian skepticism**. (The latter work includes the former.) He distinguishes between **skepticism** as a **theory** or philosophy and skepticism as a way of life. Theoretical skepticism employs the theoretical **arguments** of other philosophers in order to undermine and destroy them; indeed, theoretical skepticism even does away with itself. In examining the arguments offered in support of any position, the Pyrrhonian skeptic claims to find equally compelling arguments against it. The proper response to the resulting *isostheneia* (the state of being confronted with equally compelling arguments for contradictory positions) is to suspend **judgment** and adopt neither position. Skepticism as a practical way of life is intended to help one avoid the **errors** of **dogmatic** philosophers and allows one to attain ***ataraxia*** (tranquility, freedom from anxiety). One may act on the basis of how things appear, but one makes no judgment about whether those **appearances** are veridical. *See also* PYRRHO OF ELIS.

SHENG. Chinese term meaning "sage." *Sheng* is the ultimate stage of human perfection or enlightenment. In Confucianism, *sheng* involves attaining complete ethical **knowledge**. *See also* CONFUCIUS; MORAL EPISTEMOLOGY.

SKEPTICAL ALTERNATIVES. Descriptions of situations that are **consistent** with one's **evidence** but incompatible with the **truth** of the **belief** one has based on that evidence. For instance, the claim that one is merely a **brain in a vat** all of whose **experiences** are being caused by a computer is a skeptical alternative for beliefs based on **sense perception**. **René Descartes's** methodological **doubt** is intended to isolate any beliefs that are free of skeptical alternatives (and thus **indubitable**); these are said to qualify as **knowledge**. Some skeptics argue that in order for a belief to qualify as **knowledge** (or for it to be **epistemically justified**), the subject must be in possession of evidence that rules out all skeptical alternatives; because this is rarely possible, we have little or no knowledge. *See also* RELEVANT ALTERNATIVES; SKEPTICISM.

SKEPTICISM. The view that some specified body of **beliefs** does not qualify as **knowledge** or is not **justified**. Global skepticism is the view that no beliefs qualify as knowledge (or are justified), but most forms of skepticism are local: They make this claim only about some proper subset of beliefs. Thus, one might be a skeptic about our beliefs about history, **God**, **causation**, the **external world**, and so forth. Some philosophers take the central task of **epistemology** to be responding to skeptical challenges.

One distinction among forms of skepticism has to do with whether the skeptic proposes an epistemic criterion. *Critical* skeptics do not. Instead, they challenge one to defend one's claims to knowledge (or justified belief) and then attack that defense. This might take the form of insisting that each claim one makes in that defense also be defended. This is employed in the **epistemic regress argument**, and

foundationalism attempts to find an epistemically suitable end point. *Substantive* skepticism specifies some criterion for knowledge or justification and then argues that some or all of our beliefs fail to meet this requirement. For instance, a substantive skeptic might claim that to qualify as knowledge, the **evidence** supporting that belief must rule out all **skeptical alternatives**, and few (if any) of our beliefs meet this condition.

Cartesian skepticism takes its name from the first of **René Descartes**'s *Meditations on First Philosophy* (1641), in which he employs the Method of Doubt to set up the skeptical challenge he addresses in the remainder of that work. (Descartes himself is not a skeptic.) This form of substantive skepticism states that a belief qualifies as knowledge only if it is **indubitable** and that only one's belief that one's own mind exists ("*cogito ergo sum*") meets that requirement. From this has arisen the very widespread skeptical strategy of proposing **skeptical alternatives** for any belief ordinarily accepted as knowledge (or as a justified belief). This involves describing a situation consistent with one's **experience** and other evidence but in which the belief being assessed is false (e.g., a "**brain in a vat**" scenario). Critics claim that Cartesian skepticism sets too high a standard for knowledge; perhaps one need rule out only **relevant alternatives**.

Cartesian skepticism can also be formulated thus: Anyone who knows that *p* and recognizes that *p* entails *q* must also know that *q*. Because each **proposition** *p* entails the negation of each skeptical alternative to that proposition, in order to know that *p*, one would also have to know that each skeptical alternative is false. The Cartesian skeptic points out that one cannot reasonably be said to know the latter, so (by *modus tollens*) one cannot be said to know the former. In "Epistemic Operators" (1970), **Fred Dretske** argues that this principle at the heart of this argument is false.

Pyrrhonian skepticism is named for **Pyrrho of Elis**, a skeptic of antiquity, and included **Sextus Empiricus**; it is the form of substantive skepticism most closely related to critical skepticism. The Pyrrhonian skeptic says that a belief qualifies as knowledge only if the person who holds that belief can adequately defend it. An adequate defense would require responding satisfactorily to the regress of skeptical questions employed by the critical skeptic. Instead of finding an adequate defense, the Pyrrhonian skeptic says that the arguments in support of a knowledge claim are evenly balanced with those against it. The reasonable response, it is claimed, is to withhold **judgment**. Critics point out that this form of skepticism seems to rely on confusing the state of being justified in holding a belief with the activity of justifying it; it neglects the **fact** that one might be in the state without engaging in the activity.

Humean skepticism, another form of local, substantive skepticism, begins with the distinction between matters of fact and relations of **ideas**, the two types of subjects of thought. **David Hume**, for whom this type of skepticism is named, grants that one can have knowledge of relations of ideas, for these relations hold **necessarily** and can be ascertained without depending on anything outside the mind. One cannot, however, have knowledge of matters of fact. These are **contingent** and thus require dependence on our senses. Any beliefs regarding matters of fact that go beyond one's current sensory experience (by positing the existence of material objects, for instance) **presuppose** various relations of **cause** and effect. The problem is that sense experience can never provide adequate evidence for the **truth** of such causal claims.

The responses to skepticism are numerous and diverse. Descartes employs a mathematical model; beginning with unquestionable premises and proceeding by means of unassailable **deductive** steps, he sought to establish a firm foundation for our knowledge claims. **George Berkeley** avoided skeptical challenges employing the gap between **appearance** and **reality** by eliminating any appeal to a mind-independent external world and claiming that appearance *is* reality. **Thomas Reid**, **G. E. Moore**, and others have taken a "commonsense" approach, with the former arguing for **reliable** faculties of the mind that provide a firm foundation for our beliefs and the latter arguing that we are more certain of the falsehood of the skeptic's arguments than we are of any of the truth of any premises in those arguments. **Immanuel Kant** acknowledges that we are unable to have knowledge of things in themselves but argues that we can know about all actual and possible experiences. **Ludwig Wittgenstein** argues that skepticism is founded on a misconception of language and that most skeptical worries cannot coherently be raised. **Hilary Putnam**'s response is somewhat similar: He argues that because of the nature of language and mental content, if our beliefs were mostly false, we would be unable coherently to state the skeptical alternatives. **Donald Davidson**, taking a related position, argues that the contents of beliefs are determined by the causes of those beliefs. Therefore, one would be unable to have beliefs about material objects unless those beliefs had been caused by those objects. A brain in a vat might have beliefs about the computer causing its experiences but would be unable to share our beliefs about external objects. *See also* EPISTEMIC LEVELS; EXTERNALISM/INTERNALISM; INDUBITABILITY; PROBLEM OF THE CRITERION; TRANSCENDENTAL ARGUMENTS.

SOCIAL EPISTEMOLOGY. The branch of **epistemology** that studies the social dimension of **knowledge** and **belief** and the ways in which education, religion, social institutions, and other social factors promote or hinder the growth of knowledge. This includes the study of scientific practices, standards of **evidence**, the role of **authority** figures and power structures, and the designation of expert status. A society's epistemic division of labor is examined, as are consensus and collective knowledge. This is a normative study, to be distinguished from the descriptive work done in **sociology of knowledge**. **Thomas Kuhn**'s description of the social nature of **science** is a component of social epistemology, as are the feminist critiques of traditional epistemology. *See also* COLLECTIVE BELIEF; CONTINENTAL EPISTEMOLOGY; FEMINIST EPISTEMOLOGY; FOUCAULT, MICHEL; SCIENCE; SCIENTIFIC METHOD; TESTIMONY.

SOCIOLOGY OF KNOWLEDGE. The naturalistic, descriptive study of **knowledge** and related social structures within a society and across societies. The role of social conventions and institutions is studied, with particular emphasis on scientific endeavors. Sociologists of knowledge seek to describe the **beliefs** and knowledge claims of a society and then explore the relevance to them of various social factors. This includes examining how consensus is achieved, how the society's beliefs are passed on to new members, how beliefs are challenged and defended, and how conventional knowledge and common sense are established and defined. *See also* COLLECTIVE BELIEF; CONTINENTAL EPISTEMOLOGY; FEMINIST EPISTEMOLOGY; FOUCAULT, MICHEL.

SOCRATES (469–399 B.C.). Greek philosopher; he wrote nothing and is known largely through the writings of his student **Plato**. Socrates developed a method of **argument** known as **elenchus** ("putting to the test"). Once someone had claimed to know something, Socrates would question that individual to draw out a contradiction inherent in the position being defended. This leads to a more refined position that then becomes the new subject of examination. Plato depicts this process as leading eventually to (recollected) **knowledge** of the **Forms**. *See also* ANAMNESIS; DIALECTIC.

SOLIPSISM. A set of related views that focus on the first-person perspective. Metaphysical solipsism is the view that only oneself exists; there is no material **external world** or other minds. Methodological solipsism is the view that the content of one's mental states and the reasons for one's behavior should be explained solely in terms of one's first-person perspective, considering only the contents of the mind and not the external environment. **Epistemological** solipsism is the view that one can be certain only that oneself exists; others may exist, but one lacks sufficient **evidence** to support such a claim. **Bertrand Russell** defines (but does not endorse) a variant of epistemological solipsism he calls solipsism of the present moment (*Human Knowledge*, 1948). This is the view that only one's existence at the present moment is certain; there is no strong evidence of one's past or future existence. Epistemological solipsism is generally regarded as an undesirable (but perhaps inescapable) consequence of the failure to **justify** our common **inferential** practices. *See also* EGOCENTRIC PREDICAMENT; MENTALISM; OTHER MINDS, PROBLEM OF; SKEPTICISM; UNIFORMITY OF NATURE.

SPECIFIC RESPONSE THEORY. An attempt, developed by **Ralph Barton Perry**, to construe **belief** and **sense perception** in terms of the subject's behavior and bodily adjustments. *See also* BEHAVIORISM, ANALYTICAL; BEHAVIORISM, METHODOLOGICAL.

SPECKLED HEN PROBLEM. An objection to **A. J. Ayer**'s **sense-data analysis** of **perception**, formulated by **Gilbert Ryle**. Ryle notes that when one sees a speckled hen, the sense-data **theory** implies that one is aware of a speckled sense datum. Ayer's theory states that one is immediately aware of the properties of sense data, but Ryle argues that one is not immediately aware of the number of speckles one has seen. Either the sense datum is vague in the sense that it has speckles but lacks a determinate number of speckles, or it has properties of which one is not immediately aware. Neither horn of this dilemma is tenable for a defender of sense data. *See also* IMPRESSION; SENSE PERCEPTION; VAGUENESS.

SPENCER, HERBERT (1820–1903). English philosopher, economist, and social reformer. He endorses **positivism**, the view that the only genuine **empirical knowledge** to be found is generated by **science**.

SPINOZA, BARUCH (BENEDICT DE) (1632–1677). Dutch philosopher, psychologist, and political theorist; a central figure in seventeenth-century **rationalism**. From age twenty-two, he used "Benedict" instead of his given name, "Baruch." His **epistemology** is presented primarily in his unfinished *Treatise on the Emendation of the Intellect* (published posthumously in the *Opera postuma*, 1677). Like other rationalists, Spinoza distinguishes the **imagination** from the intellect (the two representative faculties of the mind). Using input from the senses, the imagination forms images that represent objects. The intellect forms representations that are not in the form of images.

Spinoza distinguishes three different types or levels of **knowledge**. Opinion or imagination is the lowest form; it includes hearsay and indeterminate **experience**. Reason is a higher form of knowledge and is based on an adequate understanding of the properties (although not the essences) of objects. **Intuitive** knowledge is the highest form and the only one that provides **certainty**. It begins with an understanding of **God**'s essence and uses this as a basis for drawing conclusions about the essences of things. This basis also allows one to examine **causes** and draw conclusions about their effects.

Spinoza argues that an **idea**'s **truth** can be determined directly by examining it; there is no need for other signs or criteria (such as **René Descartes**'s clearness and distinctness criterion). **Doubt** and **error** can be avoided by eliminating any obscurity in one's ideas or in the relationships among them. This is accomplished by reasoning in the appropriate order, moving from causes to effects.

In Spinoza's metaphysics, God is the only substance in existence. What we regard as separate objects are actually modes of that one universal substance. Each thing's nature or essence is its structure or pattern, and the means by which it tends to maintain its existence. Each human mind is also a mode of God, the one thinking substance. *See also* CLEAR AND DISTINCT IDEA; IMPRESSION; RATIONALISM; REPRESENTATIVE REALISM; SENSE PERCEPTION.

SPIR, AFRIKAN (1837–1890). German nonacademic philosopher who influenced **Friedrich Nietzsche**. His *Forschung nach der Gewissheit in der Erkenntnis der Wirklichkeit* (*Inquiry Concerning Certainty in the Knowledge of Actuality*, 1869) distinguishes between things as they are and reality as we **experience** it. All we can know of the former is that they must conform to the principle of identity. The only other thing of which one can be certain is the existence of time. *See also* APPEARANCE/REALITY; OBJECTIVE/SUBJECTIVE; SKEPTICISM.

STOIC EPISTEMOLOGY. Founded in Athens in the fourth century B.C. by **Zeno of Citium**, Stoicism was an influential school of thought. The Stoics' concern with **epistemology** was included in their study of **logic**, which for them was a broad examination of speech and reasoning. The mind begins as a *tabula rasa*, a blank slate; all content comes through **experience**. **Sense perception** supplies one with **impressions** about whose nature one can be **certain**. These have **propositional** content and form the foundation for all of one's **knowledge**. Knowledge is firm **belief** that one can **rationally** maintain despite contrary **arguments**. The key to avoiding **error** is to rely only on cognitive impressions. These result from perceptual contact with the world, correctly represent it, and could not arise from what is not. The human mind is naturally inclined toward such impressions, but our corrupted condition sometimes leads us to believe false sense impressions or reason fallaciously. Skeptical arguments are raised by competing schools of thought that point out that there is nothing in the content of a sense impression that could be a **reliable** indicator of **truth** and thus that the foundation described by the Stoics could not save one from error. *See also* FOUNDATIONALISM; INFORMAL FALLACIES; SKEPTICISM.

STRAWSON, PETER FREDERICK (1919–). English analytic philosopher, professor at Oxford University. He was knighted in 1977 and is the father of philosopher Galen Strawson. He has argued against both **skepticism** and the view that **beliefs** can be **justified** only by appeal to allegedly privileged (i.e., **infallible**) foundations. His *Introduction to Logical Theory* (1952) defends **induction** against skeptical challenges, saying that our inductive practices do not require **epistemic justification**; our fundamental objective categories are necessary even to describe our **experiences** and thus cannot be rejected. His *Individuals* (1959) and *The Bounds of Sense* (1966) use **transcendental arguments** against skepticism, arguing that stating and defending skepticism requires accepting that which the skeptic claims to **doubt**. *Scepticism and Naturalism* (1985) draws on work by **David Hume** and **Ludwig Wittgenstein** to contend that **arguments** for skepticism can be rejected because we are incapable of accepting their conclusion; we cannot be persuaded by them. *See also* INDUCTION.

STROUD, BARRY (1935–). American philosopher who was trained at Harvard University; he teaches at the University of California at Berkeley. He is a fellow of the American Academy of Arts and Sciences. His work in **epistemology** includes an award-winning examination of **David Hume** (*Hume*, 1977), a detailed study of **skepticism** (*The Significance of Philosophical Scepticism*, 1985), and work on the **externalism/internalism** debate. Other notable works include *Meaning Understanding, and Practice: Philosophical Essays* (2000) and *Understanding Human Knowledge: Philosophical Essays* (2000).

SUÁREZ, FRANCISCO (1548–1617). Also known as Doctor Eximius; Spanish philosopher and theologian. His *Disputationes metaphysicae* (*Metaphysical Disputations*, 1597) explains that metaphysics is the study of the **objective concept** of being, the object as conceived in the mind (rather than the thing itself). Reflection is not involved in one's **knowledge** of individual entities; instead, each substance, property, and accident is known by means of a proper and separate concept. This challenges the view common at that time that individuals are known only by means of universals. Suárez also describes **middle knowledge** (*scientia media*), which is **God**'s knowledge of what an individual with free will will do in any given situation. *See also* ACT/OBJECT ANALYSIS; DIVINE FOREKNOWLEDGE; GIVEN, THE; INTROSPECTION.

SUBSTANTIVE SKEPTICISM. *See* SKEPTICISM.

SYNESTHESIA. A rare mixing or joining of the senses so that properties ordinarily associated with one sensory system are experienced by another. For instance, someone with synesthesia may smell colors or see music. *See also* EXPERIENCE; PRIMARY AND SECONDARY QUALITIES; SENSE PERCEPTION.

– T –

TABULA RASA. Meaning "blank tablet," this phrase is often used in presenting the view that all mental contents are acquired through **experience**. **John Locke** famously presented this view in this way in his *An Essay Concerning Human Understanding* (1690). This is an important component in **empiricism**. *See also A PRIORI/A POSTERIORI* KNOWLEDGE; INNATE IDEA; STOIC EPISTEMOLOGY.

TARSKI, ALFRED (1901–1983). Polish-born mathematician and logician, most of whose work was done at the University of California at Berkeley. He is most noted for his analysis of **truth** in formal languages and his defense of the **correspondence theory of truth**. Tarskian biconditionals are sentences such as "The sentence 'There are cups on the table' is true if and only if there are cups on the table." When one has formulated a Tarskian biconditional for every sentence in a formal language, Tarski claims, one has given an account of truth for that language.

TAUTOLOGY. A logical **truth**, a statement that is true in all possible situations (or in all **possible worlds**) and whose negation is contradictory. Tautologies are those statements that are logically implied by their own negation. It is generally held that such statements can be known by reasoning alone and are often used as **examples** of *a priori* **knowledge**. *See also* CERTAINTY; IMPLICATION; INDUBITABILITY; LOGIC.

TEICHMÜLLER, GUSTAV (1832–1888). German philosopher; he taught at Göttingen and Basel. He developed perspectivism, the view that the most fundamental **reality** is the self of first-person **experience** and that the conceptual world is constituted and projected by this self. *See also* EXTERNAL WORLD; EXTERNALISM/INTERNALISM; SOLIPSISM.

TESTABILITY. A scientific **theory**'s capacity to be tested experimentally. A testable theory is one that generates a **hypothesis** that, when conjoined with a statement of initial conditions, generates a **prediction** about the **observable** outcome of an experimental situation. When such predictions are true, the theory is often said to be confirmed or made more probable. **Karl Popper** argues that testability lies only in the capacity of experiments to falsify a theory and that true predictions do not provide positive **evidence** of a theory's **truth**. *See also* CONFIRMATION; CRUCIAL EXPERIMENT; HYPOTHETICO-DEDUCTIVE METHOD; LOGICAL POSITIVISM; PROBABILITY.

TESTIMONY. Information or **evidence** gained through the statements and actions of others; a major contributor to **knowledge** and **justified true belief**. Although testimony plays a central role in our lives, epistemological **theories** have given it surprisingly little attention. Like **perception** and **memory**, testimony is **fallible** yet widely relied on. One generally gives preference to the testimony of some individuals over that of others, and this preference is often based on past **experience** or **authority**. **David Hume** argues that although there is no **causal** connection between someone's testimony that *p* and its being true that *p*, "we are accustomed to find a conformity between them," and thus our reliance on testimony is no more irrational than any of our other **doxastic** habits (*An Enquiry Concerning Human Understanding*, 1690/1975). **Thomas Reid** argues that **God** has designed human nature in such a way that we all naturally tend to tell the **truth** and to believe what others tell us (*An Enquiry into the Human Mind*, 1764).

Of the standard epistemic theories, **foundationalism** faces serious difficulties in explaining how **beliefs** based on testimony can be highly justified or qualify as knowledge. There is a paucity of connections between **basic beliefs** (e.g., about truths of **logic** or current sensory states) and testimony-based beliefs. **Reliabilism** has difficulty identifying the **belief-forming process** involved and showing how the epistemic status of one's beliefs changes when one listens to the testimony of trusted friends as opposed to politicians. **Coherentism** has the least difficulty accounting for the epistemic role of testimony (although it faces the usual challenges in connecting epistemic success with truth). *See also* SOCIAL EPISTEMOLOGY.

THEORETICAL ENTITY. An entity whose existence is posited by a **theory** to explain some **observable** phenomenon but that cannot be observed directly (e.g., subatomic particles). **Ernst Mach**, some **logical positivists**, and others claim that statements about such entities are useful tools for organizing **experiences** but are not actually meaningful; this is known as the **instrumentalist** approach. **Rudolf Carnap** ("Empiricism, Semantics, and Ontology," 1956) claims that "internal" questions about the nature and existence of theoretical entities are those raised within a context in which the theoretical framework is taken for granted; internal questions are answered by consulting the theories in question. Raising those questions outside the context of the theory makes them "external," and then the question of the existence of theoretical entities cannot meaningfully be raised; the issue, then, is whether the theory is useful in predicting, controlling, and explaining the relevant phenomena.

The most compelling **example** of **knowledge** about theoretical entities arises from attempts to calculate Avogadro's number (the number of molecules in a mole of any substance; approximately 6.02×10^{23}). Experimental methods approaching this question from different aspects all yield very similar results. This is widely viewed as compelling **evidence** that the entities being counted actually exist. *See also* ABSTRACT ENTITY; CONTEXTUALISM; INTERNALISM/EXTERNALISM; PREDICTION.

THEORY. A conceptual model of a body of phenomena; a set of principles, rules, or generalizations regarding the existence, nature, or interaction of a specified set of entities, systems, or events. A theory can also be regarded as a semiformal **axiomatic** system. Theories tend to present an idealization of phenomena and circumstances that are not found in **reality** and that make the application of the theory difficult.

David Hume argues that our theories cannot be deduced from **observation**; many radically different theories could account for one's **experiences**. Theoretical simplicity (as reflected in Ockham's razor), ease of **explanation**, and predictive power all play roles that have yet to be fully clarified. In such situations, it is not clear whether there is any **rational** means of choosing one theory over another or whether any particular one can be said to be the *true* theory.

The role of theory in **science** is disputed. Although it has been traditionally held that scientists accept one or more theories, **Thomas Kuhn, Imre Lakatos**, and others argue that what scientists accept are not theories but rather a set of procedures and assumptions. This disagreement generates corresponding disputes about the role of theories and theory change in scientific progress. *See also* ABSTRACT ENTITY; CONFIRMATION; FEYERABEND, PAUL; KUHN, THOMAS; OCKHAM, WILLIAM OF; POPPER, KARL; QUINE, W. V. O.; SCIENCE; SCIENTIFIC METHOD; THEORETICAL ENTITY; UNDERDETERMINATION OF THEORY.

THEORY LADEN. A statement or **perception** is theory laden when it makes reference to entities, forces, processes, or other theoretical **concept**s. **Rudolf Carnap** distinguishes between theoretical and **observational** terms, but **Paul Feyerabend** and others challenge this, arguing that all perceptions are theory laden. The theory ladenness of perception undermines **sense perception**'s capacity to provide **objective** information about the **external world**. *See also* OBJECTIVITY; THEORETICAL ENTITY.

THEORY OF APPEARING. The **theory** that perceiving an object consists in that object's appearing or presenting itself to one in a particular way and that these manners of appearance are unanalyzable. It is related to **direct realism** in that it holds that one is directly aware of external objects. The most common objection to it is that it has difficulty providing a plausible account of what appears to one in cases of **illusion** or hallucination. This theory has recently been revived by **William Alston**. *See also* APPEARANCE/REALITY; EXTERNAL WORLD; IMMEDIACY; SENSE PERCEPTION.

TRANSCENDENTAL ARGUMENT. An **argument**, generally deductive, regarding the conditions for the possibility of a phenomenon (e.g., **consciousness** or **rationality**) whose existence is not challenged (at least in the context in which the argument is presented). **Immanuel Kant** uses several such arguments in his *Critique of Pure Reason* (1781), concluding, for example, that the **concepts** ("categories") of cause and substance are required for any possible **experience**. This was intended to show the *a priori* nature of these concepts in response to **David Hume**'s **skepticism**.

Subsequent transcendental arguments have also been used largely as responses to skepticism. **Ludwig Wittgenstein** employs such arguments in his *Philosophical Investigations* (1953) and *On Certainty* (1969), using them to draw conclusions about the impossibility of a private language and the falsehood of global skepticism. **P. F. Strawson** responded to skepticism about other minds by arguing that one's capacity to apply mental terms to oneself is possible only if one can successfully ascribe them to others; this is a transcendental argument (*Individuals*, 1959).

Critics argue that although transcendental arguments may demonstrate that we possess various concepts, they fall short of showing that anything in the **external world** corresponds to or falls under those concepts. Therefore, the value of such arguments against skepticism is much more limited than their popularity would suggest. *See also A PRIORI/A POSTERIORI* KNOWLEDGE; CONTEXTUALISM; DEDUCTION; INNATE IDEA; OTHER MINDS, PROBLEM OF; PRIVATE LANGUAGE ARGUMENT.

TRANSCENDENTAL REDUCTION. *See* EPOCHÉ; HUSSERL, EDMUND.

TRIPARTITE THEORY OF KNOWLEDGE. *See* JTB THEORY OF KNOWLEDGE.

TRUTH. The property of **propositions** or statements that correspond to or accurately present what is the case; a central epistemic desideratum. Truth is deceptively simple, and there is ongoing debate about how best to understand it.

The *correspondence* theory of truth, which can be found in the work of **Aristotle**, says that a proposition is true if it corresponds with a **fact** or aspect of the world. This **theory** has difficulty clarifying the nature of facts and the manner in which propositions can correspond to them.

The *verificationist* theory of truth says that true propositions are those that can be proven or verified. This faces the criticism that although verification provides a good **reason for believing** a proposition, it does not seem to be **equivalent** to that proposition's truth.

The *coherence* theory of truth states that a proposition is true if and only if it stands in sufficiently strong coherence relations with other propositions so that all the propositions in the system are strongly linked in the various ways that contribute to coherence. Although there is some **vagueness** and disagreement about the nature of coherence, in general propositions are said to form a coherent system if they are **logically** and probabilistically **consistent** and stand in **explanatory** relations to one another and the propositions can be derived from or inferred from others in the set. Because the coherence of a set of propositions is a matter of degree, some argue that truth is a matter of degree also. The coherence theory of truth is often held in conjunction with the **coherentism** theory of **epistemic justification** or **knowledge**.

William James (*The Meaning of Truth*, 1909) and others developed the *pragmatic* theory of truth, according to which true propositions or beliefs are those that lead to desirable results when acted on. Critics argue that true beliefs may well have undesirable consequences and false ones desirable consequences. *See also* INFERENCE; TARSKI, ALFRED; VERIFICATIONISM.

TRUTHS OF REASON/TRUTHS OF FACT. In the work of **Gottfried Leibniz**, **truths** of reason are those that can be reduced to identity statements by means of the substitution of **equivalent** terms. The negation of a truth of reason is contradictory. When in their simplest, most explicit form, truths of reason are **self-evidently** true and can be known *a priori*. Truths of **fact** are statements that cannot be reduced to identity statements and can be known only *a posteriori*. *See also* A PRIORI/A POSTERIORI KNOWLEDGE; ANALYTICITY.

– U –

UNDERDETERMINATION OF THEORY. When two or more **theories** are compatible with the available **evidence**, that evidence is said to underdetermine theory choice. **W. V. O. Quine** (*Pursuit of Truth*, 1990) argues that such situations present **empiricism** with a dilemma: It must either find an empirical basis for preferring one of these competing theories or deny that they are in competition.

UNEXPECTED EXAMINATION PARADOX. A **paradox** about **prediction**. A teacher announces that there will be a surprise examination sometime the following week. If the exam is not given by Friday morning, the students will know that it must be that day, and the exam will not be a surprise. Therefore, if the exam is a surprise, it must be given Monday through Thursday. However, if it is not given by Thursday morning, the students will know it must be that day (because Friday has already been ruled out), and it will not be a surprise. Therefore, if the exam is a surprise, it must be given Monday through Wednesday. This pattern of reasoning is repeated to show that a surprise exam cannot be given on any day of the week. The paradox is that it is also true that the teacher can give the students a surprise exam that week.

UNGER, PETER (1942–). American philosopher who was educated at Oxford University; he is a professor at New York University. He is noted for his *Ignorance: A Case for Scepticism* (1975; 2nd ed., 2002). In this, as well as in his *Philosophical Relativity* (2002), he argues that many philosophical questions are unanswerable. Our attempts to reach answers are said to rely on ultimately indefensible assumptions about the meanings of key terms.

UNIFORMITY OF NATURE. The idea that the future will resemble the past and that unobserved instances will resemble observed ones. This is generally held to be required if **induction** is to be **reliable**. **David Hume** points out that in using induction, we are assuming the uniformity of nature and that we have no **evidence** to support this assumption. *See also* PROBLEM OF INDUCTION.

– V –

VAGUENESS. Vagueness *de dicto* is the property of statements that allows for borderline cases and difficulty in classification. Often general terms (e.g., "heap," "bald") are the source of this vagueness. Such statements do not have clear **truth** values. Vagueness *de re* is indeterminacy in objects or states of affairs themselves rather than in statements about them. It may, for instance, be indeterminate whether a particular molecule is a part of an organism. Epistemic vagueness refers to states of affairs in which one has insufficient information or **evidence** to determine the truth of a statement or **belief**. Concerns about vagueness have led to the development of many-valued and epistemic **logics**, developments in semantic **theories**, and more.

VASUBANDHU (fourth–fifth century A.D.). Mahayana **Buddhist** Indian philosopher. His *Abhidharmakosá* (*Treasure Chamber of the* Abhidharma) and *Vimsatikā* (*Proof in Twenty Verses That Everything Is Only Conception*) defend his claim that the mind is only a stream of mental contents and that there is no mind-independent existence. *See also* BERKELEY, GEORGE; DHARMAKĪRTI; IDEALISM; INDIAN EPISTEMOLOGY.

VEDAS. Early Hindu texts presenting sacred **knowledge** about the nature of **reality** and ideals for human conduct. The teachings in these scriptures are said to be timeless and uncreated (even by **God**). *See also* RELIGIOUS KNOWLEDGE; REVELATION.

VERIFICATIONISM. The view that sentences are meaningful or intelligible only if they can be verified or **falsified** or that the meaning of a sentence consists in its method of verification. *See also* LOGICAL POSITIVISM; POPPER, KARL; PRINCIPLE OF VERIFIABILITY; TESTABILITY; TRUTH.

VERSTEHEN. German: "understanding" or "interpretation." This term is used in anthropology and other social sciences to describe a method of interpreting or reconstructing meanings from the agent's or subject's point of view. This focuses on the meaning that actions have for the actor and that utterances have for the speaker. *Verstehen* is contrasted with *Erklärung* (German: "**explanation**"), which examines causes as viewed from an externalist perspective. *See also* EXTERNALISM/INTERNALISM; OBJECTIVE/ SUBJECTIVE; SOLIPSISM; WITTGENSTEIN, LUDWIG.

VICO, GIAMBATTISTA (1668–1744). Italian philosopher and historian. His *La scienza nuova* (*The New Science*, 1725; 2nd ed., 1730; 3rd ed., 1744) examines the historical development of nations and marks an advance in the philosophy of history. Vico first endorsed but later rejected **René Descartes**'s **foundationalism** and replaced it with his own *verum factum* method, according to which we can know only what we have created. Nations, cultures, and their histories are human creations, so they are knowable. *See also* HISTORICAL KNOWLEDGE; HISTORICISM.

VIENNA CIRCLE. A group of philosophers and scientists who met in Vienna in the 1920s and 1930s and whose work spawned **logical positivism** and a new way of understanding **science**. Begun by mathematician Hans Hahn, physicist Philip Frank, and philosopher **Otto Neurath**, the Vienna Circle also included Moritz Schlick, **Rudolf Carnap**, Herbert Feigl, Gustav Bergmann, and **Kurt Gödel**. This group discussed **Ludwig Wittgenstein**'s *Tractatus Logico-Philosophicus* (1921), the nature of **science**, and **analytic** philosophy.

VIJÑĀNAVĀDA. An **idealist** school of **Buddhist** thought, originating in about the fourth century A.D. In its conflicts with the Mādhyamika and **realist** schools of Buddhism, members of the Vijñānavāda school seek to identify contradictions in their opponents' views, paying particular attention to such fundamental **concepts** as substance and **causation**. Further, they argue that **reality** is **consciousness** or mind and that mind is nothing more than a stream of mental contents. *See also* BUDDHAGOSA; IDEALISM; INDIAN EPISTEMOLOGY; NĀGĀRJUNA; VASUBANDHU.

VIJÑAPTI. Hindu term meaning "representation," used in Indian **Buddhism** in **arguments** about whether **reality** is nothing more than representations or mental states and whether there is any mind-independent reality. *See also* IDEALISM; INDIAN EPISTEMOLOGY; *PRATYAKṢA*; REPRESENTATIVE REALISM.

VIRTUE EPISTEMOLOGY. The view that **knowledge** or **epistemic justification** arises from the proper functioning of the subject's cognitive faculties in a suitable environment. Epistemic virtues are characteristics of an individual that are conducive to forming true **beliefs**, avoiding **error**, and identifying or grasping the **implications** of **evidence**. Impartiality, curiosity, sound reasoning, acute eyesight, care in making calculations, and so forth are among the epistemic virtues. When approached from a naturalistic or externalist standpoint, virtue **epistemology** closely resembles **reliabilism**: Both assess beliefs by examining the reliability or **truth** conductivity of the means by which they were formed. In addition, both reliabilism (when properly formulated) and virtue-based **theories** consider the environment or circumstances in which beliefs are formed. *See also* BELIEF-FORMING PROCESS; CONTEXTUALISM; EXTERNALISM/INTERNALISM; LOGIC.

VOLUNTARISM. Also called **doxastic** voluntarism, it is the view that what one believes or the degree to which one accepts a **belief** is under one's voluntary control. Some versions of voluntarism require only that there be limited or indirect voluntary control over beliefs. Recent results in empirical **psychology** have challenged the common view that voluntarism is true. *See also* EMPIRICISM; ETHICS OF BELIEF; NATURALIZED EPISTEMOLOGY.

– W –

WANG YANG-MING (1472–1529). Chinese philosopher. He argues that people have innate **knowledge** of what is morally good and that there is a unity of knowledge and action. *See also A PRIORI/A POSTERIORI* KNOWLEDGE; INNATE IDEA; MORAL EPISTEMOLOGY.

WARRANTED ASSERTABILITY. **John Dewey** and some other **pragmatists** propose replacing our talk of *true* statements with talk of which statements have warranted assertability. Dewey argues that **truth** is mutable and that the traditional quest for **certainty** is based on a misunderstanding of truth. **Hilary Putnam** argues that truth is idealized warranted assertability. *See also* EPISTEMIC WARRANT; PRAGMATISM.

WEB OF BELIEF. W. V. O. Quine argues in his "Two Dogmas of Empiricism" (1953) and elsewhere that none of one's **beliefs** are immune from revision or rejection, not even those traditionally regarded as **analytic**. Instead, one's beliefs form a web, and any belief in that web can be maintained in the face of apparently contrary **evidence** or **experience**, provided one is willing to make sufficiently large changes elsewhere in that web. *See also* COHERENTISM; CREDULITY; DUHEM, PIERRE; HOLISM; NEURATH, OTTO.

WHITEHEAD, ALFRED NORTH (1861–1947). British philosopher and mathematician; trained at Trinity College, Cambridge, and later taught there. He and **Bertrand Russell** wrote *Principia Mathematica* (3 vols., 1910–1913), which greatly advanced symbolic **logic**. Whitehead's *Process and Reality* (1929) reflects his view that many of the **epistemological** issues that have concerned philosophers from the time of **René Descartes** arise from metaphysical **errors**, particularly mind/body dualism. He argues that this should be rejected in favor of his monistic philosophy of organism, known as process philosophy.

WITTGENSTEIN, LUDWIG (1889–1951). Austrian-born philosopher; he went to England to study at Cambridge University, where he became a protégé of **Bertrand Russell**. His early work, which includes his *Tractatus Logico-Philosophicus* (1921), was an examination of the nature and use of language. Sentences, he argues, achieve meaning because of their logical structure, a logical "picture" of a factual state of affairs; this is sometimes called the "picture **theory** of meaning." Like **logical positivism**, this approach implies that sentences about theology, ethics, and many other "philosophical" statements are meaningless.

His later work, most of which was published posthumously and includes his *Philosophical Investigations* (1953), replaces his early view of language with one that focuses on actual linguistic practice. The words that denote **concepts**, he claims, do not mark out sharply etched meanings but instead indicate family resemblances. The meanings of words are rooted in public criteria for their proper application. His famous **private language argument** draws out from this the **implication** that there could not be a language that only one person speaks. Instead, language is likened to an essentially social game or practice. His *On Certainty* (1969) argues both against global **skepticism** and against **Cartesian** foundationalist **arguments** against the skeptics. Again, these arguments are based on his claim that philosophers on both sides of this issue have misunderstood the nature of language. *See also* CONTEXTUALISM; CONVENTION; FOUNDATIONALISM; GRAMMAR; LOGICAL CONSTRUCTION; OTHER MINDS, PROBLEM OF; SOCIOLOGY OF KNOWLEDGE.

– Z –

ZENO OF CITIUM (334–262 B.C.). Greek philosopher from Cyprus; founder of Stoicism. *See also* STOIC EPISTEMOLOGY.

ZENO OF ELEA (ca. 450 B.C.). Greek philosopher noted for his **paradoxes** regarding plurality and motion.

ZETETIC ATTITUDE. An attitude of questioning, of unremitting interrogation. **Maurice Merleau-Ponty** presented this as a model for philosophy. *See also* DIALECTIC; DOUBT; SKEPTICISM.

Bibliography

CONTENTS

I. INTRODUCTION

The epistemology literature is enormous and growing rapidly. This bibliography is an attempt to pick out works that are particularly noteworthy. Readers who are new to epistemology would do well to begin with a general textbook in this field. Richard Feldman's *Epistemology* and Richard Fumerton's volume by the same title are particularly valuable. The *Companion to Epistemology* (in the Blackwell Companions to Philosophy Series) is not a textbook but provides very good overviews of particular epistemological theories and issues.

There are many good translations of the writings of the ancient and medieval philosophers; in general, the epistemological writings are included with works on other topics. Excellent discussions of these writings are also available. The *Epistemology* volume, edited by Stephen Everson, includes many particularly good essays on epistemology in ancient philosophy; Tachau's *Vision and Certitude in the Age of Ockham* is a good overview of medieval epistemology. There are also a number of works devoted to the ancient origins of skepticism; these include Burnyeat's *The Sceptical Tradition* and Stough's *Greek Scepticism*.

Epistemological issues (and their role in metaphysical debates) became more clearly delineated in the writings of the seventeenth-century rationalists and eighteenth-century empiricists. In addition to the many excellent translations of primary sources, some secondary sources are emerging as classic interpretations. In the study of Spinoza, for instance, Jonathan Bennett and Edwin Curley are particularly influential. The same can be said of John Gibson's work on Locke, Cottingham's work on Descartes, Jolley's work on Leibniz, and Fogelin's work on Hume.

Immanuel Kant and the post-Kantian idealists constitute a large and notable influence on our epistemological thinking. Bennett's *Kant's Analytic* presents an interesting but controversial interpretation of Kant's thought; Paul Guyer's *Kant and the Claims of Knowledge* is a very scholarly work and is well regarded in the field. Those who are new to Kant's epistemology may wish to begin with Peter Strawson's *The Bounds of Sense*. Although this is not a particularly sympathetic reading of Kant, it is an excellent introduction to the issues and terminology of the field. A great deal of work being done in this area is written in German and French; only a small portion of this has been translated into English. This bibliography emphasizes that latter portion.

Readers interested in logical positivism and the Vienna Circle are encouraged to begin with A. J. Ayer's *Language, Truth and Logic* and Ludwig Wittgenstein's *On Certainty* and *Tractatus Logico-Philosophicus*. Morawetz's commentary *Wittgenstein and Knowledge: The Importance of* On Certainty is an invaluable companion to these works.

The study of epistemology as it is found in the American pragmatists should begin with Thayer's collection *Pragmatism: The Classic Writings*. George Dicker's *Dewey's Theory of Knowing* and Scheffler's *Four Pragmatists* are notable commentaries in this area. Richard Rorty's *The Consequences of Pragmatism* presents an interesting but disputed approach to this body of thought.

Much of the work being done in Continental epistemology—and it is voluminous—is written in languages other than English; again, this bibliography emphasizes the English works but includes some particularly notable works in French. Foucault's *Power/Knowledge: Selected Interviews and Other Writings* provides a fairly accessible introduction to his thought. Richard Rorty's *Philosophy and the Mirror of Nature* and *The View from Nowhere* are interesting critiques of traditional analytic philosophy and have generated a great deal of controversy (and self-examination).

As one would expect, work in Indian epistemology is generally written in languages other than English; once again, this bibliography highlights those works accessible to an English-speaking audience. Datta's *Six Ways of Knowing* is valuable as an introduction to the issues and theories in this area.

Much of the scholarly work in epistemology addresses particular issues or theories. Those of greatest note are represented in this bibliography, including *a priori* knowledge, the nature of epistemic justification, the criteria for knowledge, and the role of psychology in epistemology. Classic works include W. V. O. Quine's "Two Dogmas of Empiricism," Hilary Putnam's "Two Dogmas Revisited," and Laurence BonJour's *The Structure of Empirical Knowledge*.

Feminist theorists provide a vitally important body of criticism of how epistemological issues have traditionally been understood. Lorraine Code's *What Can She Know?* is particularly notable in this connection, as are Jane Duran's *Toward a Feminist Epistemology* and Sandra Harding's *The Science Question in Feminism*. Those who seek a good introduction and overview of these issues should consult Phyllis Rooney's *Feminism and Epistemology: An Introduction*. Related issues and criticisms can be found in the bibliography's section on social epistemology.

Arguments regarding skepticism have persisted from philosophy's origins and are found in many different languages and cultures. David Hume's *Treatise of Human Nature*, Barry Stroud's *The Significance of Philosophical Scepticism*, and Peter Unger's *Ignorance: A Case for Scepticism* are notable components of the English literature in this area. Charles Landesman's *Skepticism:*

The Central Issues provides a good overview of skeptical thought in the Western tradition.

The bibliography also includes sections on mathematical knowledge, metaepistemology, moral knowledge, religious knowledge, science, induction, and sense perception. Together with the sections described previously, these cover the vast majority of the epistemic literature.

II. GENERAL EPISTEMOLOGY TEXTS

Audi, Robert. *Belief, Justification, and Knowledge*. Belmont, CA: Wadsworth, 1988.

Baergen, Ralph. *Contemporary Epistemology*. Fort Worth, TX: Harcourt Brace College Publishers, 1995.

Bernecker, Sven, and Fred Dretske. *Knowledge: Readings in Contemporary Epistemology*. Oxford: Oxford University Press, 2000.

Chisholm, Roderick. *Theory of Knowledge*. 3rd ed. Foundations of Philosophy Series. Englewood Cliffs, NJ: Prentice Hall, 1989.

Dancy, Jonathan. *Introduction to Contemporary Epistemology*. Oxford: Blackwell, 1985.

Dancy, Jonathan, and Ernest Sosa, eds. *A Companion to Epistemology*. Blackwell Companions to Philosophy Series. Oxford: Blackwell, 1992.

Feldman, Richard. *Epistemology*. Upper Saddle River, NJ: Prentice Hall, 2003.

Fumerton, Richard. *Epistemology*. First Books in Philosophy. Oxford: Blackwell, 2005.

Hill, Thomas. *Contemporary Theories of Knowledge*. New York: Macmillan, 1961.

Lehrer, Keith. *Theory of Knowledge*. Boulder, CO: Westview Press, 1990.

Morton, Adam. *A Guide through the Theory of Knowledge*. Encino, CA: Dickenson, 1977.

Moser, Paul K., and A. van der Nat, eds. *Human Knowledge: Classical and Contemporary Approaches*. New York: Oxford University Press, 1987.

Moser, Paul K., Dwayne Mulder, and J. D. Trout. *The Theory of Knowledge: A Thematic Introduction*. New York: Oxford University Press, 1998.

Nagel, Ernest, and Richard Brandt, eds. *Meaning and Knowledge: Systematic Readings in Epistemology*. New York: Harcourt, Brace, and World, 1965.

Pollock, John. *Knowledge and Justification*. Princeton, NJ: Princeton University Press, 1974.

———. *Contemporary Theories of Knowledge*. Totowa, NJ: Rowman & Littlefield, 1986.

Pollock, John, and J. Cruz. *Contemporary Theories of Knowledge*. 2nd ed. Lanham, MD: Rowman & Littlefield, 1999.

Sosa, Ernest, and Jaegwon Kim, eds. *Epistemology: An Anthology*. Blackwell Philosophy Anthology. Oxford: Blackwell, 1999.

Sosa, Ernest, and Enrique Villanueva, eds. *Epistemology*. Philosophical Issues, vol. 14. Oxford: Blackwell, 2004.

Steup, Matthias, and Ernest Sosa, eds. *Contemporary Debates in Epistemology*. Contemporary Debates in Philosophy Series. Oxford: Blackwell, 2004.

Williams, M. *Problems of Knowledge: A Critical Introduction to Epistemology*. New York: Oxford University Press, 2001.

III. ANCIENT GREECE: PRIMARY SOURCES

Aristotle. *The Complete Works of Aristotle: The Revised Oxford Translation*. 2 vols. Princeton, NJ: Princeton University Press, 1984.

———. *Nicomachean Ethics*. Translated and edited by R. Crisp. Cambridge, MA: Harvard University Press, 2000.

Diogenes Laertius. *Diogenes Laertius: Lives of Eminent Philosophers*. Edited and translated by R. Hicks. 2 vols. London: Heinemann, 1925.

Long, A. A., and D. N. Sedley, eds. and trans. *The Hellenistic Philosophers*. 2 vols. Cambridge: Cambridge University Press, 1987.

Plato. *Platonis Opera*. Edited by J. Burnett. 5 vols. Oxford: Clarendon Press, 1900–1907.

———. *The Collected Dialogues of Plato*. Translated and edited by E. Hamilton and H. Cairns. New Haven, CT: Princeton University Press, 1961.

Sextus Empiricus. *Opera*. 3 vols. Vols. 1 and 2, edited by H. Mutschmann. Leipzig: Teubner, 1912–1914. Vol. 3, edited by J. Mau. Leipzig: Teubner, 1954.

———. *Sextus Empiricus: Outlines of Pyrrhonism and against the Mathematicians*. Edited and translated by R. Bury. 4 vols. London: Heinemann, 1933–1949.

IV. ANCIENT GREECE: COMMENTARY

Annas, J. "Stoic Epistemology." In *Epistemology*, edited by S. Everson, 184–203. Cambridge: Cambridge University Press, 1990.

Barnes, J. *The Presocratics*. London: Routledge and Kegan Paul, 1979.

———. "The Beliefs of a Pyrrhonist." *Proceedings of the Cambridge Philological Society* 29 (1982): 1–29.

Bostock, D. *Plato's Theaetetus*. Oxford: Clarendon Press, 1988.

Brickhouse, T., and N. D. Smith. "Vlastos on the Elenchus." *Oxford Studies in Ancient Philosophy* 2 (1984): 185–96.

Cooper, J. H. "Plato on Sense Perception and Knowledge." *Phronesis* 15 (1970): 123–46.

Coxon, A. *The Fragments of Parmenides*. *Phronesis* Supplemental Series, III. Assen: Maastricht, 1986.

Diels, K., and W. Kranz. *Die Fragmente der Vorsokratiker*. 6th ed. Berlin, 1951.

Fine, G. "Knowledge and Belief in *Republic* V." *Archiv für Geschichte der Philosophie* 58 (1978): 121–39.

Fränkel, H. "Xenophanes' Empiricism and his Critique of Knowledge." In *The Presocratics*, edited by A. Mourelatos, 118–31. Garden City, NJ: Anchor Press/Doubleday, 1974.

Frede, M. "Stoics and Sceptics on Clear and Distinct Ideas." In *The Sceptical Tradition*, edited by M. Burnyeat, 65–93. Berkeley: University of California Press, 1983.

Gulley, N. *Plato's Theory of Knowledge*. London: Methuen, 1962.

Hussey, E. "The Beginnings of Epistemology: From Homer to Philolaus." In *Epistemology*, edited by S. Everson, 11–38. Cambridge: Cambridge University Press, 1990.

Kirk, G. S., J. E. Raven, and M. Schofield. *The Presocratic Philosophers*. 2nd ed. Cambridge: Cambridge University Press, 1983.

Lesher, J. H. "Perceiving and Knowing in the *Iliad* and *Odyssey*." *Phronesis* 26 (1981): 2–24.

———. "Heraclitus' Epistemological Vocabulary." *Hermes* 3 (1983): 155–70.

Long, A. A., and D. N. Sedley. *The Hellenistic Philosophers*. Cambridge: Cambridge University Press, 1987.

Nussbaum, Martha. "Eleatic Conventionalism and Philolaus on the Conditions of Thought." *Harvard Studies in Classical Philosophy* 83 (1979): 63–108.

Robinson, R. *Plato's Earlier Dialectic*. 2nd ed. Oxford: Oxford University Press, 1953.

Sedley, D. "The Motivation of Greek Scepticism." In *The Sceptical Tradition*, edited by M. Burnyeat, 9–29. Berkeley: University of California Press, 1983.

Sharples, R. W., ed. *Stoics, Epicureans and Sceptics: An Introduction to Hellenistic Philosophy*. New York: Routledge, 1996.

Stough, C. *Greek Scepticism*. Berkeley: University of California Press, 1969.

Vlastos, Gregory. "The Socratic Elenchus." *Oxford Studies in Ancient Philosophy* 1 (1983): 27–58.

———. "Socrates' Disavowal of Knowledge." *Philosophical Quarterly* 35 (1985): 1–31.

White, N. P. *Plato on Knowledge and Reality*. Indianapolis: Hackett, 1976.

V. MEDIEVAL EPISTEMOLOGY: PRIMARY SOURCES

Aquinas, Thomas, St. *Summa Theologiae*. Translated by the English Dominican Fathers. London: Burns, Oates, and Washburne, 1912–1936.

——. *Summa Contra Gentiles*. Translated by the English Dominican Fathers. London: Burns, Oates, and Washbourne, 1934.

——. *Questions on the Soul*. Translated by James H. Robb. Milwaukee, WI: Marquette University Press, 1984.

Augustine, St. *Opera Omnia*. Reprinted in vols. 32–47 of J. P. Migne's *Patrologiae Cursus Completus*, *Series Latina*. Paris, 1844–1864.

Ockham, William of. *Guillelmi de Ockham: Opera Philosphica et Theologica*. 10 vols. St. Bonaventure, NY: The Franciscan Institute, 1977.

VI. MEDIEVAL EPISTEMOLOGY: COMMENTARY

Adams, Marilyn McCord. *William Ockham*. Notre Dame, IN: University of Notre Dame Press, 1987.

Aertsen, J. *Nature and Creature: Thomas Aquinas's Way of Thought*. Leiden: Brill, 1988.

Day, S. *Intuitive Cognition: A Key to the Significance of the Later Scholastics*. St. Bonaventure, NY: The Franciscan Institute, 1947.

Markus, R. A. "Augustine: Reason and Illumination." In *Cambridge History of Later Greek and Early Medieval Philosophy*, edited by A. Armstrong, chapter 23. Cambridge: Cambridge University Press, 1967.

——. "Augustine: Sense and Imagination." In *Cambridge History of Later Greek and Early Medieval Philosophy*, edited by A. Armstrong, chapter 24. Cambridge: Cambridge University Press, 1967.

Nash, R. H. *The Light of the Mind: Saint Augustine's Theory of Knowledge*. Lexington: University Press of Kentucky, 1969.

Tachau, K. H. *Vision and Certitude in the Age of Ockham: Optics, Epistemology, and the Foundations of Semantics 1250–1345*. Leiden: E. J. Brill, 1988.

VII. SEVENTEENTH-CENTURY
RATIONALISM: PRIMARY SOURCES

Descartes, René. *Oeuvres de Descartes*. Edited by C. Adam and P. Tannery. 12 vols. Paris: 1887–1913. Rev. ed., Paris: Vrin/CNRS, 1964–1976.

——. *The Philosophical Writings of Descartes*. 2 vols. Translated and edited by John Cottingham, Robert Stoothoff, and Dugald Murdoch. Cambridge: Cambridge University Press, 1984.

Gassendi, Pierre. *The Selected Works of Pierre Gassendi*. Translated and edited by C. Brush. New York: Johnson Reprint, 1972.

Leibniz, G. W. *New Essays on Human Understanding*. Translated by P. Remnant and J. Bennett. Cambridge: Cambridge University Press, 1704/1981.

——. *Gottfried Wilhelm Leibniz—Philosophical Papers and Letters*. Translated and edited by L. Loemker. Dordrecht: D. Reidel, 1969.

Mersenne, M. *La Verité des Sciences Contre les Sceptiques ou Pyrrhoniens*. Paris: T. Du Bray, 1625.

Spinoza, Benedict. *Spinoza Opera*. 4 vols. Edited by C. Gebhardt. Heidelberg: Carl Winter, 1923.

——. *The Collected Works of Spinoza*. 2 vols. Edited by E. Curley. Princeton, NJ: Princeton University Press, 1985.

VIII. SEVENTEENTH-CENTURY RATIONALISM: COMMENTARY

Ariew, Roger, Dennis Des Chene, Douglas Jesseph, Tad Schmaltz, and Theo Verbeek. *Historical Dictionary of Descartes and Cartesian Philosophy*. Lanham, MD: Scarecrow Press, 2003.

Ashworth, F. J. "Descartes' Theory of Clear and Distinct Ideas." In *Cartesian Studies*, edited by R. Butler, 89–105. Oxford: Blackwell, 1972.

Bennett, Jonathan. *A Study of Spinoza's Ethics*. Indianapolis: Hackett, 1984.

Brown, Stuart, and N. J. Fox. *Historical Dictionary of Leibniz's Philosophy*. Lanham, MD: Scarecrow Press, 2006.

Clarke, Desmond. *Descartes' Philosophy of Science*. Manchester: Manchester University Press, 1982.

Cleve, James van. "Foundationalism, Epistemic Principles, and the Cartesian Circle." *Philosophical Review* 88 (1979): 55–91.

Cottingham, J. *Descartes*. Oxford: Blackwell, 1986.

——. *The Rationalists*. Oxford: Oxford University Press, 1988.

Curley, Edwin M. "Experience in Spinoza's Theory of Knowledge." In *Spinoza*, edited by M. Grene, 22–59. New York: Anchor, 1973.

——. *Descartes against the Sceptics*. Oxford: Blackwell, 1978.

——. "Spinoza's Geometric Method." *Studia Spinozana* 2 (1986): 151–68.

Frankfurt, H. *Demons, Dreams and Madmen: The Defense of Reason in Descartes' Meditations*. New York: Bobbs-Merrill, 1970.

Gibson, John. *Locke's Theory of Knowledge and Its Historical Relations*. Cambridge: Cambridge University Press, 1960.

Hintikka, J. "*Cogito Ergo Sum*: Inference or Performance?" *Philosophical Review* 72 (1964): 3–32.

Jolley, Nicholas. *Leibniz and Locke—A Study of the New Essays on Human Understanding*. Oxford: Clarendon Press, 1984.

———. *The Light of the Soul: Theories of Ideas in Leibniz, Malebranche, and Descartes*. Oxford: Clarendon Press, 1990.

Kenny, A. *Descartes*. New York: Random House, 1968.

Loeb, Louis. *From Descartes to Hume*. Ithaca, NY: Cornell University Press, 1981.

Maull, Nancy. "Spinoza in the Century of Science." In *Spinoza and the Sciences*, edited by M. Grene and D. Nails, 3–13. Dordrecht: D. Reidel, 1986.

Parkinson, G. H. R. *Spinoza's Theory of Knowledge*. Oxford: Clarendon Press, 1954.

Popkin, R. *The History of Skepticism from Erasmus to Descartes*. 4th ed. Berkeley: University of California Press, 1979.

Rescher, Nicholas. *Leibniz: An Introduction to His Philosophy*. Lanham, MD: University Press of America, 1986.

Savan, David. "Spinoza: Scientist and Theorist of Scientific Method." In *Spinoza and the Sciences*, edited by M. Grene and D. Nails, 95–123. Dordrecht: D. Reidel, 1986.

Williams, Bernard. "The Certainty of the *Cogito*." In *Descartes: A Collection of Critical Essays*, edited by W. Doney, 88–107. London: Macmillan, 1968.

———. *Descartes: The Project of Pure Enquiry*. Harmondsworth: Pelican Books, 1978.

Wilson, M. *Descartes*. London: Routledge, 1978.

———. *Leibniz's Doctrine of Necessary Truth*. New York: Garland, 1990.

Yolton, J. W. "Ideas and Knowledge in Seventeenth-Century Philosophy." *Journal of the History of Philosophy* 13 (1975): 145–65.

IX. BRITISH EMPIRICISM: PRIMARY SOURCES

Berkeley, George. *An Essay towards a New Theory of Vision*. 1709.

———. *A Treatise Concerning the Principles of Human Knowledge*. 1710.

———. *Three Dialogues between Hylas and Philonous*. 1713.

———. *De Motu*. 1721.

———. *Alciphron: or the Minute Philosopher*. 1732.

———. *The Works of George Berkeley*. 9 vols. Edited by A. A. Luce and T. E. Jessop. London: Nelson, 1948–1957.

Hobbes, Thomas. *English Works of Thomas Hobbes*. 11 vols. Edited by Sir W. Molesworth. London: J. Bohn, 1839–1845.

Hume, David. *An Enquiry Concerning Human Understanding.* Edited by P. Nidditch. Oxford: Clarendon Press, 1690/1975.

——. *A Treatise of Human Nature.* Edited by L. A. Selby-Bigge; revised by P. H. Nidditch. Oxford: Oxford University Press, 1739/1978.

Locke, John. *An Essay Concerning Human Understanding.* Edited by P. Nidditch. London: Clarendon Press, 1690/1975.

Reid, Thomas. *Essays on the Intellectual Powers of Man.* Edited by B. Brody. Cambridge, MA: MIT Press, 1785/1969.

——. *Thomas Reid's Inquiry and Essays.* Edited by K. Lehrer and R. Beanblossom. Indianapolis: Bobbs-Merrill, 1975.

X. BRITISH EMPIRICISM: COMMENTARY

Aaron, R. I. *John Locke.* 3rd ed. Oxford: Clarendon Press, 1971.

Allaire, Edwin B. "Berkeley's Idealism." *Theoria* 29 (1963): 229–44.

Alston, William P. "Thomas Reid on Epistemic Principles." *History of Philosophy Quarterly* 2 (1985): 435–52.

Bennett, Jonathan. *Locke, Berkeley, Hume: Central Themes.* Oxford: Oxford University Press, 1971.

Bracken, Harry. *Berkeley.* London: Macmillan, 1974.

Brook, Richard J. *Berkeley's Philosophy of Science.* The Hague: Nijhoff, 1973.

Craig, E. J. "Berkeley's Attack on Abstract Ideas." *Philosophical Review* 77 (1968): 425–37.

Flew, Anthony. "Was Berkeley a Precursor of Wittgenstein?" In *Hume and the Enlightenment: Essays Presented to Ernest Campbell Mossner.* Edited by W. B. Todd, 153–63. Austin: University of Texas Humanities Research Center, 1974.

Fogelin, R. *Hume's Scepticism in the Treatise of Human Nature.* London: Routledge and Kegan Paul, 1985.

Grayling, A. C. *Berkeley: The Central Arguments.* London: Routledge, 1986.

Luce, A. A. *Berkeley and Malebranche.* Oxford: Oxford University Press, 1934.

——. *Berkeley's Immaterialism.* London: Nelson, 1945.

——. *The Dialectic of Immaterialism.* London: Hodder and Stoughton, 1963.

Mackie, John L. *Problems from Locke.* Oxford: Oxford University Press, 1976.

Pappas, George. "Berkeley and Common Sense Realism." *History of Philosophy Quarterly* 8 (1991): 27–42.

Pitcher, George. *Berkeley.* London: Routledge and Kegan Paul, 1977.

Popkin, Richard H. "Berkeley and Pyrrhonianism." *Review of Metaphysics* 5 (1951–1952): 223–46.

Stove, D. C. *Probability and Hume's Inductive Scepticism*. Oxford: Oxford University Press, 1973.

Stroud, Barry. "Berkeley *v.* Locke on Primary Qualities." *Philosophy* 55 (1980): 149–66.

Taylor, C. C. W. "Berkeley's Theory of Abstract Ideas." *Philosophical Quarterly* 28 (1978): 97–115.

Tipton, Ian C. *Berkeley: The Philosophy of Immaterialism*. London: Methuen, 1974.

———, ed. *Locke and Human Understanding*. Oxford: Oxford University Press, 1977.

Weinberg, Julius. "The Nominalism of Berkeley and Hume." In *Abstraction, Relation, and Induction: Three Essays in the History of Thought*, edited by J. Weinberg, 3–60. Madison: University of Wisconsin Press, 1965.

Yolton, J. W. *Locke and the Compass of Human Understanding*. Cambridge: Cambridge University Press, 1970.

XI. KANT AND POST-KANTIAN IDEALISM: PRIMARY SOURCES

Hegel, G. W. F. *Die Phänomenologie des Geistes*. Bamberg and Würtzburg, 1807. Translated by A. Miller, *The Phenomenology of Spirit*. Oxford: Clarendon Press, 1977.

———. *Wissenschaft der Logik*. 2 vols. Nürnberg, 1812–1816; Berlin, 1831. Translated by A. Miller, *Hegel's Science of Logic*. London: Allen and Unwin, 1969.

Heidegger, Martin. *Sein und Zeit*. Tübingen, 1927. Translated by J. Macquarrie and E. Robinson, *Being and Time*. New York: Harper and Row, 1962.

Husserl, Edmund. *Logische Untersuchungen* I–II. *Husserliana*, vols. 18 and 19. The Hague: Martinus Nijhoff, 1960. Translated by J. Findlay, *Logical Investigations*. 2 vols. London: Routledge and Kegan Paul, 1970.

Kant, Immanuel. *Kritik der reinen Vernunft*. Riga, 1781. 2nd ed. Riga, 1787. Translated by N. Kemp Smith, *Critique of Pure Reason*. London: Macmillan, 1964.

XII. KANT AND POST-KANTIAN IDEALISM: COMMENTARY

Allison, H. *Kant's Transcendental Idealism*. New Haven, CT: Yale University Press, 1973.

Aquila, R. *Representational Mind: A Study of Kant's Theory of Knowledge*. Bloomington: Indiana University Press, 1983.

Beiser, F., ed. *The Cambridge Companion to Hegel*. Cambridge: Cambridge University Press, 1992.

Bennett, Jonathan. *Kant's Analytic*. Cambridge: Cambridge University Press, 1966.

Bird, G. *Kant's Theory of Knowledge*. London: Routledge and Kegan Paul, 1962.

Broad, C. D. *Kant: An Introduction*. Cambridge: Cambridge University Press, 1978.

Burbidge, John. *Historical Dictionary of Hegelian Philosophy*. Lanham, MD: Scarecrow Press, 2001.

Denker, Alfred. *Historical Dictionary of Heidegger's Philosophy*. Lanham, MD: Scarecrow Press, 2000.

Diethe, Carol. *Historical Dictionary of Nietzscheanism*. Lanham, MD: Scarecrow Press, 1999.

Guignon, C. *Heidegger and the Problem of Knowledge*. Indianapolis: Hackett, 1983.

Guyer, Paul. *Kant and the Claims of Knowledge*. Cambridge: Cambridge University Press, 1987.

Holzheg, Helmut, and Vilem Mudrock. *Historical Dictionary of Kant and Kantianism*. Lanham, MD: Scarecrow Press, 2005.

Kemp Smith, Norman. *A Commentary on Kant's Critique of Pure Reason*. 2nd ed. London: Routledge and Kegan Paul, 1923.

Miller, I. *Husserl, Perception and Temporal Awareness*. Cambridge, MA: MIT Press, 1984.

Müller, G. E. "The Hegel Legend of 'Thesis, Antithesis and Synthesis.'" *Journal for the History of Ideas* 19 (1958): 411–14.

Pritchard, H. A. *Kant's Theory of Knowledge*. Oxford: Clarendon Press, 1909.

Strawson, Peter F. *The Bounds of Sense*. London: Methuen, 1966.

Watkin, Julia. *Historical Dictionary of Kierkegaard's Philosophy*. Lanham, MD: Scarecrow Press, 2001.

Westphal, K. R. "Hegel's Solution to the Dilemma of the Criterion." *History of Philosophy Quarterly* 5 (1988): 173–88.

———. *Hegel's Epistemological Realism: A Study of the Aim and Method of Hegel's Phenomenology of Spirit*. Dordrecht: Kluwer, 1989.

XIII. LOGICAL POSITIVISM, WITTGENSTEIN, AND THE VIENNA CIRCLE: PRIMARY SOURCES

Ayer, Alfred Jules. *Language, Truth and Logic*. London: Gollancz, 1946.

———, ed. *Logical Positivism*. Glencoe: Free Press, 1959.

Carnap, Rudolf. *Der Logische Aufbau der Welt*. 1928. Translated by R. George, *The Logical Structure of the World: Pseudoproblems in Philosophy*. London: Routledge and Kegan Paul, 1967.

Neurath, Otto. *Otto Neurath, Empiricism and Sociology*. Edited by M. Neurath and R. Cohen. Dordrecht: Reidel, 1973.

Reichenbach, Hans. *Relativitätstheorie und Erkenntnis Apriori*. Berlin, 1920. Translated by M. Reichenbach, *The Theory of Relativity and A Priori Knowledge*. Berkeley: University of California Press, 1965.

———. *Wahrscheinlichkeitslehre*. Leiden, 1935. Translated by E. Hutten and M. Reichenbach, *The Theory of Probability*, 2nd ed. Berkeley: University of California Press, 1949.

———. *Experience and Prediction*. Chicago: University of Chicago Press, 1938.

Wittgenstein, Ludwig. *Tractatus Logico-Philosophicus*. Translated by C. Ogden. London: Routledge and Kegan Paul, 1922.

———. *Philosophical Investigations*. Translated by G. E. M. Anscombe. Oxford: Blackwell, 1953.

———. *On Certainty*. Translated by D. Paul and G. Anscombe; edited by D. Paul, G. Anscombe, and G. von Wright. New York: Harper Torchbooks, 1969.

XIV. LOGICAL POSITIVISM, WITTGENSTEIN, AND THE VIENNA CIRCLE: COMMENTARY

Jacob, P. "The Neurath-Schlick Controversy." *Fundamenta Scientae* 5 (1984): 351–66.

Kober, Michael. "Certainties of a World-Picture: The Epistemological Investigations of *On Certainty*." In *The Cambridge Companion to Wittgenstein*, edited by H. Sluga and D. G. Stern, 411–41. Cambridge Companions Series. Cambridge: Cambridge University Press, 1996.

Lycan, William. "Non-Inductive Evidence: Recent Work on Wittgenstein's 'Criteria.'" *American Philosophical Quarterly* 8 (1971): 109–25.

Morawetz, Thomas. *Wittgenstein and Knowledge: The Importance of* On Certainty. Atlantic Highlands, NJ: Humanities Press, 1978.

Richter, Duncan. *Historical Dictionary of Wittgenstein's Philosophy*. Lanham, MD: Scarecrow Press, 2004.

Salmon, W. C. *Hans Reichenbach: Logical Empiricist*. Dordrecht: Reidel, 1979.

XV. AMERICAN PRAGMATISM: PRIMARY SOURCES

Dewey, James. *Logic, the Theory of Inquiry*. New York: Henry Holt, 1938.

———. *The Quest for Certainty*. New York: Putnam, 1960.

Hookway, C. *Peirce*. London: Routledge and Kegan Paul, 1985.

James, William. *The Will to Believe and Other Essays in Popular Philosophy*. New York: Dover, 1897/1956.

———. *Pragmatism: A New Name for Some Old Ways of Thinking*. Cambridge, MA: Harvard University Press, 1907/1975.

———. *The Meaning of Truth: A Sequel to Pragmatism*. Cambridge, MA: Harvard University Press, 1909/1975.

———. *Essays in Radical Empiricism*. Cambridge, MA: Harvard University Press, 1976.

Peirce, Charles S. *Collected Papers*. 8 vols. Cambridge, MA: Belknap Press, 1931–1958.

Schiller, F. C. S. *Studies in Humanism*. London: Macmillan, 1907.

Thayer, H. S., ed. *Pragmatism: The Classic Writings*. New York: New American Library, 1970.

XVI. AMERICAN PRAGMATISM: COMMENTARY

Dewey, James. "The Development of American Pragmatism." In *Philosophy and Civilization*, edited by J. Dewey, 13–35. New York: Minton, Balch, 1931.

Dicker, George. *Dewey's Theory of Knowing*. Philadelphia: Philosophical Monographs, 1976.

Giuffrida, R., and E. H. Madden. "James on Meaning and Significance." *Transactions of the C. S. Peirce Society* 11 (1975): 18–35.

Haack, Susan. "'Extreme Scholastic Realism': Its Relevance to Philosophy of Science Today." *Transactions of the Charles S. Peirce Society* 28, no. 1 (1992): 19–50.

Hare, Peter H., and Chakrabarti, C. "The Development of William James's Epistemological Realism." In *History, Religion and Spiritual Democracy*, edited by M. Wohlgelernter, 231–45. New York: Columbia University Press, 1980.

Madden, E. H., and Chakrabarti, C. "James' 'Pure Experience' versus Ayer's 'Weak Phenomenalism.'" *Transactions of the C. S. Peirce Society* 12 (1976): 3–17.

Migotti, M. "Recent Work in Pragmatism: Revolution or Reform in the Theory of Knowledge?" *Philosophical Books* 29 (1988): 65–73.

Murphy, A. E. "Dewey's Epistemology and Metaphysics." In *The Philosophy of John Dewey*, 3rd ed., edited by P. Schilpp and L. Hahn, 193–226. Carbondale: Southern Illinois University Press, 1989.

Myers, G. E. *William James: His Life and Thought*. New Haven, CT: Yale University Press, 1986.

Rorty, Richard. *The Consequences of Pragmatism*. Hassocks: Harvester, 1982.
Scheffler, I. *Four Pragmatists*. London: Routledge and Kegan Paul, 1974.
Thayer, H. S. "Dewey and the Theory of Knowledge." *Transactions of the C. S. Peirce Society* 26 (1990): 443–58.

XVII. CONTINENTAL EPISTEMOLOGY

Adorno, T., and M. Horkheimer. *Dialective of Enlightenment*. Translated by J. Cumming. New York: Continuum, 1987.
Bayes, K., J. Bohman, and T. McCarthy, eds. *After Philosophy: End or Transformation*. Cambridge, MA: MIT Press, 1987.
Derrida, Jacques. *La Voix et le Phénomène*. Paris: Presses Universitaires de France, 1967. Translated by D. Allison, *Speech and Phenomenon*. Evanston, IL: Northwestern University Press, 1973.
——. *Marges de la Philosophie*. Paris: Editions de Minuit, 1972. Translated by A. Bass, *Margins of Philosophy*. Chicago: University of Chicago Press, 1982.
Dreyfus, Herbert, and P. Rabinow. *Michel Foucault: Beyond Structuralism and Hermeneutics*. 2nd ed. Chicago: University of Chicago Press, 1983.
Foucault, Michel. *Power/Knowledge: Selected Interviews and Other Writings, 1972–1977*. Edited by C. Gordon. New York: Pantheon, 1980.
Habermas, Jürgen. *Knowledge and Human Interests*. London: Heinemann, 1971.
Heidegger, Martin. *Being and Time*. Translated by M. O'Connell. New York: Continuum, 1962.
Horkheimer, M. *Critical Theory*. Translated by M. O'Connell. New York: Continuum, 1972.
Lyotard. J.-F. *The Postmodern Condition: A Report on Knowledge*. Translated by G. Bennington and B. Massumi. Minneapolis: University of Minnesota Press, 1985.
Madison, G. *The Phenomenology of Merleau-Ponty*. Athens: Ohio University Press, 1981.
Merleau-Ponty, Maurice. *Phénoménologie de la Perception*. Paris: Gallimard, 1945. Translated by C. Smith, *The Phenomenology of Perception*. New York: Humanities Press, 1962.
——. *The Primacy of Perception*. Edited by J. M. Edie. Evanston, IL: Northwestern University Press, 1964.
——. *Le Visible et l'Invisible*. Paris: Gallimard, 1964. Translated by A. Lingis, *The Visible and the Invisible*. Evanston, IL: Northwestern University Press, 1968.

Rorty, Richard. *Philosophy and the Mirror of Nature*. Princeton, NJ: Princeton University Press, 1979.
———. *The View from Nowhere*. New York: Oxford University Press, 1986.

XVIII. INDIAN EPISTEMOLOGY

Annambhatta. *Tarkasmgraha*. Translated with notes by G. Bhattacharya. Calcutta: Progressive Publishers, 1976.
Bhattacharya, S. "Some Features of the Technical Language of the Navya-Nyāya." *Philosophy East and West* 40 (1990): 129–40.
Chatterjee, S. C. *Nyāya Theory of Knowledge*. Calcutta: Calcutta University Press, 1978.
Chattopadhyaya, D., and M. Gangopadhyaya. *Nyāya Philosophy and Vatsyāyana Bhasya*. Calcutta: Calcutta University Press, 1975.
Datta, D. M. *Six Ways of Knowing*. Calcutta: Calcutta University Press, 1972.
Flintoff, E. "Pyrrho and India." *Phronesis* 25 (1980): 88–108.
Hattori Masaaki, D. *On Perception*. Cambridge, MA: Harvard University Press, 1968.
Jayatilleke, K. N. *Early Buddhist Theory of Knowledge*. London: Allen and Unwin, 1963.
Matilal, B. K. *Perception: An Essay on Classical Indian Theories of Knowledge*. Oxford: Cambridge University Press, 1986.
Mohanty, J. N. *Gangesa's Theory of Truth*. 2nd ed., revised. Delhi: Motilal Banarasidass, 1989.
———. "Indian Epistemology." In *A Companion to Epistemology*, edited by J. Dancy and E. Sosa, 196–200. Blackwell Companions to Philosophy Series. Oxford: Blackwell, 1992.
Potter, K. H., ed. *Encyclopedia of Indian Philosophies*. Vol. 2: *Indian Metaphysics and Epistemology: The Tradition of Nyāya-Vaisesika up to Gangesa*. Princeton, NJ: Princeton University Press, 1977.

XIX. CURRENT ISSUES: *A PRIORI* KNOWLEDGE

Ayer, Alfred J. *Language, Truth and Logic*. 2nd ed. London: Gollancz, 1946.
———. "Basic Propositions." In *Philosophical Analysis*, edited by M. Black, 60–74. Englewood Cliffs, NJ: Prentice Hall, 1950.
Casullo, Albert. "Kripke on the *A Priori* and the Necessary." *Analysis* 37 (1977): 152–59.
———. "Necessity, Certainty, and the *A Priori*." *Canadian Journal of Philosophy* 18 (1988): 43–66.

———. "Revisability, Reliabilism, and *A Priori* Knowledge." *Philosophy and Phenomenological Research* 49 (1988): 187–213.

Edidin, A. "*A Priori* Knowledge for Fallibilists." *Philosophical Studies* 46 (1984): 189–97.

Harman, Gilbert. "Unger on Knowledge." *Journal of Philosophy* 64 (1967): 390–95.

Kitcher, Philip. "*A Priori* Knowledge." *Philosophical Review* 89 (1980): 3–23.

Kripke, Saul. *Naming and Necessity*. Cambridge: Cambridge University Press, 1980.

Moser, Paul, ed. *A Priori Knowledge*. Oxford: Oxford University Press, 1987.

Pap, A. *Semantics and Necessary Truth*. New Haven, CT: Yale University Press, 1958.

Putnam, Hilary. "'Two Dogmas' Revisited." In *Philosophical Papers*. Vol. 3: *Realism and Reason*, edited by H. Putnam, 87–97. Cambridge: Cambridge University Press, 1983.

Quine, W. V. O. "Two Dogmas of Empiricism." In *From a Logical Point of View*, 2nd ed., edited by W. Quine, 20–46. New York: Harper & Row, 1963.

Sober, Elliott. "Revisability, *A Priori* Truth, and Evolution." *Australasian Journal of Philosophy* 59 (1981): 68–85.

Thompson, Manley. "Epistemic Priority, Analytic Truth, and Naturalized Epistemology." *American Philosophical Quarterly* 18 (1981): 1–12.

Unger, Peter. "Experience and Factual Knowledge." *Journal of Philosophy* 64 (1967): 152–73.

XX. CURRENT ISSUES: EPISTEMIC JUSTIFICATION

Alston, William P. "Varieties of Privileged Access." *American Philosophical Quarterly* 8 (1971): 223–41.

———. *Epistemic Justification: Essays in the Theory of Knowledge*. Ithaca, NY: Cornell University Press, 1988.

Annis, D. B. "A Contextualist Theory of Epistemic Justification." *American Philosophical Quarterly* 15 (1978): 213–19.

Audi, Robert. *The Structure of Justification*. Cambridge: Cambridge University Press, 1993.

Bishop, M. "In Praise of Epistemic Irresponsibility: How Lazy and Ignorant Can You Be?" *Synthese* 122 (2000): 179–208.

Black, O. "Infinite Regresses of Justification." *International Philosophical Quarterly* 28 (1988): 421–37.

Christleib, Terry. "Coherence and Truth: BonJour's Metajustification." *Southern Journal of Philosophy* 24 (1986): 397–413.

Cleve, James van. "Epistemic Supervenience and the Rule of Belief." *The Monist* 68 (1985): 90–104.

Coady, C. A. J. *Testimony: A Philosophical Study.* Oxford: Oxford University Press, 1992.

Cornman, James. *Skepticism, Justification, and Explanation.* Dordrecht: Kluwer, 1980.

Feldman, Richard. "Reliability and Justification." *The Monist* 68, no. 2 (1985): 159–74.

——. "Having Evidence." In *Essays Presented to Edmund Gettier*, edited by D. Austin, 83–104. Dordrecht: Reidel, 1988.

Feldman, Richard, and Earl Conee. "Evidentialism." *Philosophical Studies* 48 (1985): 15–34.

Foley, Richard. "What's Wrong with Reliabilism?" *The Monist* 68, no. 2 (1985): 188–200.

——. *The Theory of Epistemic Rationality.* Cambridge, MA: Harvard University Press, 1987.

Freeman, James B. *Acceptable Premises: An Epistemic Approach to an Informal Logic Problem.* Cambridge: Cambridge University Press, 2005.

Ginet, Carl. "Justification: It Need Not Cause, but It Must Be Accessible." *Journal of Philosophical Research* 15 (1990): 105–17.

Goldman, Alvin. "What Is Justified Belief?" In *Knowledge and Justification*, edited by G. Pappas, 1–23. Dordrecht: Reidel, 1979.

——. "Strong and Weak Justification." In *Philosophical Perspectives*. Vol. 2: *Epistemology*, edited by J. Tomberlin, 51–70. Atascadero, CA: Ridgeview Publishing, 1988.

Kornblith, Hilary. "Justified Belief and Epistemically Responsible Action." *Philosophical Review* 92 (1983): 33–48.

Lycan, William. *Judgment and Justification.* Cambridge Studies in Philosophy. Cambridge: Cambridge University Press, 1988.

Moser, Paul. *Empirical Justification.* Dordrecht: D. Reidel, 1985.

——. "Whither Infinite Regresses of Justification?" *Southern Journal of Philosophy* 23 (1985): 65–74.

Plantinga, Alvin. "Positive Epistemic Status and Proper Function." *Philosophical Perspectives*. Vol. 2: *Epistemology*, edited by J. Tomberlin, 1–50. Atascadero, CA: Ridgeview Publishing, 1988.

——. *Warrant: The Current Debate.* New York: Oxford University Press, 1993.

——. *Warrant and Proper Function.* New York: Oxford University Press, 1993.

Pollock, John. "Reliability and Justified Belief." *Canadian Journal of Philosophy* 14, no. 1 (1984): 103–14.

Post, J. F. "Infinite Regresses of Justification and of Explanation." *Philosophical Studies* 38 (1980): 31–52.

Talbot, W. J. *The Reliability of the Cognitive Mechanism*. New York: Garland Publishing, 1990.

Thalberg, I. "Is Justification Transmissible through Deduction?" *Philosophical Studies* 25 (1974): 357–64.

Will, Michael. *Groundless Belief*. New Haven, CT: Yale University Press, 1977.

XXI. CURRENT ISSUES: FEMINIST EPISTEMOLOGY

Campbell, Kristen. *Jacques Lacan and Feminist Epistemology*. New York: Routledge, 2004.

Code, Lorraine. *Epistemic Responsibility*. Hanover, NH: University of New England Press, 1987.

———. *What Can She Know? Feminist Theory and the Construction of Knowledge*. Ithaca, NY: Cornell University Press, 1991.

Le Doeff, Michèle. *The Sex of Knowing*. New York: Routledge, 2003.

Duran, Jane. *Toward a Feminist Epistemology*. Savage, MD: Rowman & Littlefield, 1990.

Gardner, Catherine Vellanueva. *Historical Dictionary of Feminist Philosophy*. Lanham, MD: Scarecrow Press, 2006.

Haraway, D. "Situated Knowledges: The Science Question in Feminism and the Privilege of Partial Perspective." *Feminist Studies* 14 (1988): 575–99.

Harding, Sandra. "Why Has the Sex/Gender System Become Visible Only Now?" In *Discovering Reality: Feminist Perspectives on Epistemology, Methodology, and Philosophy of Science*, edited by S. Harding and M. Hintikka, 311–24. Boston: D. Reidel, 1983.

———. *The Science Question in Feminism*. Ithaca, NY: Cornell University Press, 1986.

Nelson, L. H. *Who Knows: From Quine to a Feminist Empiricism*. Philadelphia: Temple University Press, 1990.

Potter, Elizabeth. *Feminism and Philosophy of Science: An Introduction*. New York: Routledge, 2005.

Rooney, Phyllis. *Feminism and Epistemology: An Introduction*. New York: Routledge, 2005.

von Morstein, Petra. "Epistemology and Women in Philosophy: Feminism Is a Humanism." In *Gender Bias in Scholarship: The Pervasive Prejudice*, edited by W. Tomm and G. Hamilton, 147–65. Toronto: Wilfred Laurier Press, 1988.

XXII. CURRENT ISSUES: INTERNALISM AND EXTERNALISM

Alston, William P. "Internalism and Externalism in Epistemology." In *Epistemic Justification: Essays in the Theory of Knowledge*, edited by W. Alston, 185–226. Ithaca, NY: Cornell University Press, 1988.

———. "An Internalist Externalism." In *Epistemic Justification: Essays in the Theory of Knowledge*, edited by W. Alston, 227–47. Ithaca, NY: Cornell University Press, 1988.

Baergen, Ralph. "The Influence of Cognition upon Perception: The Empirical Story." *Australasian Journal of Philosophy* 71, no. 1 (1993): 13–23.

BonJour, Lawrence. "Externalist Theories of Empirical Knowledge." In *Studies in Epistemology*, edited by P. A. French, T. E. Uehling Jr., and H. K. Wettstein, 53–73. Midwest Studies in Philosophy, vol. 5. Minneapolis: University of Minnesota Press, 1980.

BonJour, Lawrence, and Ernest Sosa. *Epistemic Justification: Internalism vs. Externalism, Foundations vs. Virtues*. Great Debates in Philosophy. Oxford: Blackwell, 2003.

Fumerton, Richard. "The Internalism/Externalism Controversy." *Philosophical Perspectives* 2 (1988): 442–59.

Goldman, Alvin I. "The Internalist Conception of Justification." *Midwest Studies in Philosophy* 5 (1980): 27–51.

Greco, John. "Internalism and Epistemically Responsible Belief." *Synthese* 85 (1990): 245–77.

Kornblith, Hilary. "Justified Belief and Epistemically Responsible Action." *Philosophical Review* 92 (1983): 33–48.

———. "How Internal Can You Get?" *Synthese* 74 (1988): 313–27.

Kvanvig, Jonathan L. "Subjective Justification." *Mind* 93 (1984): 71–84.

Luper-Foy, S. "The Reliabilist Theory of Rational Belief." *The Monist* 68 (1985): 203–25.

Nisbett, Richard, and Timothy Wilson. "Telling More Than We Can Know: Verbal Reports on Mental Processes." *Psychological Review* 84, no. 3 (1977): 231–59.

Shoemaker, Sidney. "On Knowing Your Own Mind." In *Philosophical Perspectives*. Vol. 2: *Epistemology*, edited by J. Tomberlin, 183–209. Atascadero, CA: Ridgeview Publishing, 1988.

XXIII. CURRENT ISSUES: KNOWLEDGE AND SKEPTICISM

Amico, Robert P. *The Problem of the Criterion*. Lanham, MD: Rowman & Littlefield, 1993.

Annas, J., and J. Barnes. *The Modes of Scepticism*. Cambridge: Cambridge University Press, 1985.

Annis, David. "Knowledge and Defeasibility." In *Essays on Knowledge and Justification*, edited by G. Pappas and M. Swain, 155–59. Ithaca, NY: Cornell University Press, 1978.

Armstrong, David. "Is Introspective Knowledge Incorrigible?" *Philosophical Review* 72 (1963): 417–32.

———. *A Materialist Theory of Mind*. London: Routledge and Kegan Paul, 1968.

———. *Belief, Truth and Knowledge*. Cambridge: Cambridge University Press, 1973.

Aune, Bruce. *Knowledge, Mind, and Nature*. New York: Random House, 1967.

Ayer, Alfred Jules. *The Foundations of Empirical Knowledge*. London: Macmillan, 1940.

———. *Language, Truth and Logic*. 2nd ed. New York: Dover, 1946.

———. *The Problem of Knowledge*. Edinburgh: Penguin, 1956.

Bender, J., ed. *The Current State of the Coherence Theory*. Dordrecht: Kluwer, 1989.

Boër, S. E., and William Lycan. *Knowing Who*. Cambridge, MA: MIT Press, 1986.

BonJour, Laurence. *The Structure of Empirical Knowledge*. Cambridge, MA: Harvard University Press, 1985.

Burnyeat, M. "Can the Sceptic Live His Scepticism?" In *Doubt and Dogmatism*, edited by M. Schofield, M. Burnyeat, and J. Barnes, 20–53. Oxford: Clarendon Press, 1980.

———, ed. *The Sceptical Tradition*. Berkeley: University of California Press, 1983.

Butchvarov, P. *The Concept of Knowledge*. Evanston, IL: Northwestern University Press, 1970.

Cargile, J. "In Reply to 'A Defense of Scepticism.'" *Philosophical Review* 81 (1972): 229–36.

Carruthers, Peter. *Human Knowledge and Human Nature*. Oxford: Oxford University Press, 1992.

Casullo, Albert. "Necessity, Certainty, and the *A Priori*." *Canadian Journal of Philosophy* 18 (1988): 43–66.

———. "Revisability, Reliabilism, and *A Priori* Knowledge." *Philosophy and Phenomenological Research* 49 (1988): 87–113.

Chisholm, Roderick M. "The Problem of Empiricism." *Journal of Philosophy* 45 (1948): 512–17.

———. *The Foundations of Knowing*. Minneapolis: University of Minnesota Press, 1982.

Clay, M., and Keith Lehrer, eds. *Knowledge and Skepticism*. Boulder, CO: Westview, 1989.

Cleve, J. van. "Foundationalism, Epistemic Principles, and the Cartesian Circle." *Philosophical Review* 88 (1979): 55–91.

Cohen, S. "How to Be a Fallibilist." *Philosophical Perspectives* 2 (1988): 91–123.

Conee, Earl, and Richard Feldman. "The Generality Problem for Reliabilism." *Philosophical Studies* 89 (1998): 1–29.

Craig, E. *Knowledge and the State of Nature: An Essay in Conceptual Synthesis*. Oxford: Clarendon Press, 1990.

Davidson, Donald. "A Coherence Theory of Truth and Knowledge." In *Truth and Interpretation*, edited by E. LePore, 307–19. New York: Blackwell, 1986.

DeRose, K. "Solving the Skeptical Problem." *Philosophical Review* 104, no. 1 (1995): 1–52.

DeRose, K., and T. A. Warfield, eds. *Skepticism: A Contemporary Reader*. Oxford: Oxford University Press, 1999.

Dretske, Fred. "Epistemic Operators." *Journal of Philosophy* 67, no. 24 (1970): 1007–23.

———. "Conclusive Reasons." *Australasian Journal of Philosophy* 49 (1971): 1–22.

———. *Knowledge and the Flow of Information*. Cambridge, MA: Bradford Books/MIT Press, 1981.

———. "The Pragmatic Dimension of Knowledge." *Philosophical Studies* 40 (1981): 363–78.

Dretske, Fred, and B. Enc. "Causal Theories of Knowledge." *Midwest Studies in Philosophy* 9 (1984): 517–28.

Ducasse, Curt J. *Nature, Mind, and Death*. Carus Lectures, eighth series. La Salle, IL: Open Court, 1949.

Feldman, Richard. "An Alleged Defect in Gettier Counter-Examples." *Australasian Journal of Philosophy* 52 (1974): 68–69.

Firth, Roderick. "Coherence, Certainty, and Epistemic Priority." *Journal of Philosophy* 61 (1964): 545–57.

———. "The Anatomy of Certainty." *Philosophical Review* 76 (1976): 3–27.

Fogelin, Robert J. *Pyrrhonian Reflections on Knowledge and Justification*. New York: Oxford University Press, 1994.

Geertz, Clifford. *Local Knowledge*. New York: Basic Books, 1983.

Gertler, Brie, ed. *Privileged Access: Philosophical Accounts of Self-Knowledge*. Ashgate Epistemology and Mind Series. Burlington, VT: Ashgate, 2003.

Gettier, Edmund. "Is Justified True Belief Knowledge?" *Analysis* 23, no. 6 (1963): 121–23.

Ginet, Carl. "*Contra* Reliabilism." *The Monist* 68, no. 2 (1985): 175–87.

———. "The Fourth Condition." *Philosophical Analysis*, edited by D. F. Austin, 105–17. Amsterdam: Kluwer, 1988.

Goldman, Alvin. "A Causal Theory of Knowing." *The Journal of Philosophy* 64, no. 2 (1967): 355–72.

———. *Epistemology and Cognition*. Cambridge, MA: Harvard University Press, 1986.

———. *Empirical Knowledge*. Berkeley: University of California Press, 1988.

Griffiths, A. P., ed. *Knowledge and Belief*. Oxford: Oxford University Press, 1967.

Gunderson, Lars Bo. *Dispositional Theories of Knowledge: A Defense of Aetiological Foundationalism*. Burlington, VT: Ashgate, 2003.

Heidelberger, H. "Knowledge, Certainty, and Probability." *Inquiry* 6 (1963): 242–50.

Heller, Mark. "Relevant Alternatives." *Philosophical Studies* 55 (1989): 23–40.

Hintikka, Jaakko. *Knowledge and Belief: An Introduction to the Logic of the Two Notions*. Ithaca, NY: Cornell University Press, 1962.

———. *Knowledge and the Known: Historical Perspectives in Epistemology*. Dordrecht: Reidel, 1974.

Klein, Peter D. "Knowledge, Causality, and Defeasibility." *Journal of Philosophy* 73 (1976): 792–812.

———. *Certainty: A Refutation of Scepticism*. Brighton: The Harvester Press, 1981.

———. "Radical Interpretation and Global Scepticism." *Truth and Interpretation*, edited by E. LePore, 369–86. New York: Blackwell, 1986.

———. "Epistemic Compatibilism and Canonical Beliefs." In *Doubting: Contemporary Perspectives on Scepticism*, edited by M. Roth and G. Ross, 99–117. Boston: Kluwer, 1990.

Kornblith, Hilary. "Beyond Foundationalism and the Coherence Theory." In *Naturalizing Epistemology*, edited by H. Kornblith, 115–28. Cambridge, MA: Bradford Books/MIT Press, 1985.

———. *Knowledge and Its Place in Nature*. Cambridge, MA: MIT Press, 2002.

Kvanvig, Jonathan L. *The Value of Knowledge and the Pursuit of Understanding*. Cambridge Studies in Philosophy. Cambridge: Cambridge University Press, 2003.

Landesman, Charles. *Skepticism: The Central Issues*. Oxford: Blackwell, 2002.

Lehrer, Keith. "Knowledge, Truth, and Evidence." *Analysis* 25 (1965): 168–75.

———. *Knowledge*. Oxford: Clarendon Press, 1974.

Lehrer, Keith, and Thomas Paxson. "Knowledge: Undefeated Justified True Belief." In *Essays on Knowledge and Justification*, edited by G. Pappas and M. Swain, 146–54. Ithaca, NY: Cornell University Press, 1978.

Lewis, C. I. *An Analysis of Knowledge and Valuation*. La Salle, IL: Open Court, 1946.

Lewis, David. "Elusive Knowledge." *Australasian Journal of Philosophy* 74 (1996): 549–57.

Luper, Steven, ed. *The Skeptics: Contemporary Essays*. Ashgate Epistemology and Mind Series. Burlington, VT: Ashgate, 2003.

Luper-Foy, Steven, ed. *The Possibility of Knowledge*. Lanham, MD: Rowman & Littlefield, 1987.

Malcolm, Norman. *Knowledge and Certainty*. Englewood Cliffs, NJ: Prentice Hall, 1963.

McDowell, J. "Criteria, Defeasibility, and Knowledge." *Proceedings of the British Academy* 68 (1983): 455–79.

Meyers, Robert. *The Likelihood of Knowledge*. Philosophical Studies Series, no. 38. Dordrecht: Kluwer Academic Publishers, 1988.

Miller, R. "Absolute Certainty." *Mind* 87 (1978): 46–65.

Moore, G. E. "Four Forms of Scepticism." In *Philosophical Papers*, 193–223. New York: Macmillan, 1959.

Moser, Paul. *Knowledge and Evidence*. Cambridge: Cambridge University Press, 1989.

Nozick, Robert. *Philosophical Explanations*. Cambridge, MA: Harvard University Press, 1981.

Pappas, George, and Marshall Swain. "Some Conclusive Reasons against 'Conclusive Reasons.'" In *Essays on Knowledge and Justification*, edited by G. Pappas and M. Swain, 62–66. Ithaca, NY: Cornell University Press, 1973.

Popkin, R. *The History of Skepticism from Erasmus to Spinoza*. Berkeley: University of California Press, 1979.

Radford, C. "Knowledge—by Examples." *Analysis* 27 (1966): 1–11.

Ramsey, Frank P. "Knowledge." In *The Foundations of Mathematics and Other Essays*, edited by R. Braithwaite, 258–59. New York: Harcourt Brace, 1931.

Rescher, Nicholas. *Scepticism*. Oxford: Blackwell, 1980.

Rockmore, Tom. *On Constructivist Epistemology*. Lanham, MD: Rowman & Littlefield, 2005.

Rosenberg, J. *One World and Our Knowledge of It*. Dordrecht: Reidel, 1980.

Roth, M. D., and L. Galis, eds. *Essays in the Analysis of Knowledge*. New York: Random House, 1970.

Roth, M. D., and Glenn Ross, eds. *Doubting: Contemporary Perspectives on Skepticism*. Dordrecht: Kluwer, 1990.

Russell, Bertrand. "Knowledge by Acquaintance and Knowledge by Description." *Proceedings of the Aristotelian Society* 11 (1910–1911): 108–28.

———. *Our Knowledge of the External World*. Rev. ed. London: Allen and Unwin, 1929.

——. *Human Knowledge: Its Scope and Limits*. London: Allen and Unwin, 1948.

Sanford, David. "Knowledge and Relevant Alternatives: Comments on Dretske." *Philosophical Studies* 40 (1981): 379–88.

Schmitt, Frederick F. *Knowledge and Belief*. New York: Routledge, Chapman, and Hall, 1992.

Shope, R. K. *The Analysis of Knowing: A Decade of Research*. Princeton, NJ: Princeton University Press, 1983.

——. "Cognitive Abilities, Conditionals, and Knowledge: A Response to Nozick." *Journal of Philosophy* 81 (1984): 29–48.

Sinnott-Armstrong, Walter, ed. *Pyrrhonian Skepticism*. Oxford: Oxford University Press, 2004.

Sorensen, R. A. "Knowing, Believing, and Guessing." *Analysis* 42 (1982): 212–13.

Sosa, Ernst. "How Do You Know?" *Noûs* 14 (1980): 547–64.

——. "The Raft and the Pyramid: Coherence versus Foundations in the Theory of Knowledge." *Midwest Studies in Philosophy* 5 (1980): 3–25.

——. "Some Foundations of Foundationalism." *Noûs* 14 (1980): 547–64.

——. "Knowledge and Intellectual Virtue." *The Monist* 68 (1985): 226–44.

——. "Beyond Scepticism, to the Best of Our Knowledge." *Mind* 97 (1988): 153–88.

——. "Knowledge in Context, Scepticism in Doubt." *Philosophical Perspectives* 2 (1988): 139–56.

——. *Knowledge in Perspective*. Cambridge: Cambridge University Press, 1991.

Stemmer, Nathan. *The Roots of Knowledge*. New York: St. Martin's Press, 1984.

Stern, Robert. *Transcendental Arguments and Scepticism: Answering the Question of Justification*. Oxford: Oxford University Press, 2004.

Stine, G. C. "Scepticism, Relevant Alternatives, and Deductive Closure." *Philosophical Studies* 29 (1976): 249–61.

Strawson, Peter F. *Skepticism and Naturalism: Some Varieties*. New York: Columbia University Press, 1985.

Stroud, Barry. *The Significance of Philosophical Scepticism*. Oxford: Oxford University Press, 1985.

Swain, Michael. *Reasons and Knowledge*. Ithaca, NY: Cornell University Press, 1981.

Unger, Peter. "An Analysis of Factual Knowledge." *Journal of Philosophy* 65 (1968): 157–70.

——. *Ignorance: A Case for Scepticism*. Oxford: Oxford University Press, 1975.

Vendler, Zeno. *Res Cogitans*. Ithaca, NY: Cornell University Press, 1978.

White, A. R. *The Nature of Knowledge*. Totowa, NJ: Rowman & Littlefield, 1982.

Woozley, A. D. "Knowing and Not Knowing." *Proceedings of the Aristotelian Society* 53 (1952–1953): 151–72.

Wright, C. J. G. "Second Thoughts about Criteria." *Synthese* 58 (1984): 383–405.

XXIV. CURRENT ISSUES: MATHEMATICAL KNOWLEDGE

Benaceraf, P. "Mathematical Truth." *Journal of Philosophy* 70 (1973): 661–79.

Benaceraf, P., and Hilary Putnam, eds. *Philosophy of Mathematics: Selected Readings*. Cambridge: Cambridge University Press, 1984.

Frege, Gottlob. *Foundations of Arithmetic*. Oxford: Blackwell, 1953.

Hardy, G. H. "Mathematical Proof." *Mind* 38 (1929): 1–25.

Kessler, G. "Frege, Mill, and the Foundations of Arithmetic." *Journal of Philosophy* 76 (1980): 65–74.

Kitcher, Philip. *The Nature of Mathematical Knowledge*. Oxford: Oxford University Press, 1983.

Maddy, Penelope. "Perception and Mathematical Intuition." *The Philosophical Review* 89, no. 2 (1980): 163–96.

Mill, John Stuart. *A System of Logic*. London: Longmans, 1843.

Parsons, Charles. "Mathematical Intuition." *Proceedings of the Aristotelian Society* 80 (1980): 163–96.

Putnam, Hilary. "What Is Mathematical Truth?" *Philosophical Papers*. Vol. 1: *Mathematics, Matter and Method*, edited by H. Putnam, 60–78. Cambridge: Cambridge University Press, 1979.

Resnik, Michael. "Mathematical Knowledge and Pattern Recognition." *Canadian Journal of Philosophy* 5, no. 1 (1975): 25–39.

———. "Mathematics as a Science of Patterns: Ontology and Reference." *Noûs* (1981): 529–50.

———. "Mathematics as a Science of Patterns: Epistemology." *Noûs* (1982): 95–105.

Steiner, Mark. *Mathematical Knowledge*. Ithaca, NY: Cornell University Press, 1975.

Wittgenstein, Ludwig. *Remarks on the Foundations of Mathematics*. Oxford: Blackwell, 1956.

XXV. CURRENT ISSUES: METAEPISTEMOLOGY

Alston, William P. "Meta-Ethics and Meta-Epistemology." In *Values and Morals*, edited by A. Goldman and J. Kim, 275–97. Dordrecht: Reidel, 1978.

Baker, Lynn Rudder. *Saving Belief*. Princeton, NJ: Princeton University Press, 1987.

Bogdan, Radu, ed. *Belief*. Oxford: Oxford University Press, 1985.

Bradie, M. "Assessing Evolutionary Epistemology." *Biology and Philosophy* 1 (1986): 401–59.

Brady, Michael S., and Duncan Pritchard. *Moral and Epistemic Virtues*. Metaphilosophy Series in Philosophy. Oxford: Blackwell, 2003.

Cherniak, Christopher. *Minimal Rationality*. Computational Models of Cognition and Perception Series. Cambridge, MA: Bradford Books/MIT Press, 1986.

Churchland, Paul M. "Eliminative Materialism and the Propositional Attitudes." *Journal of Philosophy* 78 (1981): 67–90.

———. "Is *Thinker* a Natural Kind?" *Dialogue* 21 (1982): 223–38.

Clifford, William K. "The Ethics of Belief." In *Lectures and Essays*, 177–211. Volume 2. London: Macmillan, 1879.

Cohen, L. J. *An Essay on Belief and Acceptance*. Oxford: Oxford University Press, 1992.

Dancy, Jonathan. "Intuitionism and Meta-Epistemology." *Philosophical Studies* 42 (1982): 395–408.

Foley, R. *The Theory of Epistemic Rationality*. Cambridge, MA: Harvard University Press, 1987.

Fumerton, Richard. *Metaepistemology and Skepticism*. Lanham, MD: Rowman & Littlefield, 1995.

Garfield, Jay L. *Belief in Psychology: A Study in the Ontology of Mind*. Cambridge, MA: MIT Press, 1988.

Gensler, Harry J. *Historical Dictionary of Logic*. Lanham, MD: Scarecrow Press, 2006.

Gilbert, M. "Modeling Collective Belief." *Synthese* 73 (1987): 185–204.

Goldman, Alvin. "Epistemics: The Regulative Theory of Cognition." *Journal of Philosophy* 75 (1978): 509–23.

Hintikka, J., and M. B. Hintikka. *The Logic of Epistemology and the Epistemology of Logic*. Dordrecht: Kluwer Academic, 1989.

Levi, Isaac. *Mild Contraction: Evaluating Loss of Information Due to Loss of Belief*. Oxford: Oxford University Press, 2004.

Machan, Tibor R. *Objectivity: Rediscovering Determinate Reality in Philosophy, Science, and Everyday Life*. Burlington, VT: Ashgate, 2004.

McGinn, Colin. "Radical Interpretation and Epistemology." In *Truth and Interpretation*, edited by E. LePore, 356–68. New York: Blackwell, 1986.

Montmarquet, J. A. "Epistemic Virtue." *Mind* 96 (1987): 482–97.

Moser, Paul K. *Philosophy after Objectivity*. New York: Oxford University Press, 1993.

Peacocke, Christopher. *The Realm of Reason*. Oxford: Oxford University Press, 2003.

Salmon, N., and S. Soames, eds. *Propositions and Attitudes*. Oxford: Oxford University Press, 1977.

Sellars, Wilfrid. "On Accepting First Principles." *Philosophical Perspectives* 2 (1989): 301–14.

Stich, S. P. *From Folk Psychology to Cognitive Science: The Case against Belief*. Cambridge, MA: Bradford Books/MIT Press, 1983.

——. "Reflective Equilibrium, Analytic Epistemology and the Problem of Cognitive Diversity." *Synthese* 74 (1988): 391–413.

Stroud, Barry. "Transcendental Arguments." *Journal of Philosophy* 65 (1968): 241–56.

Weinberg, Jonathan, S. Nichols, and S. Stich. "Normativity and Epistemic Intuitions." *Philosophical Topics* 29, no. 1 (2001): 429–60.

Wigner, E. P. "The Limits of Science." *Proceedings of the American Philosophical Society* 94 (1950): 422–27.

XXVI. CURRENT ISSUES: MORAL KNOWLEDGE

Brinks, D. O. *Moral Realism and the Foundations of Ethics*. Cambridge: Cambridge University Press, 1989.

Broad, C. D. "Some Reflections on Moral-Sense Theories in Ethics." Reprinted in W. S. Sellars and J. Hospers *Readings in Ethical Theory*. New York: Appleton-Century-Crofts, 1952: 363–88.

Daniels, Norman. "Wide Reflective Equilibrium and Theory Acceptance in Ethics." *Journal of Philosophy* 76 (1979): 256–82.

Gert, Bernard. *The Moral Rules*. New York: Harper and Row, 1966.

Gewirth, Alan. *Reason and Morality*. Chicago: University of Chicago Press, 1978.

Goldman, Alvin. "Ethics and Cognitive Science." *Ethics* 103 (1993): 337–60.

Sidgwick, Henry. *Methods of Ethics*. 6th ed. London: Macmillan, 1874.

Sinnott-Armstrong, Walter, and Mark Timmons, eds. *Moral Knowledge? New Readings in Moral Epistemology*. New York: Oxford University Press, 1996.

XXVII. CURRENT ISSUES: NATURALIZED EPISTEMOLOGY

Bogdan, R. J., ed. *Belief: Form, Content, and Function*. Oxford: Oxford University Press, 1986.

Cherniak, C. *Minimal Rationality*. Cambridge, MA: Bradford Books/MIT Press, 1986.

Churchland, Paul. *A Neurocomputational Perspective*. Cambridge: Cambridge University Press, 1989.

Churchland, Paul, and Patricia Churchland. "Stalking the Wild Epistemic Engine." *Noûs* 17 (1983): 5–18.

Duran, Jane. *Epistemics: Epistemic Justification Theory Naturalized and the Computational Model of Mind.* Lanham, MD: University Press of America, 1989.

Goldman, Alvin. *Epistemology and Cognition.* Cambridge, MA: Harvard University Press, 1986.

———. "Epistemic Folkways and Scientific Epistemology." In *Liaisons: Philosophy Meets the Cognitive and Social Sciences*, 155–75. Cambridge, MA: MIT Press, 1992.

Greenwood, John D. *The Future of Folk Psychology.* Cambridge: Cambridge University Press, 1991.

Haack, Susan. "The Relevance of Psychology to Epistemology." *Metaphilosophy* 6 (1975): 161–76.

Kahnemann, David, P. Slovic, and A. Tversky, eds. *Judgment under Uncertainty: Heuristics and Biases.* Cambridge: Cambridge University Press, 1982.

Kahnemann, David, and A. Tversky. "On the Reality of Cognitive Illusions." *Psychological Review* 103 (1996): 582–91.

Kim, Jaegwon. "What Is Naturalized Epistemology?" *Philosophical Perspectives* 2 (1988): 381–405.

Kitchener, Richard F. "Genetic Epistemology, Normative Epistemology, and Psychologism." *Synthese* 45 (1980): 257–80.

Kornblith, Hilary. "The Psychological Turn." *Australasian Journal of Philosophy* 60 (1982): 238–53.

———, ed. *Naturalizing Epistemology.* Cambridge, MA: Bradford Books/MIT Press, 1987.

Maffie, James. "Recent Work on Naturalized Epistemology." *American Philosophical Quarterly* 27, no. 4 (1990): 281–93.

Mischel, Theodore. *Cognitive Development and Epistemology.* New York: Academic Press, 1971.

Nisbett, Richard, and Lee Ross. *Human Inference: Strategies and Shortcomings of Social Judgment.* Century Psychology Series. Englewood Cliffs, NJ: Prentice Hall, 1980.

Nisbett, Richard, and Timothy Wilson. "Telling More Than We Can Know: Verbal Reports on Mental Processes." *Psychological Review* 84, no. 3 (1977): 231–59.

Putnam, Hilary. "Why Reason Cannot Be Naturalized." *Synthese* 52 (1982): 3–23.

Quine, W. V. O. "Epistemology Naturalized." In *Ontological Relativity and Other Essays*, 69–90. New York: Columbia University Press, 1969.

———. "Reply to Morton White." In *The Philosophy of W. V. Quine*, edited by L. E. Hahn and P. A. Schilpp, 663–65. La Salle, IL: Open Court, 1986.

Ricketts, Thomas G. "Rationality, Translation, and Epistemology Naturalized." *Journal of Philosophy* 79 (1982): 117–36.

Roth, Paul. "Siegel on Naturalizing Epistemology and Natural Science." *Philosophy of Science* 50 (1983): 482–93.

Sheehan, P. "Quine on Revision: A Critique." *Australasian Journal of Philosophy* 51 (1973): 95–104.

Siegel, Harvey. "Justification, Discovery, and the Naturalizing of Epistemology." *Philosophy of Science* 47 (1980): 297–321.

Sosa, Ernest. Nature Unmirrored, Epistemology Naturalized." *Synthese* 55 (1983): 49–72.

Stich, Stephen. "Belief and Subdoxastic States." *Philosophy of Science* 45 (1978): 499–518.

———. *From Folk Psychology to Cognitive Science: The Case against Belief.* Cambridge, MA: MIT Press, 1983.

Stroud, Barry. "The Significance of Naturalized Epistemology." *Midwest Studies in Philosophy* 6 (1981): 455–71.

Taylor, James. "Epistemic Justification and Psychological Realism." *Synthese* 85 (1990): 199–230.

White, M. "Normative Ethics, Normative Epistemology, and Quine's Holism." In *The Philosophy of W. V. Quine*, edited by L. E. Hahn and P. A. Schilpp, 649–62. La Salle, IL: Open Court, 1986.

Woods, Michel. "Scepticism and Natural Knowledge." *Proceedings of the Aristotelian Society* 54 (1980): 231–48.

XXVIII. CURRENT ISSUES: RELIGIOUS KNOWLEDGE

Alston, William P. "Perceiving God." *Journal of Philosophy* 83 (1986): 655–65.

———. *Perceiving God.* Ithaca, NY: Cornell University Press, 1991.

Atran, Scott. *In Gods We Trust: The Evolutionary Landscape of Religion.* Evolution and Cognition Series. New York: Oxford University Press, 2002.

Blanshard, Brand. *Reason and Belief.* London: Allen and Unwin, 1974.

Freud, Sigmund. *Die Zukunft einer Illusion.* Vienna: Internationaler Psychoanalytischer Verlag, 1927. Translated by W. Robson-Scott; revised and edited by J. Strachey. The International Psycho-Analytical Library, 15. London: Hogarth, 1973.

Hick, J. *Faith and Knowledge.* 2nd ed. London: Macmillan, 1967.

Mackie, John. *The Miracle of Theism.* Oxford: Oxford University Press, 1982.

Mavrodes, George. *Belief in God: A Study in the Epistemology of Religion.* New York: Random House, 1970.

Penelum, Terence. "On 'Perceiving God.'" *Journal of Philosophy* 83 (1986): 665–66.

Plantinga, Alvin. "Reason and Belief in God." In *Faith and Rationality*, edited by A. Plantinga and N. Wolterstorff, 16–93. Notre Dame, IN: University of Notre Dame Press, 1983.

Price, Henry H. *Belief*. London: George Allen and Unwin, 1945.

Shermer, Michael. *How We Believe: The Search for God in an Age of Science*. New York: W. H. Freeman, 2000.

Swinburne, Richard. *The Existence of God*. Oxford: Clarendon Press, 1979.

XXIX. CURRENT ISSUES: SCIENCE AND INDUCTION

Alexander, H. G. "The Paradoxes of Confirmation." *British Journal for the Philosophy of Science* 9 (1958): 227–33.

BonJour, Laurence. "A Reconsideration of the Problem of Induction." *Philosophical Topics* 14 (1986): 93–124.

Bovens, Luc, and Stephan Hartmann. *Bayesian Epistemology*. Oxford: Oxford University Press, 2004.

Duhem, P. *The Aim and Structure of Physical Theory*. New York: Atheneum, 1962.

Fraassen, B. van. *The Scientific Image*. Oxford: Oxford University Press, 1980.

Friedman, Michael. "Explanation and Scientific Understanding." *Journal of Philosophy* 71 (1974): 5–19.

Glymour, C. *Theory and Evidence*. Princeton, NJ: Princeton University Press, 1988.

Goodman, Nelson. *Fact, Fiction, and Forecast*. Indianapolis: Bobbs-Merrill, 1965.

Hanson, N. R. *Patterns of Discovery*. Cambridge: Cambridge University Press, 1958.

Harman, Gilbert. "The Inference to the Best Explanation." *Philosophical Review* 74 (1965): 88–95.

———. *Change in View: Principles of Reasoning*. Cambridge, MA: Bradford Books/MIT Press, 1986.

Hempel, Carl Gustav. *Aspects of Scientific Explanation*. New York: Free Press, 1965.

Hesse, M. *The Structure of Scientific Inference*. Berkeley: University of California Press, 1974.

Howson, C., and F. Urbach. *Scientific Inference: The Bayesian Approach*. La Salle, IL: Open Court, 1989.

Jeffry, R. C. *The Logic of Decision*. Chicago: University of Chicago Press, 1983.

Keller, E. F. *Reflections on Gender and Science*. New Haven, CT: Yale University Press, 1985.

Kitcher, Philip. "Explanatory Unification." *Philosophy of Science* 48 (1981): 507-31.

——. *The Advancement of Science*. New York: Oxford University Press, 1993.

Kornblith, Hilary. *Inductive Inference and its Natural Ground*. Cambridge, MA: MIT Press, 1993.

Kuhn, Thomas. *The Structure of Scientific Revolutions*. 2nd ed. Chicago: University of Chicago Press, 1970.

Lehrer, Keith. "Justification, Explanation, and Induction." In *Induction, Acceptance, and Rational Belief*, edited by M. Swain, 100–133. Dordrecht: Reidel, 1970.

Lipton, P. *Inference to the Best Explanation*. London: Routledge, 1991.

Popper, Karl. *The Logic of Scientific Discovery*. London: Hutchinson, 1959.

——. *Conjectures and Refutations*. London: Routledge and Kegan Paul, 1963.

——. "Conjectural Knowledge: My Solution to the Problem of Induction." In *Objective Knowledge*, 1–31. Oxford: Clarendon Press, 1972.

——. *Objective Knowledge*. Oxford: Clarendon Press, 1972.

Putnam, Hilary. "The 'Corroboration' of Scientific Theories." In *The Philosophy of Karl Popper*, vol. 1, edited by P. Schilpp, 221–40. The Library of the Living Philosophers. La Salle, IL: Open Court, 1974.

——. *Reason, Truth, and History*. London: Cambridge University Press, 1981.

Reichenbach, Hans. *Experience and Prediction*. Chicago: University of Chicago Press, 1949.

Salmon, W. C. *The Foundations of Scientific Inference*. Pittsburgh: University of Pittsburgh Press, 1967.

——. "Rational Prediction." *British Journal for the Philosophy of Science* 32 (1981): 115–25.

Sellars, Wilfrid. *Science, Perception and Reality*. London: Routledge and Kegan Paul, 1963.

Thagard, P. "The Best Explanation: Criterion for Theory Choice." *Journal of Philosophy* 75 (1978): 76–92.

Trout, J. D. "Scientific Explanation and the Sense of Understanding." *Philosophy of Science* 69, no. 2 (2002): 212–33.

von Wright, G. H. *The Logical Problem of Induction*. Oxford: Blackwell, 1957.

Will, Frederick. *Induction and Justification*. Ithaca, NY: Cornell University Press, 1974.

XXX. CURRENT ISSUES: SENSORY PERCEPTION

Akins, Kathleen, ed. *Perception*. New York: Oxford University Press, 1995.

Alston, William P. *The Reliability of Sense Perception*. Ithaca, NY: Cornell University Press, 1993.

Armstrong, David. *Perception and the Physical World*. London: Penguin, 1961.

Austin, J. L. *Sense and Sensibilia*. Oxford: Oxford University Press, 1968.

Barnes, W. H. F. "The Myth of Sense-Data." In *Perceiving, Sensing, Knowing*, edited by R. Swartz, 138–67. Garden City, NJ: Anchor, 1965.

Boyle, Robert. "Experiments and Observations upon Colors." In *Works*, vol. 1, 2132–36. Volume 6. London: Birch, 1772.

Broad, C. D. "The Theory of Sensa." In *Perceiving, Sensing, and Knowing*, edited by R. Swartz, 85–129. Berkeley: University of California Press, 1965.

Carrier, L. S. *Experience and the Objects of Perception*. Washington, DC: University Press of America, 1981.

Chisholm, Roderick. *Perceiving: A Philosophical Study*. Ithaca, NY: Cornell University Press, 1957.

Coates, Paul. *The Metaphysics of Perception: Wilfrid Sellars, Critical Realism and the Nature of Experience*. New York: Routledge, 2005.

Cornman, J. *Materialism and Sensations*. New Haven, CT: Yale University Press, 1971.

———. *Perception, Commonsense and Science*. New Haven, CT: Yale University Press, 1975.

Dancy, Jonathan, ed. *Perceptual Knowledge*. Oxford: Oxford University Press, 1988.

Dretske, Fred I. *Seeing and Knowing*. Chicago: University of Chicago Press, 1969.

Gibson, J. *The Perception of the Visual World*. Boston: Houghton Mifflin, 1950.

Goldman, Alvin. "Discrimination and Perceptual Knowledge." *Journal of Philosophy* 73 (1976): 771–91.

———. "Epistemology and the Psychology of Perception." *American Philosophical Quarterly* 18 (1981): 43–51.

Goodman, Nelson. *The Structure of Appearance*. Cambridge, MA: Harvard University Press, 1951.

Grice, Paul. "The Causal Theory of Perception." *Proceedings of the Aristotelian Society* suppl. vol. (1961): 121–52.

Hamlyn, D. W. *Sensation and Perception*. London: Routledge and Kegan Paul, 1961.

Jackson, Frank. "On the Adverbial Analysis of Visual Experience." *Metaphilosophy* 6, no. 2 (1975): 127–35.

——. *Perception: A Representative Theory*. Cambridge: Cambridge University Press, 1977.

Leon, M. "Character, Content, and the Ontology of Experience." *Australasian Journal of Philosophy* 65 (1987): 377–99.

Marr, David. *Vision*. New York: Freeman, 1982.

Moore, G. E. "Sense-Data." In *Some Main Problems of Philosophy*, 28–51. London: Allen and Unwin, 1953.

Peacocke, C. *Sense and Content: Experience, Thought, and Their Relations*. Oxford: Clarendon Press, 1983.

Pendlebury, Michael. "Sense Experiences and Their Contents: A Defense of the Propositional View." *Inquiry* 33 (1990): 215–30.

Perkins, M. *Sensing the World*. Indianapolis: Hackett, 1983.

Pitcher, G. *A Theory of Perception*. Princeton, NJ: Princeton University Press, 1971.

Price, H. H. *Perception*. New York: McBride, 1933.

Prichard, H. A. *Knowledge and Perception*. Oxford: Clarendon Press, 1950.

Rock, Irwin. *The Logic of Perception*. Cambridge, MA: Bradford Books/MIT Press, 1983.

Russell, Bertrand. *Our Knowledge of the External World*. London: Allen and Unwin, 1914.

Sellars, Wilfrid. *Science, Perception, and Reality*. London: Routledge and Kegan Paul, 1963.

——. "The Adverbial Theory of Objects of Sensation." *Metaphilosophy* 6 (1975): 144–60.

Swartz, R. J., ed. *Perceiving, Sensing, and Knowing*. Berkeley: University of California Press, 1965.

Tye, Michael. "The Adverbial Theory: A Defense of Sellars against Jackson." *Metaphilosophy* 6, no. 2 (1975): 136–43.

XXXI. CURRENT ISSUES: SOCIAL EPISTEMOLOGY

Annis, David B. "A Contextualist Theory of Justification." *American Philosophical Quarterly* 15 (1978): 213–19.

Bloor, David. *Knowledge and Social Imagery*. London: Routledge and Kegan Paul, 1976.

Campbell, Donald T. "A Tribal Model of the Social System Vehicle Carrying Scientific Knowledge." *Knowledge: Creation, Diffusion, Utilization* 1 (1979): 181–201.

Coady, C. A. "Testimony and Observation." *American Philosophical Quarterly* 10 (1973): 149–55.

Goldman, Alvin. *Knowledge in a Social World*. New York: Oxford University Press, 1999.

———. *Pathways to Knowledge: Private and Public*. Oxford: Oxford University Press, 2004.

Hacking, Ian. *The Social Construction of What?* Cambridge, MA: Harvard University Press, 1999.

Harman, Gilbert. "Moral Philosophy Meets Social Psychology: Virtue Ethics and the Fundamental Attribution Error." *Proceedings of the Aristotelian Society* 99 (1998–1999): 315–31.

Kantorovich, A. "The Collective *A Priori* in Science." *Nature and System* 5 (1983): 77–96.

Kusch, Martin. *Knowledge by Agreement: The Programme of Communitarian Epistemology*. Oxford: Oxford University Press, 2004.

Lehrer, Keith. "Personal and Social Knowledge." *Synthese* 73 (1987): 87–107.

Longino, H. *Science as Social Knowledge*. Princeton, NJ: Princeton University Press, 1990.

Rouse, J. *Knowledge and Power*. Ithaca, NY: Cornell University Press, 1956.

Schmitt, Frederick F., ed. *Socializing Epistemology: The Social Dimension of Knowledge*. Lanham, MD: Rowman & Littlefield, 1994.

Wellbourne, Michael. "The Transmission of Knowledge." *Philosophical Quarterly* 29 (1979): 1–9.

———. "The Community of Knowledge." *Philosophical Quarterly* 31 (1981): 302–14.

———. "A Cognitive Thoroughfare." *Mind* 92 (1983): 410–12.

About the Author

Ralph Baergen (B.A., University of Manitoba; M.A. and Ph.D., Syracuse University) wrote his dissertation (directed by William P. Alston) on epistemic reliabilism and worked on various aspects of applying psychological research to traditional epistemic issues. He is also the author of *Contemporary Epistemology* (1995) and a number of epistemological articles. He is a professor at Idaho State University and does research in medical ethics.